I0210534

The way I see it, love is an amusement park,
and food its souvenir.
Stephanie Klein

Dedication

To James, my favorite writing partner and ghost hunting buddy. You can turn the lights off on me any time. (Just warn a girl first, okay?)

OTHER AMERICAN HAUNTINGS INK TITLES BY SYLVIA SHULTS

HUNTING DEMONS
A True Story of the Dark Side of the Paranormal (2015)

44 YEARS IN DARKNESS
A True Story of Madness, Tragedy & Shattered Love (2016)

THE SPIRITS OF CHRISTMAS
The Dark Side of the Holidays (2017)

GONE ON VACATION
Haunted Zoos, Museums & Amusement Parks (2022)

GONE ON VACATION
ENDLESS SUMMER

SYLVIA SHULTS

An American Hauntings Ink Book

GONE ON VACATION
Endless Summer

© Copyright 2025 by Sylvia Shults

All Rights Reserved.
ISBN: 978-1-958589-26-7
First Edition

Published by American Hauntings Ink
201 East Broadway – Alton IL – 62002
www.americanhauntingsink.com

Publisher's Note:
No part of this publication may be reproduced, distributed, or transmitted in any form or
by any means, including photocopying, recording, or other electronic or mechanical
methods, without the prior written consent
of the publisher, except in case of brief quotations embodied in critical reviews or other
noncommercial uses permitted by copyright law.

Cover Design by April Slaughter
Interior Design by Troy Taylor

Printed in the United States of America

ADMIT ONE **TICKET** ★ 102378945637 ★

102378945637

INTRODUCTION

So, vacation time has rolled around again. The kids are out of school, and it's the perfect time to plan a road trip. Where will you take the family?

How about someplace haunted?

Oh, I'm not talking about a drafty old house where a breeze with no source stirs tattered curtains through broken windows. I'm not talking about a derelict prison, its abandoned hallways still echoing with the groans and cries of prisoners forgotten by the world. I'm not talking about cemeteries, or battlefields, or Southern mansions, the trees in their front yards festooned with the gray-green drapery of Spanish moss. (Although admittedly, any one of these places would be a fantastic setting for a haunting.)

No, I'm picturing somewhere much cheerier, brighter, friendlier … but even bright, cheery, friendly places can be home to restless spirits.

In the first volume of *Gone On Vacation*, we visited haunted zoos, museums, and amusement parks, and we had an absolute blast. In this second book, we're going to explore even more haunted places. We're going to hunt up more museums and amusement parks. We'll stroll the streets of historic villages, streets that still echo with the daily business of the folks who lived there many decades before. We'll even stretch our vacation into the spooky season and visit haunted house attractions that are actually haunted.

So, pack your bags - leave plenty of room for spooky souvenirs - and let's hit the road in search of history and hauntings. An endless summer awaits!

Sylvia Shults
Summer 2025

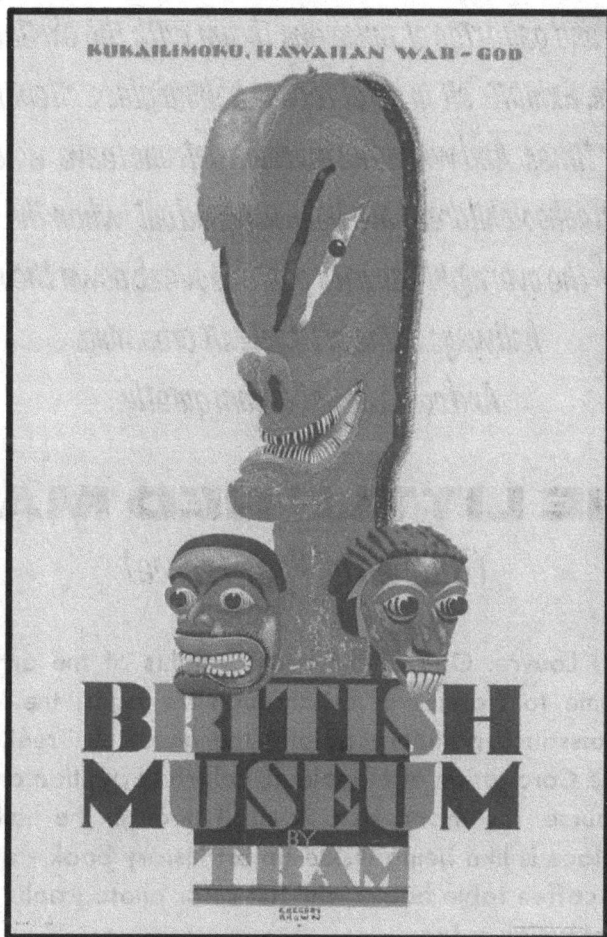
KUKAILIMOKU, HAWAIIAN WAR-GOD
BRITISH MUSEUM BY TRAM

BEYOND THE VELVET ROPE
Haunted Museums

The halls and galleries of museums thrum with the excited babble of visitors. Exhibits sit in quiet repose behind glass, silent relics of earlier times. And when the museum patrons leave, when the chattering schoolchildren have been ushered out, when the sensible shoes of the overnight security guards squeak down the marble hallways ... the artifacts sit dreaming.

And some do not dream quietly.

THE LITTLE RED MAN
(The Louvre, Paris, France)

The Louvre. One of the heavyweights of the art museum world. Home to classics of art through the ages: the Venus de Milo, Renaissance paintings galore, the graceful Greek Winged Victory, the Coronation of Napoleon, colorful Egyptian antiquities, and of course, the Mona Lisa. A stroll through the halls of this former palace is like being inside an art history book - one of the really big coffee table books with full color photographs and slick pages, that weigh a ton.

The Louvre is by far the biggest and most visited museum in the world. Nearly 10 million people wander through its 16 acres of galleries every year, which works out to just about 28,000 visitors a day. On busy days in the last few years, 45,000 people have come through the doors every single day, prompting museum officials to quietly pump the brakes. Since June 2022, daily attendance has been capped at 30,000. If you are one of these lucky thousands, you'll be treated to the sight of some of the greatest hits of the art world. If you glanced at every single one of the museum's artworks - there are half a million of them in the collection, of which 38,000 are on display - taking just thirty seconds to drool over each one, it would take you 100 days to work your way through the entire building. And that's not including stopping to eat expensive croissants, sleep a bit, or take any bathroom breaks. At all. So, you know, maybe pace yourself, huh?

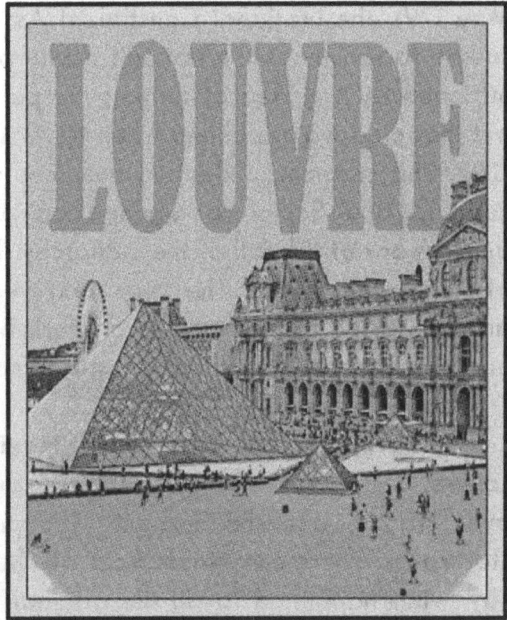

And as you walk, do keep an eye out for the ghosts.

The Louvre Palace began life as a fortress. In the late 12th century, England still held the territory of Normandy, so King Philip Auguste had the fort built in 1190 to protect Paris from attack from the west. He basically built a fortified wall around the city, and the fort itself was a defensive tower. Over the next several centuries, the palace went through several renovations. In the 14th century, King Charles V turned the fortress into a royal residence. In 1546, King Francis I decided to redecorate, remodeling the palace in the French Renaissance style. Louis XIV moved the royal headquarters to Versailles in May 1682.

With the move to the countryside, the Louvre was turned into a residence for artists. The Sun King was an enthusiastic supporter of the arts; he himself excelled at both dance and music (he played the guitar). The Louvre became a haven for artists to create under the patronage of the king. After the Revolution, in

May 1791, the National Constituent Assembly decided to use the Louvre to showcase the nation's masterpieces. Louis XVI had been intrigued by the idea of turning the palace into a royal museum, but that plan was sidelined when he was imprisoned on August 10, 1792. The museum, under the auspices of the Royal Academy of Painting and Sculpture, opened on August 10, 1793, the first anniversary of the fall of the monarchy. That first display consisted of 721 works of art. The very next year, France's revolutionary armies started bringing more artwork back from their exploits in northern Europe. The Vatican contributed artwork too, through the Treaty of Tolentino in 1797.

During World War II, the Nazis set their sights on the Louvre. They'd already been looting art from private homes all over France, and the museum was pressed into service as a storeroom where the Nazis kept all their stolen goods. But, you say, what happened to all the art that was in the Louvre before the Germans showed up?

I'm so glad you asked. The director of the Louvre, one Jacques Jaujard, saw the systemic looting of homes and businesses in Germany as the Nazis searched for plunder. He realized it was only a matter of time before the Nazis turned their greedy gaze towards Paris, and the crown jewel of Europe's museums. Jaujard had his staff pack everything up and move it to safety. Two hundred trucks were loaded up with nearly 2,000 boxes of art, which was squirreled away to more secure locations. By the time Hitler's soldiers reached the museum, they were greeted by empty frames. Despite having to move the works of art several times, staying a step or two ahead of the Nazis and keeping the artwork out of the grasp of enemy hands, none of the priceless treasures of the Louvre were damaged or went missing.

So, whose ghost is it that wanders these world-famous halls?

Well, some visitors have reported seeing the ghostly apparitions of a few of the artists whose work resides at the museum, such as Leonardo da Vinci and Eugene Delacroix. But the most famous ghost of the Louvre is a creepy phantom named Jean L'Ecorcheur, or Jack the Skinner. To tell his story, we have to travel back several centuries, to 1564.

In the 1560s, Queen Catherine de Medici, wife of Henry II, decided to have a palace built for herself. Her architects chose a spot near the Louvre, a site that was occupied by several tile factories. In remembrance of this, the new palace was referred to as the Tuileries.

But there were people working in those factories, and living in the area, who had to be displaced so the palace could be built. The project necessarily involved the eviction of several area residents, including Jean L'Ecorcheur. Jean worked as a butcher, which is how he got his grisly nickname. He landed on his feet, though, and for a time, he served Queen Catherine as one of her most efficient assassins.

Soon, however, Jack the Skinner got too big for his culottes. He realized that he knew quite a few juicy secrets about the royal family, and he started to get a bit cocky. Catherine asked the chevalier Neuville, one of her trusted men-at-arms, to take care of the problem by silencing the rebel by any means necessary. Neuville decided to make that silence permanent. Jean L'Ecorcheur was himself assassinated.

Just before he died, Jean threatened, "I'll be back." With his last breaths, he predicted that the queen would die "near Saint-Germain." Catherine subsequently avoided going to places with this name for the rest of her life ... but she couldn't escape the butcher's premonition. As she lay on her deathbed many years later in 1589, she asked for a priest to be brought to her, so she could confess her sins.

The name of her confessor was Julien de Saint-Germain.

Since the 16th century, a creepy spook has been seen skulking around the Tuileries gardens, which are all that remain of the palace complex. He's known as the Little Red Man of the Tuileries. The spirit, dressed in red, is seen both in the gardens and in the Louvre. The ominous ghost has visited some of the most important figures of French history ... right before the biggest tragedies of their lives. He allegedly appeared to Marie Antoinette before the fall of the monarchy. Napoleon claimed to have seen the Little Red Man in 1815, before the battle of Waterloo. King Louis XVIII supposedly saw the spirit a few days before his death.

The last time the ghost was actually seen was when the Tuileries Palace burned, in May 1871. It's said, though, that the Little Red Man of the Tuileries still wanders the underground passages of the Louvre. Is he in search of redemption? Absolution? Or vengeance?

MORE THAN JUST MUMMIES
(The British Museum, London, England)

At the height of British colonial power, in the 19th and early 20th centuries, the Crown controlled vast areas of the globe. A beautifully descriptive phrase arose from that era of history: "The sun never sets on the British Empire." The British military spread out from the small island, and extended the reach of the Empire throughout the known world. Scientists and explorers followed, both in search of knowledge about the cultures the military had encountered.

And where there are travelers and explorers, there are

folks in search of souvenirs.

The vast collection of the British Museum began with Sir Hans Sloane. Sloane was a well-read and well-educated man, a doctor, who was able to indulge a passion for collecting. He was helped in this pursuit by British imperial expansion. Unfortunately, he financed these purchases with income partly derived from enslaved labor on Jamaican sugar plantations. (Sloane held investments in both the Royal African Company and the South Sea Company, which traded in enslaved people. He also married Elizabeth Langley Rose, a wealthy widow and heiress of sugar plantations in Jamaica. So ... yeah. We'd definitely consider that dirty money today.)

Setting aside the unpleasant reality of where Sloane got his fortune, later generations certainly reaped the benefit of his travels and his curiosity. And interestingly, I'm not just referring to Sloane's extensive artifact collecting (more than 80,000 "natural and artificial rarities") or his impressive library (over 40,000 books and manuscripts). I'm also talking about another fun fact. Sir Hans Sloane is often credited with inventing chocolate milk.

In 1687, Sloane went to Jamaica as the personal physician to the new governor of the island, Christopher Monck. (Monck ended up dying the next year, but I'm sure it wasn't Sloane's fault.)

While there, Sloane was able to indulge his passion for learning. He wrote a book in 1707 called *A Voyage to the Islands Madera, Barbados, Nieves, St. Christophers, and Jamaica*, and followed it with a second volume in 1725. He encountered the locals enjoying a drink made from cocoa beans brewed up with water, which he thought was pretty gross. There were recipes already concocted for mixing cocoa with sugar, milk, eggs, and spices, and the Jamaicans were making hot chocolate with milk and cinnamon as far back as 1494. But Sloane was influential enough that his recipe got noticed. By the 1750s, a grocer named Nicholas Sanderson was marketing "Sir Hans Sloane's Milk Chocolate" as a medicinal elixir, and the Cadbury brothers referenced Sloane's recipe when they sold tins of drinking chocolate in the 19th century.

But chocolate milk wasn't Sloane's only contribution to the finer aspects of life for future generations. He had a generous charitable streak; he helped to establish London's Foundling Hospital, the first institution in England to care for abandoned children. Every child in the hospital's care was vaccinated, as Sloane was an early adopter of inoculation. He also worked at Christ's Hospital, a private school in West Sussex, from 1694 to 1730, and donated his salary back. He ran a free surgery every morning, doing physical examinations and consulting pro bono for the Royal College of Physicians, and supported their dispensary of easily affordable medications.

But his most lasting legacy - aside from chocolate milk (yum!) -- was his extensive collection of stuff. In addition to his own assemblage of plant specimens, coins, medals, and drawings, he also acquired the holdings of several other collectors. He died in January 1753, and gave instructions that all of his curiosities should be gifted to the public. He stated in his will that he would bequeath his entire collection to the nation on the condition that Parliament pay his heirs 20,000 pounds. This was quite a bargain; some sources say the collection was valued at 80,000 pounds (the equivalent of 15,387,173 pounds today).

Sloane's will also expressly stated that he wanted his collection to be made available to anyone who wanted to see it. The curators were uncomfortable with this stipulation. They thought that only scholars and members of the upper class should have the privilege of seeing the artifacts. But Sloane's will made it clear: anyone, even ordinary members of the public, would have the opportunity to visit the museum and learn from the collection. Sloane's last wishes were honored, and his collection provided the foundation for the British Museum's vast displays. Even today, admission to the British Museum is free to the public.

The museum's holdings were expanded over the centuries, with explorers, connoisseurs, aficionados, and other enthusiasts making their contributions. But all of this came at a cost.

The British Museum's collection of anthropological artifacts is massive. More than six million people wander through the museum annually; that's an average of 17,000 visitors every day. The collections include around 8 million objects that cover 2 million years of human history. Some of the most iconic artifacts in the world are housed here, like the Rosetta Stone, the Elgin Marbles, the winged lion sculptures from Assyria, and the Sutton Hoo burial treasure. Here's the thing, though ... most of them came from places other than England. Most of these artifacts are very far from home.

And the spirits attached to them are not at all happy about it.

The Elgin Marbles were brought from Athens starting in 1801 by Thomas Bruce, the seventh earl of Elgin (hence the name). These beautiful ancient Greek sculptures once graced the Parthenon and other buildings on the Acropolis. Crafted between 447 and 42 BCE, they were placed on the temple dedicated to the goddess Athena. The sculptures represent the Greeks' careful study and rendering of the human form, the foundation of classical art.

Lord Elgin was a great lover of ancient art and antiquities. At the time he was visiting Greece, the country was occupied by the Ottoman Turks. Elgin was the British ambassador to the Ottoman Empire. He feared that the lovely, irreplaceable sculptures, two thousand years old, would not survive the Turkish occupation. He asked permission to have artists sketch and copy the most important pieces of architectural detail for posterity. The government granted the request, and eventually gave Elgin permission to take the lot.

Elgin was thrilled, and started packing up the Parthenon Marbles for shipment to England. By 1812, the last of the sculptures had been taken, and all of the artwork was in its new home. (In 1804, HMS *Mentor* made it as far as the Greek island of Cythera, then sank in a storm. The entire cargo was recovered, though.) There were quite a few people, including Englishmen, who accused Elgin of being dishonest and flat-out greedy. These detractors pointed out that taking the sculptures from their home in the Parthenon was nothing short of vandalism. The whole situation was even debated in Parliament. Admittedly, 1802 was not the most culturally enlightened time. But even back then, people realize that Lord Elgin had no authority to take the artwork from its rightful home in Greece. Elgin, you may be happy to know, didn't profit from this venture. In 1816, the British crown bought the collection for 35,000 pounds - about half of what it cost him to bring the sculptures to England.

The government of Greece periodically demands that the Parthenon Marbles be returned. With just as much regularity, the British Museum refuses to return them. Museum officials point out that having them on display has saved the sculptures from deterioration and the ravages of time. There is, actually, a museum in Athens next to the Acropolis. It opened in 2009, with a large section of the museum devoted to the Parthenon. The artwork and details that Elgin removed over 200 years ago are represented - in the Acropolis Museum - by plaster replicas.

But there are still original sculptures in the Acropolis Museum. And if stone can be said to feel - if the lifelike statues of the Greeks can convey emotion - then I have a sad story for you.

The graceful female figures that served as supports for the Erechtheion, one of the temples on the Acropolis, are called caryatids. The temple was dedicated to the gods Athena and Poseidon, and was considered the most sacred part of the complex. The six caryatids who supported the southern roof of the temple were carved from fine marble over several years, from 421 BCE to 406 BCE.

The caryatids still stand at the entrance to the temple. Each one is dressed in a flowing peplum, the simple, elegant tunic worn by Greek women. They stand easily hipshot, relaxed, effortlessly bearing the weight of the building on their heads.

But these six statues are just copies. Five of the originals now stand in the Acropolis Museum, right there in Athens. A space is left open for the sixth one, in the hopes that someday she will return from England and rejoin her sisters. But the sixth one is still in exile. Legend has it that as she was packed up to make the long, cold journey to the North, people heard the other five statues weeping for their sister as she was taken away.

The British Museum is full of artifacts that seem to have some sort of attachment. Some of them are rather benign; just as at the Field Museum in Chicago, people leave offerings at the statues of Sekhmet, the lion-headed Egyptian goddess of love and romance. Where the Field has only one statue of Sekhmet, who graciously receives offerings of fruit, flowers, even a dish of honey now and then, the British Museum has thirty statues of the goddess, mostly from the temple complex at Karnak.

The statues of Sekhmet are just a tiny part of the museum's

Egyptian holdings. If some people think that the statues are imbued with some sort of other-worldly power, that belief pales in comparison to the mystique of the Egyptian mummies.

In *Gone On Vacation*, I wrote about the coffin lid of the priestess of Amun, an artifact that had a decades-long reputation for being cursed. Ever since the "Unlucky Mummy" was donated to the museum in July 1889, it has been blamed for causing all kinds of disasters, injury, and death. (Spoiler alert: most of that tale was made up out of whole cloth. The mummy did not go down with the *Titanic*. In fact, the "Unlucky Mummy" wasn't even a body. It was just the lid of a coffin. The artifact was not responsible for most of the supernatural shenanigans attributed to it.)

But there are plenty of other mummies at the museum, and they do give people the clownies. At one time, a rumor made the rounds of the museum's janitorial staff - they swore that as they cleaned and dusted the glass cases, they could see the mummies moving. Museum officials soon came up with an explanation.

Long-time Collections Manager Jim Peters says, "The fact that the cleaners said they'd seen their wrappings rippling ... the museum said, 'Oh that was just the cleaners over-cleaning the cases! They'd caused a build up of static 'cause the cases hadn't been opened for a while, so it built up the static charge in the air, and it meant things seemed to be moving, but they weren't really.' Everyone just went, 'Ahh thanks for explaining that, we can go back to work now ...' But you know, you'd have to be quite close, and they'd have to be quite light fabrics ... I never really bought that, but that was the resolution." (I have to agree. Mummy wrappings are usually linen strips, bound tightly around the body, and hardened with oils and unguents that have had centuries to set. Rippling from static electricity? No way. Just no way. I'm not buying that for a second.)

Another museum employee, Phil Heary, worked there for 29 years, and reported something strange in the Ancient Egypt gallery. At the time, 19 mummies were on display there. He reported that he once felt the temperature fall dramatically in the hall for no reason at all.

"It was like walking into a freezer," he said. "My stomach turned over. The feel of the gallery was - you wanted to get out."

It's not only the Egyptian artifacts that seem to be the source of paranormal energy. There are a pair of massive human-headed winged bulls flanking the entrance to the Assyrian gallery. Wandering cold spots have been reported here, too.

In the Queen Elizabeth II Great Court, a couple of weird things happened at 3 am one night. The overnight security team heard a fire alarm blaring from the handicapped restroom. They went to check it out but didn't find anything out of place. But as they were walking on a staircase in the Great Court, security guards watching their camera feeds radioed to the team, telling them they could see large balls of white light glowing around them. The guards on the staircase saw nothing. A theory was proposed about this particular incident. An exhibit that ran from October 2014 to January 2015 included a white wrought-iron gate from Buchenwald concentration camp. Could the presence of the eerie glowing orbs be connected to that grim relic?

One of the most alarming reports of paranormal activity at the British Museum comes from the Sutton Hoo gallery. The Sutton Hoo treasures came from an Anglo-Saxon ship burial that was discovered in Suffolk in 1939. This discovery formed the bedrock of modern knowledge of that period in English history and turned out to be the most spectacular treasure hoard ever unearthed in the United Kingdom. And even the discovery of the burial mound had a ghostly element to it.

The Suffolk estate of Edith Pretty was the site of eighteen Anglo-Saxon burial mounds. The existence of these mounds was hardly a secret; in fact, they'd been dug up and looted so much over the centuries that by the 1930s, everyone just assumed that any treasure that had been buried there had to be long gone. But Edith wasn't dissuaded. She came by her interest in archaeology honestly. She'd been to Egypt and had watched excavations in the Nile Valley. And her father, Robert Dempster, an archaeologist himself, had unearthed a Cistercian abbey on the grounds of Edith's childhood home.

Edith was convinced that there was still treasure to be found under the green English grass. Why? Well, it depends on which story you believe. Because there are several.

The first is that a friend of Edith's, Dorothy Cox, would see the ghosts of Anglo-Saxon warriors marching around one of the burial mounds. She saw the soldiers every time she came to visit, and she was certain that the mound held treasure, which the ghosts were still guarding. Another story involves a different friend of Edith's, a medium by the name of William Parish. This tale says that Parish held a séance in which a phantom warrior, dressed in black and riding a black horse, appeared holding a drawn sword and told Edith to dig at the mounds.

The third story - and keep in mind that we really don't know which if any of these are the truth - says that Edith herself had a dream about a rider on a large white horse. In this dream, she watched the helmeted rider being buried and saw the flash of gold as the treasure was laid to rest with him. The dream made such an impression on her that she shared it with a local historian, Vincent Redstone. Redstone introduced her to Basil Brown, a fellow archaeologist.

Edith invited Basil to excavate three of the mounds, and he began work on the site in June 1938. One of the mounds revealed a ship burial over the course of one excavating season. The next spring, the workers dug into the largest of the mounds and found iron rivets from the hull of a ship that was 27 meters long. Basil realized he needed more help, and called in expert archaeologist Peggy Piggott. She cut her vacation short to pitch in, and soon arrived at the dig with her husband, Stuart. It was Peggy who was the first to discover treasure at the dig site - a tiny gold trinket inlaid with red garnets that glinted up at her from the soil.

The mound soon gave up its secrets. The archaeologists found 263 artifacts, including weapons, coins, gold buckles, and silver cutlery. The prize of the entire hoard was a distinctive full-face helmet, with the features of the face picked out in gold and silver, the only one of its kind ever found in England. It's believed that the treasure is the burial of Raedwald, a ruler of the East Angles who died in 624. The first night after it was unearthed, Edith slept with it under her bed, to keep it secure. She later donated the entire collection to the British Museum. The Sutton Hoo treasure was so significant that during World War II, there was talk of hiding it in the London Underground to keep it safe from German bombing raids.

The ghosts who led Edith Pretty to excavate the burial mounds are not the only spirits connected to the treasure. Security guards assigned to the gallery often encounter unexplained noises or see flashes of movement out of the corner of the eye. Sometimes it's not even that much, just a creepy feeling in the pit of the stomach.

The heavy doors that lead to the gallery often open on their own. Some people try to blame it on a passing gust of wind ... inside a museum? But one museum docent had a pretty serious run-in with whatever likes to play with those doors.

The doors between Galleries 41 and 42 were notoriously old and warped, and really hard to shut anyway. The two docents doing their rounds were able to get one door shut, but the second door wouldn't quite meet the other. One of the docents slammed the door, and kept on slamming it, trying to get it to seat properly. Suddenly, the door that had been closed was flung back open. Then things got physical. He felt something push against his chest, and then he got knocked right off his feet. He tumbled backwards and landed on his backside. Then the doors slammed shut with a loud crash.

Interestingly, Patsy Sorenti, a historian of the Anglo-Saxon period who also happens to be a medium, has a fascinating theory as to why these disturbances center on Gallery 42, where the Sutton Hoo treasure is displayed. The Medieval Christian Relics collection, right next door, was recently converted into the Islamic gallery. And that caused some serious upset in the supernatural realm.

"Whoever was linked to those objects, maybe more than one person, [is terribly upset] because you swapped Christianity for Islam, and in the Medieval world, in those times, that was the devil … That's why [he] was thrown. That's what it is - you've replaced Christianity, you have replaced it with something that's a devil to us. You displaced us for that."

This tracks with the research done by Noah Angell, author of *Ghosts of the British Museum: A True Story of Colonial Loot and Restless Objects*. He started researching hauntings at the museum in 2016, and has collected hundreds of stories, mostly from security guards who walk the museum's halls after it closes to visitors. In an article about his book in *The Economist*, Angell said, "Most of the people that I've gathered these stories from … don't self-identify as believing in ghosts. For the most part, these visitor-services and security people are working-class blokes and they don't make a fuss unless something really serious is going on."

All of Angell's witnesses though, do seem to agree that objects hold energy. This is a "sort of folk belief of the museum worker," he says. He is the first to admit the possibility that the objects themselves may be uneasy in their current settings, especially when artifacts that were once used in ritual and ceremonial settings are no longer used, and simply sit idle and forgotten on museum shelves, with no purpose any more except to look pretty.

That would certainly help to explain the disturbances in the former Medieval Christian Relics gallery. To artifacts imbued with the all-consuming sense of the sacred of the average medieval Christian, being shunted aside in favor of Islamic culture has got to be a shock to the system, as well as a horrific insult. And the poor Egyptian mummies; instead of resting comfortably in their tombs, with funerary priests burning incense and making offerings in their memory, they are out on display in glass cases for everyone to stare at.

Maybe these artifacts do hold some sort of sense memory. Maybe the objects, steeped in history, have held on to the thoughts and emotions of the people who once used them.

Or maybe, the spirits of those people still linger, drawn to the halls of the British Museum by the relics of their lives long past.

A PALACE FIT FOR
AN EMPEROR
(The Forbidden City, Beijing, China)

Every culture has its own unique way of relating to the supernatural. American culture is fascinated with the concept of ghosts, and every region of the United States has its own flavor of spooks. Europeans have an easy familiarity with the paranormal - after all, so many castles in the United Kingdom and in continental Europe are home to spirits.

The Chinese take their ghosts very seriously. I mean, *real* seriously. According to Chinese tradition, ghosts are to be avoided at all costs. Confucius, that master of Oriental wisdom, said, "Respect the ghosts and gods, but keep away from them." Wise

advice for a people steeped in thousands of years of history and superstition.

On many a doorstep in China, you'll find two statues flanking the doorway. These are the famous guardian lions, originating in Chinese Buddhism. They'll always be depicted as a pair, the visual representation of yin and yang. The male lion has his right paw on a ball, representing the energy of the material world, while the female lion rests her left paw gently on a tiny cub, denoting the world of nature. The symbolism is powerful: the male lion guards the building and the material objects inside it, while the female protects the living beings inside the home.

The guardians were there not only for protection, but also to prevent any evil spirits from entering the home. Traditionally, the guardian statues were cast from bronze or iron or carved out of decorative stone such as marble or granite. In other words, they were expensive, both in the cost of the material used to make them, and the skilled labor that went into producing these works of art. As such, guardian lions were, for centuries, reserved for the wealthy and the elite. So of course, the doorsteps of buildings in the Forbidden City in Beijing are guarded by these exquisite sculptures.

The architects of the Forbidden City also had another trick up their sleeves. All the doorways of the buildings have high thresholds - visitors must pick up their feet to step over them. This seems like kind of a pain, until a tour guide explains ... ghosts can't jump. So, a human can easily exit a room, but a ghost would be trapped inside.

The Forbidden City is one of the most popular tourist sites in the world. Between 16 and 19 million people visit each year. Entry is limited to 40,000 visitors per day. (So, I guess, if you're visitor number 40,001, it really *is* the Forbidden City. Sorry, I couldn't resist.)

There's a good reason for the place's popularity. It's a World Heritage site, home to the largest and best-preserved collection of ancient wooden structures in the world, over 900 of them. The Palace Museum holds over one million priceless Chinese artifacts and works of art.

But there is a much darker side to this famous city within a city. Built between 1406 and 1420 by the Ming dynasty Emperor Yongle, the Forbidden City was home to twenty-four emperors, whose rule stretched over two dynasties. For nearly six centuries, the royal families lived in these buildings, attended by a city's worth of servants, guards, administrators, eunuchs, and concubines. The Qing dynasty was overthrown in 1911, and the last emperor, Puyi, was booted out of the Inner Court of the palace complex in 1924. The palace was opened to the public the very next year.

It was Emperor Yongle, who ordered this magnificent palace to be built, who is responsible for the paranormal activity here, activity so extreme that visitors are not allowed to stay in the city after nightfall. In 1421, Yongle succumbed to a fit of paranoia, and ordered his soldiers to kill thousands of palace residents because he thought they could reveal his secrets. Most of the victims were his concubines.

Yongle wasn't the only cruel, capricious emperor to abuse his power. One of the eeriest spots in the Forbidden City is the Hall of Supreme Harmony. In direct opposition to its peaceful name, this is where numerous executions were carried out. The palace was a hotbed of intrigue and betrayal, and many courtiers got caught up in the complex politics of the imperial court. Again, by virtue of their proximity to the emperor - and his secrets - many of these victims were concubines. Visitors to the Hall of Supreme Harmony report sudden drops in temperature, seeing shadowy figures dart through the massive hall, and have even witnessed apparitions of what appear to be silken scarves drifting in midair. Many of the young female victims were dispatched by being strangled with scarves of white silk. (Classy, I know.) Other unfortunate victims were beheaded, and their headless ghosts still drift, desolate, in the Hall of Supreme Harmony.

Most of the reports of paranormal activity here are vague - a feeling of being watched, doors that open and close by themselves, shadowy figures seen out of the corner of the eye. But a museum guard was part of a spectral encounter in 1995. He was watching TV in the security office one night when two other guards burst into the room. The two had been patrolling the grounds when they'd seen a woman, dressed all in black, walking away from them. They called out to her, but she simply ignored them. Then she started to run. The guards easily caught up to her, cornering her at a locked door, thinking they'd soon apprehend the trespasser. As they skidded to a stop behind her, yelling for her to turn around, she turned - and the guards were horrified to see that she had no face.

The men dropped their flashlights and pounded back to the security office. All three of the men grabbed firearms and returned to the scene. They found the flashlights on the floor, still on. But the woman was gone.

Chinese ghosts hold a unique place in supernatural folklore. Many of them, just like European ghosts, are earthbound because they are seeking revenge or absolution, or are tied to this plane due to unfinished business. But Chinese ghosts also have a special purpose: they are believed to have a connection to the imperial family. They're seen as acting as guardians or protectors of the dynasty.

If that is indeed the case, the spirits that haunt the Forbidden City are about a century too late.

"GHOST HILL"
(Penang War Museum, Bukit Batu Maung, Malaysia)

Here's a question for you to ponder. If you're running a war museum attraction, and National Geographic does a documentary on it, and calls it one of the most haunted places in Asia, do you lean into it?

Even if it might not be true?

The Penang War Museum was featured on the National Geographic show *I Wouldn't Go In There*. (And just as an aside, how cool a name is that for a TV show?) It has gained the reputation of being one of Asia's most haunted locations. Curious explorers, fans of dark tourism, adventurers of all stripes, and of course paranormal investigators, all make the trek to Buki Hantu ... or in English, Ghost Hill.

Remember how we talked a couple chapters ago about the sun never setting on the British Empire? Thousands of miles away from England, on the other side of the world, in fact, lay "British Malaysia", an area on the Malay Peninsula controlled by the Crown. This region included some of the most important and profitable territories in the Empire. The British only held the area from 1909 to 1946, but that was a crucial time in Malaysian history.

In the 1930s, the British built a fort on Bukit Batu Maung (or "Batu Maung Hill".) The fort was intended to protect British shipping routes around the Malay Peninsula, and to provide a

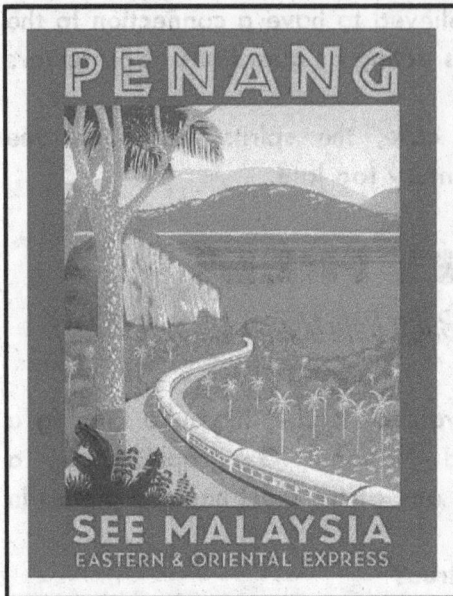
PENANG

SEE MALAYSIA
EASTERN & ORIENTAL EXPRESS

defense for the Royal Air Force base at Butterworth, just across the Penang Channel. However, the British only held the fort for five years.

The Japanese began their invasion of Malaya on December 8, 1941. The British made a valiant effort to hold the crucial fort, but they had a huge strike against them.

The fort had been designed to repel attacks from the sea. After all, that was one of its intended functions, to protect the shipping interests of the Empire. Two six-inch batteries faced out towards the channel ... but the fort's anti-aircraft defenses weren't yet finished. When the Imperial Japanese Army launched an airborne attack on Penang Island, targeting the fort, the British were caught unprepared. By December 15, just a week after the invasion had begun, most of the British and Commonwealth troops that made up the garrison were evacuated. The fort was left to the Japanese.

The Japanese occupation of Penang Island lasted from December 17, 1941, to September 1945, when they finally surrendered. Some historians believe that the Japanese moved into the fort and used it to defend their own shipping routes, just as the previous tenants had done. The British had destroyed the two six-inch guns before their retreat, so the Japanese couldn't use them, but other than that, it seemed to be business as usual at the fort, with a change in administration, of course.

But there are others who speak of a much darker past.

There are some who say that when the Japanese took over Penang Fort, they turned it into a POW camp. Cruelty reigned here, with ceremonial beheadings a daily occurrence. The camp was ruled with an iron fist by a sadistic executioner, Tadashi Suzuki. Prisoners lived in fear of this tyrant, who oversaw the torture with appalling glee. According to the whispered stories, Suzuki carried out the beheadings using a samurai sword. After each execution, they said, he would wash his sword in a bottle of whiskey. It was even rumored that he drank the whiskey afterwards.

After the Japanese emperor surrendered in 1945, Penang Fort was abandoned. The jungle soon encroached on the compound, nature reclaiming what humans had built. Thick green vines curled over the concrete, and the humid air began to erode the rusting anti-aircraft gun batteries. The locals kept well away from the decaying ruins, and the tales of horror grew with each passing year. Soon, Bukit Batu Maung became Bukit Hantu - "Ghost Hill."

In 2002, the Penang War Museum opened to the public. Knowing full well the grisly reputation of the place, the museum has really embraced the fear factor. Bat-filled tunnels await those daring enough to explore underground. Nature abounds in the jungle surrounding the fort. Signs warn "Beware of Wild Animal (snakes, centipedes, scorpions, bats, wildcats, eagle, etc.)." (The "etc." is particularly unsettling.) Skeletons dance in wall paintings, and a sign that simply says "Guillotine" hangs from a tree, spattered with faded red drops that look an awful lot like blood. And eerie sculptures fashioned from wood, wire, and dirty rags haunt the jungle around the fort. These are, a sign explains, "Giant Effigies." The sign goes on to say that the figures represent apparitions witnessed by the workers who helped restore the fort, turning it into the war museum.

Whether or not these figures, and the menacing ghost of

Tadashi Suzuki, were actually seen is a matter of pure conjecture. After all, the museum is well-known as a dark tourism destination, and they do play up the macabre at the expense of real history. (I mean, a sign at the entrance points visitors towards the War Museum Paintball Park, so how serious can it actually be?) But museum guards and paranormal investigators alike have had plenty of experiences there. A security guard on the overnight shift once saw a full-bodied apparition of a soldier who held a rifle with a bayonet in one hand - and in the other hand it brandished a samurai sword, the fearsome Suzuki's weapon of choice. And a ghost hunter who visited the museum claims he had a short conversation with a spirit. The investigator asked if the ghost wanted him to do anything.

"To die," came the chilling reply.

A GRAY LADY, A MASS GRAVE, AND A TOILET GHOST

(Simon's Town, Cape Town, South Africa)

Simon's Town is a naval base for the South African Navy. It's tucked into the shelter of False Bay, on the eastern side of the very bottom of the continent. It's pretty much a suburb of Cape Town, South Africa.

And the whole town is a playground for ghosts.

To start with, there was a spot of trouble in 2019 at a construction site. Officials wanted to build apartments to house Navy officers, but since the place they planned to build was a historically protected area, archaeologists were called in to do a survey of the site.

And they found a mass grave.

Construction on the housing project was immediately halted, and the shallow grave was investigated. If the bodies turned out to be indigenous people, the higher-ups knew the site would be locked down, and the project would be killed. After some study, though, the archaeologists had more information.

In the 1780s, an expedition consisting of ten ships was making its way around the cape. The problem was that nearly half of the sailors aboard this flotilla were sick with one disease or another. The ships docked at Simon's Town in search of help for the ill sailors. A hospital had been built there by the Dutch East India Company about twenty years before. The hospital could accommodate about 250 patients, but the facility was overrun by the sudden influx of men, some of whom were quite desperately sick. Many of the sailors died without getting the help they needed. About 90 men were buried in a common grave, to rest there until being dug up in 2019. Once their provenance was established, they were given reburial, and construction on the apartment block continued.

Surprisingly, this interruption of the sailors' eternal rest doesn't seem to have contributed to the hauntings in Simon's Town. No matter - there are still plenty of spooks to go around. The Palace Barracks is the stomping grounds of an old sea captain

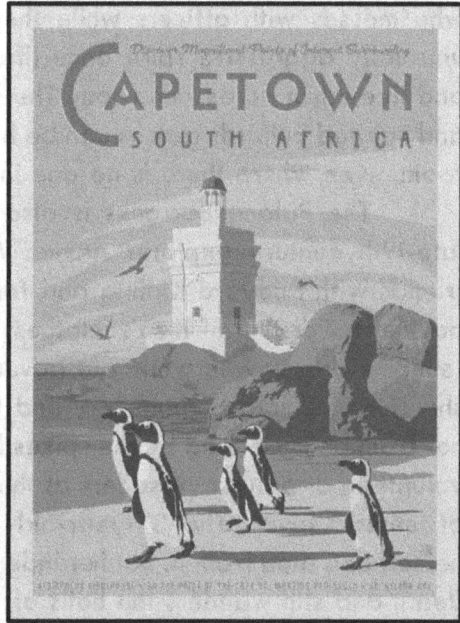

who messes with officers while they're trying to sleep. Another unusually aggressive spirit once lifted an officer out of his chair and threw him across the room. The sounds of drinking, carousing, and spirited billiards games can be heard coming from the billiards room, even where there is no one in there.

The Palace Barracks is also the home of the ghost of a late-19th century explorer named Mary Kingsley. Kingsley was friends with Rudyard Kipling and famously ignored well-meaning advice to dress in men's clothes. This insistence on wearing feminine dress, even while out adventuring, served her well when she stumbled into a game pit, and the fabric of her skirts saved her from being injured by the spikes lining the pit. In 1900, Kingsley volunteered to nurse prisoners at the Barracks during an outbreak of enteric fever. The 37-year-old Kingsley caught the disease herself and died from it. But her independent spirit refuses to admit death and still wanders the halls of the barracks.

The Ibeka building was built in 1816 by P.J. Truter Jr, who was a customs collector. He owned it until 1842. In 1840, the government leased the building from Truter and used it as a temporary isolation hospital for smallpox patients. Ghosts here include a nurse who may have hanged herself in a stairwell ... and an old man who sits on a toilet. And no, I'm not making this up.

The Admiralty House, built in 1740, was the first permanent structure in Simon's Town. The Admiralty House, Ibeka, and another building, the Residency, are all said to be linked by tunnels. This may be why all of them are haunted by the same ghost, of a woman with brown hair.

This spirit is known by several names, so you can take your pick. She appears in a gray dress, so she is sometimes called the Gray Lady. But! She is also known as the Lilac Lady or the Lavender Lady. That tickles me - to think that this particular Gray Lady comes in a variety of other pleasant colors.

The Residency is really the focus of this story, and I'll tell you why very shortly. It was originally built in 1771 for the use of governors of the Dutch East India Company. But when Britain's Royal Navy occupied Simon's Town in 1814, the Residency became the headquarters of the town's magistrates and remained so until 1980.

The Residency was a deeply unpleasant place for most of that time. It was basically the town jail, its hallways lined with cells where prisoners were kept, sometimes in chains. Interesting fact - some of the doors in the building are repurposed cabin doors from old sailing ships. Is that why some of them bang shut on their own sometimes, because they still remember the shifting waves underneath them, or the violence of a storm at sea?

Or is there a more sinister explanation behind the hauntings in this place? Visitors claim that freezing winds sometimes blast through the rooms, and people have seen the shadowy forms of prisoners long dead skulking around the cells. One of these unfortunate souls is believed to be a sailor who was flogged to death. The use of the cat o'nine tails was illegal during the British occupation, but that doesn't mean it didn't happen. Another sour-faced ghost haunts these halls, said to be the spirit of a guard's wife who abused her position of authority and mistreated the prisoners in her care. You might ask, why are so many people wandering through this particular building?

Because the Residency became the Simon's Town Museum in 1982, that's why. And museum workers have had many experiences with the ghosts of the place - and those experiences began well before the building's conversion into a museum.

In the Bar Room at the Simon's Town Museum, there hangs a portrait of a lovely young woman. No one knows exactly who she is, but it's suggested that her ghost is one of the friendlier spirits of the building. She was often seen by the wives of the magistrates who lived and worked here between 1814 and 1980.

She picked up the nickname "the Gray Lady" because she was often seen wearing a gray dress. One magistrate, Duncan Neethling, saw the Gray Lady following his wife around the kitchen. She has been seen both inside and outside the building. This spirit is usually quiet and agreeable, but she does have her moments of pique. Once, she surprised a museum staff member by slamming a door on his fingers.

Who, exactly, the Gray (or Lilac or Lavender) Lady is remains a mystery to this day, and we may never know for sure. There are several candidates, though. Of course, there is the "servant girl who worked at the Residency in the 1700s" theory. What is much more interesting is that there are a couple of historical possibilities for the identity of the Gray Lady.

The spirit may be the ghost of a teenage girl who once lived at the Residency. This could be Eleanor Macartney, the daughter of the first British governor of Simon's Town.

Or it could be one of the daughters of Gideon Rousseau. As mentioned earlier, the Residency was built in 1771 for the governors of the Dutch East India Company. But in 1776, the building was sold to Rousseau, a wealthy entrepreneur and the father of twelve children. It's said that one of his daughters fell in love with a sailor, quite possibly the British Admiral Horatio Nelson. Rousseau, as a wealthy businessman, would have been delighted to host such a luminary in his home. But when Nelson had to leave, heeding the call of duty and of the sea, the distraught young woman drowned herself rather than live without his love.

There is one more resident of Simon's Town who deserves a mention ... but this one wasn't human.

We don't know the exact date of his birth, but it's usually given as April 1, 1937. He didn't really care when his birthday was, as even he didn't know for sure. He just happily accepted that April Fool's Day was his birthday. Somehow, it suited him. He moved to Simon's Town with a guy named Benjamin Chaney, who took care of him. He started hanging around the sailors at the naval base and dockyards and quickly picked up a nickname.

Nuisance.

He was a big boy, over six and a half feet tall when he was standing up, and his favorite place to rest was at the top of the gangplank of whatever ship was currently moored at the wharf. The other sailors got tired of stepping over him and affectionately started calling him Nuisance.

He did get into trouble at one point, because he liked to follow the sailors around. He would take day trips by train as far as Cape Town, 22 miles away. But he would never pay his train fare. Even though the sailors tried to cover for him and hide him, the conductors caught him every time. They would kick him off the train, but he would simply wait for the next one or walk to the nearest station and get on the next train that came along.

Other passengers thought this was hilarious, and some of them would even offer to buy his ticket. But the officials of the South African Railways & Harbours company were not amused. They warned Chaney, Nuisance's good friend, that if he didn't stop riding the train for free, Nuisance would have to be executed.

This caused an absolute uproar among both the locals and the sailors of Simon's Town. They wrote to the Navy, pleading for something to be done. Someone offered to buy Nuisance a season pass for the train, but naval command had a better solution. Again, this was highly unusual, but they figured this was a good way to save Nuisance. They enlisted him in the Navy. As a member of the armed forces, he was entitled to free rail travel, so he would no longer get in trouble for fare-dodging. Instead, he would serve his country. And what would his job be, as a member of the Royal Navy? Would he be a gunner, or a ship's cook, or even a lowly cabin boy?

Nope.

His only job was to be a morale booster for the troops serving in World War II. He was very well-suited to the task. All the sailors in the port already loved him.

After all, who wouldn't love a goofy, adorable, big friendly dog?

Yes, Nuisance was a Great Dane.

He was enlisted on August 25, 1939. His last name was written down in the intake notebook as "Nuisance", and rather than leaving the space for his first name blank, some wit wrote in "Just." His civilian trade was listed as "Bonecrusher." The newly minted sailor Just Nuisance was quickly promoted from Ordinary Seaman to Able Seaman, so that he could draw rations.

Just Nuisance continued to ride with sailors on train trips, and would go with them on leave, escorting them back to base when the pubs closed. One of his promotional appearances was at his "wedding" to another Great Dane, Adinda. Adinda later had a litter of five pups. Two of the pups, named Victor and Wilhelmina, were auctioned off to raise money for the war effort.

Nuisance's war record was … not exemplary. He would regularly forget his free pass but ride the train anyway. He would lose his collar, fight with other mascots, and refuse to leave the pub at closing time. Once, he was sentenced to seven days with no access to bones because he was caught sleeping in an improper place - the bed of one of the petty officers.

Sadly, Nuisance was involved in a car accident, which caused a blood clot. The presence of the clot eventually paralyzed him, so on January 1, 1944, he was discharged from the Navy. His condition continued to deteriorate, and he was taken to Simon's Town Naval Hospital. There, on April 1, 1944, his seventh birthday, the veterinarian put him to sleep.

Just Nuisance's body was draped with a flag of the Royal Navy, and he was buried with full military honors, including a gun salute. His grave, at Klawer Camp, is marked with a granite headstone, and a statue of him stands in Jubilee Square in Simon's Town. His life and military service are commemorated with an exhibit at the Simon's Town Museum.

No one has ever mentioned seeing the ghost of Just Nuisance, either in the town square or at the museum. So he is probably resting in peace.

It is fun, though, to imagine a spectral Great Dane still lounging on the decks of ships in False Bay, just being a nuisance.

THE PRISON THAT MADE A NAME FOR ITSELF ... AND ALL THE OTHERS
(The Clink, London, England)

Jail. The slammer. The big house. The pen. The joint. Lockup. Corrections.

The Clink.

There are loads of slang terms for prison, and one of them happens to have deep roots in history. English history, to be precise. Let's hop in the WABAC machine and investigate this.

Winchester Palace was built in 1144 in the London neighborhood of Southwark, on the banks of the Thames. Henry of Blois was the Bishop of Winchester, second in power only to the king. As such, he was responsible for keeping law and order in the area. Henry had two prisons built on the grounds of the palace, one for men, and one for women.

It was distressingly easy to get yourself thrown into prison in those days. Thieves, pickpockets, con men, prostitutes, and

The Clink Prison
London Bridge
1144 - 1780

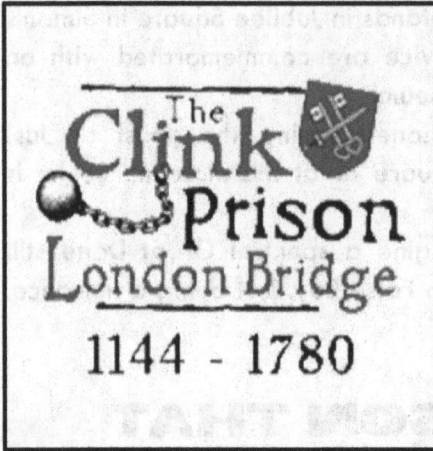

madams all found themselves locked in filthy cells in the squalid half-light. Others who had the misfortune of finding themselves on the wrong side of the bars included debtors and religious dissenters. The Puritans, of Mayflower fame, spent time here, imprisoned for their Separatist beliefs.

This particular jail was said to be one of the most brutal prisons of the Middle Ages. It got its nickname sometime in the 14th century, and no one is really sure how. It may have been that someone really focused on the sound of a blacksmith's hammer fastening a lock closed on a set of leg irons. Or the sound of a bolt being thrown, sealing a prisoner to their fate. It's been pointed out that the Flemish word for "latch" (as in the latch on a jail cell door) is "klink", although I'm not sure what the Flemish had to do with a London lockup. However it happened, this prison eventually became known as the Clink.

And it was freaking *awful*.

It was dark and dreary, and smelled horrible. There were no bathroom facilities, and prisoners were locked in their cells. Obviously, they weren't let out to use the privy or outhouse, so they just ... they just ... okay, they went in the corner of their cells. Like a kitty litter box without the litter. This lack of sanitation meant that the Clink was crawling with diseases like dysentery, cholera, typhoid fever, and malaria.

To add insult to injury, prisoners paid for the privilege of being incarcerated. When admitted to the Clink, a prisoner had to pay rent to use their cell. And they paid to rent their bed. And paid more to rent the bedding to go on the bed. Of course, they paid for food and fuel to keep warm, and for water (which wasn't clean, pure drinking water - far from it). Those who couldn't pay for all these basic human needs had to beg through the bars of their cell, and hope that passers-by would take pity on them. Some prisoners even sold their clothes to get the money to pay for food. And if you didn't have any money at all, tough toenails. There was zero sympathy to be had within the walls of the Clink. One judge wrote in 1550, "The prisoner should live on his own goods, and if he had no goods he should live on the charity of others, and if others will give him nothing then let him die in the name of God." Harsh.

Cruelest of all, they had to pay to have a blacksmith put irons on them ... *and* pay to have them taken off when their sentence was up. (That is, if they survived their stay in prison. Lots of folks didn't.) Then, before they could walk out the door as a free man or woman, they had to settle their bill with the jailer ...

Yeah, a stay in the Clink was pretty miserable. And I haven't even mentioned the torture yet. Prisoners were beaten, starved, stabbed to death, drawn and quartered, and subjected to many other excruciating forms of agony.

It's no wonder, then, that the Clink is a hotbed of paranormal activity. The Clink Prison Museum is located pretty much on the same site as the original prison - as a matter of fact, one of the exhibits at the museum is a chunk of the original wall. The prison has been burned down by rioters several times during its 600-year history. It fell into disrepair before being burned down one final time in 1780. It wasn't rebuilt after that, but the museum now stands on the site where so much misery was endured by so many desperate people.

Appropriate for such a dark theme, the Clink Prison Museum is housed in a building of black-painted brick. A skeleton hangs grinning in a gibbet at the door. There are no jump scares here by costumed actors; it's hardly necessary, given the awful history of the place.

Many paranormal groups have investigated the museum, and they've had many strange experiences there. A shadowy figure has been seen pacing around an exhibit called the Bishop's Room. Mannequins can be found in many of the displays, stand-ins for the real human beings who suffered and died in the prison over the centuries. But visitors have taken photographs that have shown figures that are most definitely *not* the mannequins. Ghost hunters have seen the apparition of a woman trying in vain to remove the shackles that still chafe her ankles in the afterlife. Poltergeist activity is common during ghost hunts at the Clink, including cell doors slamming closed. Could this be an effort by the spirits to give visitors a tiny taste of the desolate horrors they endured?

GIVING STREET URCHINS A CHANCE
(Ragged School Museum, London, England)

Just a few short miles from the Clink Prison Museum is another place well worth a visit, both for its paranormal activity and for its history.

In 1866, Thomas John Barnardo left his native Dublin and traveled to London. He intended to train as a doctor, then go on to China to serve as a missionary. That's not at all the way things turned out for him, though.

As Barnardo began his education as a physician, he was struck - hard - by the abject poverty he saw all around him in the East End of London. Victorian London was a wretched time and place to be poor. Overcrowded living conditions led to squalor, and disease was rampant. Bernardo was appalled and heartbroken by the sight of poverty-stricken children begging in the streets. He quickly realized that the poorest citizens of London had no opportunities to make a better life for themselves. The filthy streets were breeding grounds for disease. Shortly after Barnardo's arrival, a cholera epidemic swept through the East End, killing 3,000 people in a matter of weeks.

Thomas Barnardo soon decided that his life would be much better spent ministering to the needs of English children, rather than folks on the other side of the world in China. He gave up his medical studies, and threw himself into service to London's poorest, most vulnerable citizens: the children. He rented several warehouses near the Thames, and set up "ragged" schools, or free schools. He started the first one in 1867, just a year after his arrival, providing free education, food, and even lodging to many children.

Barnardo converted more warehouses into school buildings, and in 1871, the Copperfield Road Free School opened. This was the largest ragged school in London, and for the next 31 years, it educated tens of thousands of children. It closed in 1908; by that time, enough government-funded schools had opened to serve the area. The buildings of the Copperfield Road Free School went back to being used as warehouses.

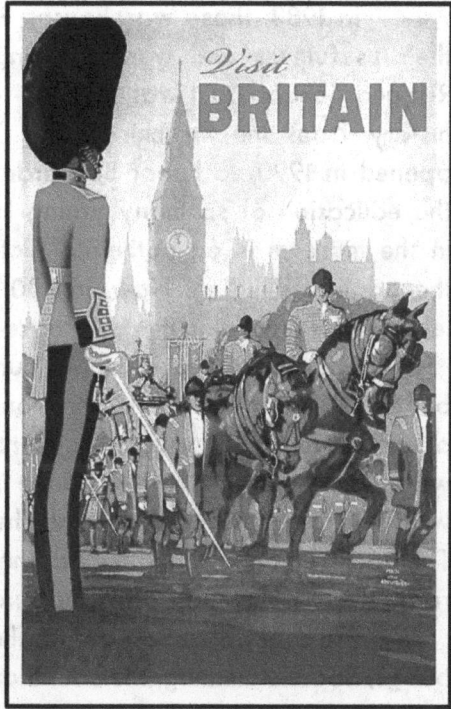

In 1983, those warehouses were assumed to have outlived their usefulness and were in danger of being demolished. The Ragged School Trust was formed, to save this wonderful piece of history from the wrecking ball. The Ragged School Museum opened in 1990, to honor Barnardo's efforts and to acknowledge the education of so many young Londoners. One of the exhibits in the museum is an authentic Victorian-era classroom set up in the original building. Now, 16,000 kids can experience a school lesson every year as it would have been taught 150 years ago.

The Ragged School Museum is one of the most haunted buildings in Britain. We might wonder why; after all, this was a place of learning, where desperately underprivileged children were finally given a better chance in life, a chance to escape their wretched circumstances through the power of a good education. The fact remains, though, that the spirits of many children still roam these halls, long after the final bell has rung.

Paranormal investigators have encountered unexplained bangs, doors slamming, the sound of running footsteps - you know, the sounds you'd expect to find echoing in the corridors of any grade school filled with rambunctious kids. But the screams and children's laughter reverberate in empty rooms. Balls of light have been reported glowing in dark corners of the building. A dark, lonely shadow figure lurks in the basement of the museum, waiting for visitors to stumble into its domain.

The child ghosts at the Ragged School Museum are not at all shy about interacting with visitors. In July 2019, Alison Oborn, founder and owner of the Australian paranormal investigation group Adelaide's Haunted Horizons, took her team on a field trip to the United Kingdom. She'd heard stories of the haunted museum and was fascinated by the paranormal possibilities of the place. Alison had been talking with Beth Darlington of Access Paranormal, who told Alison about a table tipping session at the school that got a little out of hand. Table tipping involves investigators placing their fingertips on the flat surface of a small, lightweight table, and encouraging the spirits to use the investigators' energy to move it. Table tipping originated with Victorian seances, so it stands to reason that using it in a Victorian-era setting would get great results. And it did - Beth told Alison that she'd watched a table "walk" down a hallway, with the ghost hunters trotting alongside it, trying desperately to maintain their fingertip contact with the table's top. Alison was impressed with this report from the highly respected Beth, whom she knew to be level-headed and rational. Alison was eager for her team to experience the museum too.

The Ragged School Museum exceeded Alison's expectations.

Strange things began to happen even as the group was setting up for the night's investigation. The team consisted of Alison, Kag, and Craig. They decided to use the basement as command central. The two women began to set up, as Craig wandered off by himself to do a bit of exploring. He came back a short time later.

"What did you want?" he asked.

Alison and Kag gave him blank stares in return. Why on earth was he asking?

"You called me," he insisted.

The women both shook their heads. Craig's voice lost its certainty as he continued. He'd heard a female voice calling his name and assumed one of the women wanted him to return to command central. He'd cut his exploring short ... only to find that whoever had called his name, it wasn't Kag or Alison.

They began their investigation in the room set up to look like a Victorian kitchen. As they settled in, they heard a few strange noises from the darkness around them, which just increased their excitement. The team did a short EVP session, attempting to capture ghost voices on their recorders. They'd come armed with trigger objects designed to appeal to children: cat balls, which flash colored lights when moved or even touched, were scattered around the kitchen. Alison encouraged the little spirits, asking them to move the cat balls, and promising them chocolate if they did.

The cat ball that had been placed on a bar of chocolate flashed with movement, rolling off the candy bar and prompting a startled "Shit!" from Alison. The team had a short conversation with the spirits in the room by means of a ghost box, a device that spits out words in response to the energy swirling in a room. Alison asked if the kids had enjoyed chocolate back in their day, and got a quick affirmation: "*Yes we did.*" But when a spirit voice came through the ghost box ordering "*Turn it off,*" the team decided to move to another part of the building.

It was time to explore the recreated Victorian schoolroom, and the team had big plans for this part of the evening. It was time for some roleplaying. Kag stood at the podium at the front of the room, armed with a whippy cane. Her role was to act the part of a strict 19th-century schoolmarm, and she leaned into the character with gusto. She introduced herself with half a dozen sharp raps of the cane on the podium.

"Children! My name is Mrs. Albert." She stated firmly that she wanted everyone in the schoolroom to try their hardest, but she made it clear that wrong answers would be punished.

"Those who get the sums wrong" - more smacks with the stick on the long-suffering podium - "you're getting some of the cane." She pointed with the cane at the far corner of the classroom and waggled it a bit. "Including you, over there." There was no one visible in the corner, but she was acknowledging and including any spirits that happened to be in the room.

I've got to break into the story at this point and say that Adelaide's Haunted Horizons has made their investigation of the

Ragged School Museum available on YouTube; you can find it on their website, www.adelaidehauntedhorizons.com.au/haunted/ragged-school-museum-ghost-hunt/

It is a sheer delight to watch this interaction. It's always interesting to watch another team work, to see their methods in action, and examine their techniques. Alison is fascinated by history, and her team respects the places they investigate and the spirits with whom they are trying to communicate. When Kag smacked the podium with the cane, playing the role of aggressive disciplinarian, she wasn't provoking the spirits; she was simply roleplaying, getting into the mindset of another era to communicate with the people who experienced that time.

Kag's questions were designed to move the investigation forward. "First I want to know, how many children have I got in the room with me tonight?"

"Ooh! Ooh!" Craig was behind the camera filming, but you can almost imagine his arm waving in the air, frantically trying to get the teacher's attention. Kag couldn't help but grin at Craig's childlike enthusiasm. She snapped back into character and pointed at him, demanding the answer.

"Three, miss."

"Three," Kag mused. "How d'you get three?"

"Well there's that one over there," Craig replied, indicating Alison, "there's me, and the one behind me." Again, he was bringing any spirits in the room into the conversation. Kag readily played along.

"Oh, the one in the back of the room."

"Yes," Craig said. "She's naughty," he added, with the self-righteous air of a grade-schooler tattling on a classmate.

Kag kept the investigation rolling. "We've got some lights around the room. If there's any children with us, your job is to go around and light all the lights up. You have to go to all of them and touch them."

Immediately the cat ball in front of the podium - again, the only cat ball the team had placed on a bar of chocolate - lit up. "Thank you!" Kag acknowledged, her stern character slipping a bit. Alison noted that the cat balls had been quiet the entire time they'd been in the classroom, until Kag had requested the spirit children touch one of them.

The lesson moved on to math. "You get it wrong," Kag warned, "you get the cane." (Craig cheekily blurted, "Yay!") "Are you ready?"

The ghost box was switched on. Kag upped the ante, saying that the living people would surely get the sums wrong, so if the ghost children didn't help them answer the questions, "They're gonna get the cane," she threatened with menace.

"I need you to try really, really hard to help these stupid pupils," Kag warned, in an effort to get the ghosts to speak through the spirit box.

"Spirit children, help me!" Craig pleaded.

It was time to see what the ghosts had to say. Kag began: "Two plus two equals ...", prompting the spirits to finish the equation.

The spirit box responded with "*Four*".

Trying for more interaction, Kag shifted to an encouraging tone. "Two ... plus two ..."

"*Too hard,*" the spirit box complained.

Kag waved the cane, threatening to beat Craig. The spirit box jumped to life. "*Help me.*" Then the box whimpered "*Ow ow.*" Startled, Alison asked, "Did that just say 'ow ow'?"

"*Please miss!*" came a high, panicked child's voice from the spirit box.

Kag, buoyed by the responses, pushed on. She moved on to English lessons. "What's the next letter of the alphabet?" she pressed. This is another technique that can get results - start off with a pattern, in the hopes that the spirits will respond with an answer.

"A, B, C ..." Kag began. The spirit box was silent.

"Do you guys want me to get caned?" Craig asked. An indistinct "*yeah*" came from the box. Then came an adult male voice, startlingly clear.

"*Authorize the hurt.*"

Alison and her team were thrilled with the interaction they had with the young ghosts at the Ragged School Museum. The Copperfield Road Free School educated tens of thousands of London's most vulnerable population and improved the lives of children who otherwise would have been doomed to lives of poverty, sickness, and desperation. Why are their spirits still reliving those bygone days? Maybe that experience left a lasting impression on their developing minds.

Whatever the reason, it's clear that the classrooms of the Ragged School Museum still echo with the footsteps and chatter of students whose school days ended long ago.

AN ARTIST'S INSPIRATION
(Casa Azul, Mexico City, Mexico)

It's easy to lionize Frida Kahlo. Her art is colorful, vibrant, instantly recognizable. She painted many self-portraits - she admitted that she was her own most familiar subject - and there's no mistaking those dark eyes, tight bun, flowery headdresses, and iconic unibrow. Frida Kahlo the person is just as intriguing as Frida Kahlo the artist.

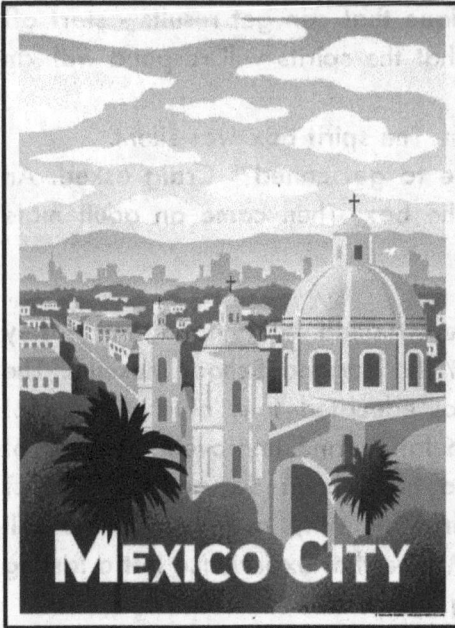
MEXICO CITY

She was born July 6, 1907, in Coyoacan, Mexico City, in a house that her father had built in 1904. She and her sisters were the product of a blended marriage. Her Hungarian-German father, Guillermo Kahlo, emigrated from Germany in 1891. He met and married Matilde Calderon y Gonzalez. Frida's mother was Mexican, but her family background was American Indian and Spanish.

Frida grew up in a house where art was appreciated. Matilde's father had been a photographer, and she talked Guillermo into giving it a go. He turned out to be very good at it, and traveled all around Mexico for about four years, taking pictures of landscapes and historic buildings. Frida would gaze, entranced, at the art her father had made. Through his photographs, she learned about her Mexican heritage, the history, art, and architecture that made up her ancestral culture. She also watched her father as he indulged in his hobby of painting. Young Frida thought she might dabble in painting as well, when she grew up.

Frida's health was not great. When she was six years old, she contracted polio. The nine months she spent bedridden with the serious illness left her right leg damaged. She was finally allowed to go back to school, where the other children saddled her with a cruel nickname: "puta de palo," or "Peg Leg." Frida's quick mind easily helped her catch up with her peers. She was very smart and got good grades. Her favorite subjects were science and math, and she planned to become a doctor.

Her grades were good enough to get her into the Escuela Nacional Prepatoria. She was a vital, vibrant student with plenty of friends. She loved the challenge of her studies, but she wasn't above a little mischief. The artist Diego Rivera came to the high school to paint a mural. Frida took great delight in pestering Rivera, calling him "Old Fatso," stealing his lunch, and putting soap on the stairs to make him slip. These rather mean-spirited antics ended up getting Frida expelled. She sobered up in a hurry and took her case to the minister of public education. She was allowed to return to school.

Every day, Frida would make the trip from Coyoacan to Mexico City to attend classes at the Escuela. On September 17, 1925, she was on her way home, riding the bus with her boyfriend Alejandro. The two had gotten on the bus and made their way to the back to sit together. As the bus slowed down to make a turn, it was hit by a streetcar. The larger vehicle was crushed, passengers killed, metal mangled by the impact. The jolt of the crash threw Alejandro under the streetcar, and Frida was trapped inside the mangled wreckage of the bus.

Frida was eventually freed from the twisted jumble of metal and rushed to the hospital. She had been impaled by a handrail that had speared straight through her pelvis. Her injuries were extensive and horrifying: a broken spinal column, a broken collarbone, several broken ribs, a broken pelvis, and her right leg had been shattered with eleven fractures. Her right foot had been dislocated and crushed, and her shoulder was also dislocated.

The vibrant 18-year-old was suddenly immobilized in a body cast. She spent many months in the hospital, wearily waiting for her broken body to heal. To try to take her mind off her pain, her parents encouraged Frida to return to the hobby she'd enjoyed as a child: painting. Her father set up a special easel above her bed, so she could paint while lying on her back. First, she decorated her white plaster cast with cheerful colors. Then she started painting the first of the self-portraits that would later bring her such fame.

Once again, serious medical issues changed Frida's life. She would undergo multiple surgeries to assuage the damage from the accident, and she would suffer from chronic pain for the rest of her short life. Her right leg would eventually be amputated due to gangrene.

To hide her damaged legs, one already twisted and deformed from her childhood bout with polio, Frida dressed in traditional long Mexican skirts. She took great care in choosing her outfits; she realized that her manner of dress was one of the only ways she could control the image she presented to the world. She embraced the colorful fabrics and indigenous designs of her Mexican heritage.

Her path and Diego Rivera's crossed once more. Frida was no longer the flighty schoolgirl who'd nicked Old Fatso's lunch. The young woman and the older man - he was twenty years her senior - fell in love and eventually married. People saw the difference between the petite Frida and the much taller (and heavier) Diego and laughingly referred to the mismatched couple as "the elephant and the dove."

Their relationship was fraught, to say the least. They both had fiery artistic temperaments. Frida chafed at being known simply as the wife of Diego Rivera, and longed to make her own mark on the world of art. She continued to paint, eventually gaining recognition as an artist in her own right.

They also both had numerous affairs. The passionately political Frida was devoted to the Communist Revolutionary movement, even writing in her diary that it was her true reason to live. (One of the men she messed around with was Leon Trotsky, if that tells you anything.) She even fudged her origins a bit, and began claiming July 7, 1910, as her birthday. She did this not to shave a couple of years off her age, but as a way to honor the date of the Mexican revolution.

Diego's infidelity hurt Frida deeply, even as she indulged in extramarital relationships of her own, with both men and women. She admitted, "I have suffered two serious accidents in my life. One in which a streetcar ran over me ... The other accident is Diego." Frida's 1935 painting "A Few Small Nips (Passionately In Love)", which depicts a woman who has been violently stabbed to death by her lover, was painted after she discovered that Diego had been having an affair with her younger sister Cristina. The couple divorced in 1939 but remarried the next year. The passion they felt for each other overpowered their disappointment and betrayal.

Frida threw herself into life, embracing every aspect of her personality with gusto. In addition to fiddling with her birth date to honor the Mexican revolution, she was truly infatuated with the cultural heritage she'd inherited from her mother's side of the family. She dressed herself in the colorful fabrics of indigenous Mexico, she used those same bright colors in her art, and she kept a menagerie of pets, including many that were sacred to the Mayans and Aztecs. Birds of all kinds, spider monkeys, even the small hairless Xoloitzcuintli dogs (sort of like Chihuahuas) shared Frida's home and reminded her every day of her heritage.

Frida eventually came out from under the giant shadow of her husband, and became Frida Kahlo, not just Mrs. Diego Rivera. A show of her artwork in New York City in October 1938 led to a show in Paris. This recognition boosted her confidence as an artist and as a person, and she sailed to Europe alone in January 1939 to show seventeen paintings at the Louvre. The prestigious museum bought Frida's painting "The Frame" - the first work of art by a 20th century Mexican artist to become part of the Louvre's permanent collection.

Frida's serious health issues finally got the better of her, and she came back to Mexico, back to Casa Azul, her childhood home. She and Diego were now living there, the blue walls that gave the home its name encompassing their art, their hunger for life, their passion for each other. She passed away in her home in 1954, at the age of 47.

A few years later, a grieving Diego set up Casa Azul, still full of Frida's art, as a museum. The Frida Kahlo Museum in Mexico City opened in 1958, and it is still kept as a riotous, colorful celebration of her life. Birds still flit through the courtyard, filling the warm air with song, perching on the flowering bushes that fill the garden. Frida is still there, literally, in the home where she grew up, the home she shared with the love of her life. Her ashes are kept in an urn at the museum.

Her spirit is still very much alive at Casa Azul, too. The spookiest story told about her is this: legend has it that when her body was being cremated, she sat up on the bier, smiling. As her hair caught fire, it appeared to create a corona of flames around her head, looking very much like her signature flowered crown headdress, rendered in tongues of flame.

But honestly, that's as creepy as it gets. The museum is a testament to Frida's "fearless spirit, boundless creativity, and tireless embrace of self-expression" (from the museum's website) - all the things that draw so many people to celebrate her memory. And it seems Frida herself has returned in spirit to her old home, a place where she was so happy in life. Curators who are in the museum after dark have reported that her clothes seem to fill out with her form, as though she is borrowing her corsets and skirts for the evening.

The museum's director, Hilda Trujillo Soto, has every confidence that her patron is still in residence. She told a reporter that she had occasionally heard the sound of labored footsteps coming from Frida's office in the basement when no one was there.

Frida had had difficulty walking ever since her childhood bout with polio, when little "Peg Leg" would struggle to keep up with the other children. The streetcar accident, subsequent surgeries, and eventual amputation of her right leg - the one already damaged by polio - only made her limp worse. She took to wearing voluminous, colorful skirts in part to hide her weakened legs.

Trujillo Soto also mentioned witnessing supernatural phenomena, as well as hearing the limping footsteps. She spoke of seeing footprints appear out of nowhere in the damp soil of the garden, as if Frida was once more wandering among the flowers she loved. The director is quick to point out, though, that none of these ghostly manifestations are the least bit frightening. Trujillo Soto says that "her sense of Frida's presence is benign, playful, and ever welcome."

In September 2025, the Frida Kahlo Museum basically doubled in size. Right next door to Casa Azul is Casa Roja, also named for its vibrant color (this one's red). Frida's parents owned both the Red House and the Blue House. Frida bought Casa Roja from her parents as a home for her sister Cristina and her family. (In case you were wondering, yes, this was the sister that Diego Rivera had the affair with, the death blow to their marriage the first time. But whatever their differences, the sisters loved each other. Cristina was loyal to Frida - she traveled with her big sister to New York City for Frida's first major art exhibition, and she was a source of comfort and moral support through Frida's many surgeries and recoveries. So, Frida showed her sincere appreciation for their sisterly bond.)

The Museo Casa Kahlo, or Casa Roja, explores Frida's early years, and traces her beginnings as an artist. There are many mementos from her childhood: dolls, photographs of Frida as a young girl, clothes, and a piece of embroidery she did when she was five. There are also pieces of Frida's history that hold more weight, such as the only Frida Kahlo mural known to exist.

The museum also has the very first oil painting Frida ever did ... the one she showed to Diego Rivera, asking his opinion if she indeed had the skill to be a painter.

Time will tell if Casa Roja is also haunted by Frida's spirit, just like Casa Azul. But in the meantime, she is content to stay in the home where she grew up. What better afterlife fate for an artist, to wander the grounds and the rooms of her home, the colorful, welcoming Casa Azul?

TEMPLE OF DOOM
(Templo Mayor Museum, Mexico City, Mexico)

December 19, 1487, was a momentous day in Tenochtitlan, the capital of the Aztec empire. It was the first day of the opening ceremony of the dedication of Huei Teocalli, the Great Temple of Tenochtitlan. Flutes tweetled as drums throbbed in a hypnotic, menacing rhythm, setting the spirits of those in the crowd ablaze with savage excitement. Knights of the realm, resplendent in jaguar skins and cloaks made of brightly colored feathers, stood at attention along the route leading to the temple. At the center of the temple complex was a gleaming white step pyramid, with two shrines at the very top.

Those pure white steps would soon run red with blood.

Prisoners of war were taken to the top of the temple. There, they were held down on stone altars, their bare chests arched and exposed. The priests, working with chilling efficiency, would slice a prisoner's chest open with a razor-sharp obsidian blade, reach in and yank the still-beating heart out, and heave the lifeless corpse off the altar and shove it to tumble down the stairs. After the first dozen bodies flopped bonelessly down, the top of the stairs would be smeared with blood. After several hundred sacrifices, the pristine white stone would be awash with a shocking red slick of gore.

It would take four days and the murder of some 4,000 prisoners to dedicate the temple.

Huei Teocalli was the pinnacle of Aztec religious life in the capital city. Tenochtitlan was founded in 1325 by the Mexica tribe, also known as the Tenochla. The city grew quickly and soon established itself as the center of the Aztec empire. Quite literally so - the temple was built on what is thought to be the exact spot where the earliest Aztecs saw their holy eagle perched on a cactus. They figured this to be the center of the universe. So of course they built a temple there.

And they kept on building it. It was rebuilt and expanded six times by the time the conquistador Hernan Cortez saw it in 1519. The basic form and function stayed the same, though: it was a huge, stepped pyramid, with two staircases, built to honor Huitzilopochtli (the god of war) and Tlaloc (the god of rain and fertility). The temple Cortez saw was the seventh incarnation of the Great Temple - known as Huei Teocalli in the Nahuatl language of the Aztecs, the Spaniards referred to it as Templo Mayor. The temple, with its twin shrines, was the centerpiece of a sacred complex that encompassed 78 buildings.

The Aztecs were gleefully savage in their religious

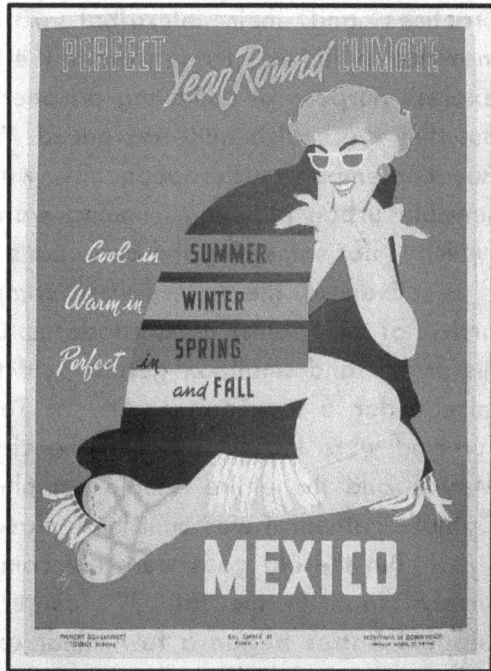

practices and their intertribal warfare (which really were inextricably linked - many wars in the empire were fought for the express purpose of collecting prisoners to sacrifice to the gods). But they were also quite advanced. They had cities larger than any contemporary European city, with sophisticated sanitation, sensible urban planning, running water, and they bathed daily (which is not something the Europeans of the day could claim).

Even so, the Aztecs were completely unprepared for the arrival of the Spanish conquistadores. Cortez and his armies - and his priests and smallpox germs - cut the Aztecs down like field mice under a lawnmower. Any of Tenochtitlan's populace who survived were kicked out, and the city was demolished. Templo Mayor, and the entire temple complex, was torn down, and a Catholic cathedral was built in its place.

But the old gods were not completely extinguished - they simply slept. In the late 19th century, Mexican archaeologist Leopold Batres began a few minor excavations at the site. The exploration continued until World War II. These digs were seen as a huge inconvenience by the residents of the area, since it was now an elegant neighborhood of Mexico City.

In the last part of the 20th century, though, people began to get excited about the possibility of archaeological discovery at the site. In 1978, a massive circular stone sculpture was discovered which depicted the moon goddess Coyolxauhqui. She was shown decapitated and with her limbs hacked off and scattered; according to Aztec legend, she and her 400 brothers were murdered by their brother Huitzilopochtli, the god of war, in his quest to become the supreme god.

This discovery kicked off a new era of archaeology at the site. Scientists were encouraged to excavate the temple grounds. This involved tearing down residential buildings dating back to the Spanish conquest, but at last, the indigenous people's heritage was recognized and respected. (Frida Kahlo would have been thrilled; Casa Azul is only five miles away from Templo Mayor.) So many Aztec artifacts were unearthed that the temple complex was named a UNESCO World Heritage site, and the Templo Mayor Museum was built to house the treasures.

The discoveries here have been extraordinary; archaeologists have excavated palace rooms with baths, the House of the Eagle Warriors, a school for priests, and temple areas dating back to the early 14th century. The museum in which the artifacts are preserved is home to several flavors of supernatural spookiness. Paranormal activity allegedly includes unexplained shadows, eerie cries, and disembodied voices.

Oh yeah, and the cihuateteo are said to roam the temple precinct too.

What are the cihuateteo, you ask? Are they ghosts? Oh no, they're much more terrifying than ghosts.

They're revenants. The undead.

Vampires.

Cihuateteo, in the Nahuatl language of the Aztecs, means Divine Women. They are the souls of women who have died in childbirth. Their souls are transformed, becoming reanimated after death. In Aztec culture, childbirth was seen as a battle, with a woman fighting to bring her child into the world. If a woman lost that battle, she was revered as a hero for her struggle and her sacrifice. Women who died in childbirth were given lavish funeral rites, and their bodies were considered to have special, mystical powers. The corpse had to be guarded until burial, with her husband and other family members protecting the body against looters. And no, these potential ghouls weren't grave robbers in search of jewelry. Nope, these looters were after body parts. Warriors were known to chop off the fingers of a woman who'd died giving birth, seeking to use her supernatural powers. They would attach trophy fingers to their shields, in the belief that the talisman would blind their enemies.

The Aztec calendar had 365 days, just like ours. They divided those days differently, though. Their year had eighteen months of twenty days each, which meant there were five days left over. These extra days really freaked the Aztecs out. They were considered extremely unlucky; people avoided conducting any business, they barely went outside, they just hunkered down and waited for the cursed days to pass.

And that's when the monsters came out.

The cihuateteo roamed the earth during those five unlucky days of the year. They would steal children away, or seduce men, only to drive them insane before slaughtering them. The cihuateteo were constantly in search of another soul to replace the one they'd lost during childbirth. Sometimes they haunted crossroads, hoping to lure living victims coming from any direction. Even in modern times, people in Mexico will leave cakes made of maize at crossroads to placate the cihuateteo. Sometimes, the cakes are left as a distraction, in the hope that the revenants will stay in one place until sunrise. Just like a vampire, the sun's rays will kill a cihuateotl instantly.

In Mexico City, ancient home of the Aztecs, a land steeped in a proud, savage heritage, there are more creatures than just ghosts that prowl the grounds of the Great Temple of Tenochtitlan.

THE MUMMY MUSEUM
(Museo de las Momias, Guanajuato City, Mexico)

Imagine yourself in a room full of mummies.

That sentence, I will admit, is one that gives me the cold shivers. The thought of walking down a corridor that has desiccated corpses propped up all the way down its entire length ... yeah, I wouldn't just nope out of there, you couldn't get me to go in there in the first place.

But that's exactly what is inside the Museo de las Momias in Guanajuato City, Mexico. And the museum is surprisingly popular. More than 4,000 visitors tour the museum every week, which is, you know, pretty good for a place that displays only one thing. The museum also has an intriguing backstory, which is worth looking into.

The museum's story really starts back in the 19th century. In 1865, the city passed a "burial tax" ordinance. The people of Guanajuato paid a yearly fee - 170 pesos - to have their dead relatives buried in the city cemetery. This wasn't a one-time thing: they had to keep up on the payments to keep the bodies buried. If they couldn't cough up the dough, their relative was removed from the cemetery crypts.

The first body to be turfed out of their not-so-final resting place was a French doctor named Remigio Leroy. He was evicted from his grave in 1865. He was a foreigner, with no local relatives to pay the burial fee. So out he went. Cemetery workers were surprised to see that Dr. Leroy was in great shape for a dead guy.

Many of these bodies were buried during a cholera epidemic that raged in the area in 1833. The epidemic was worldwide, with millions falling sick with the disease. Health officials and physicians still weren't quite sure, at the time, how cholera spread, so they were virtually powerless against the pandemic.

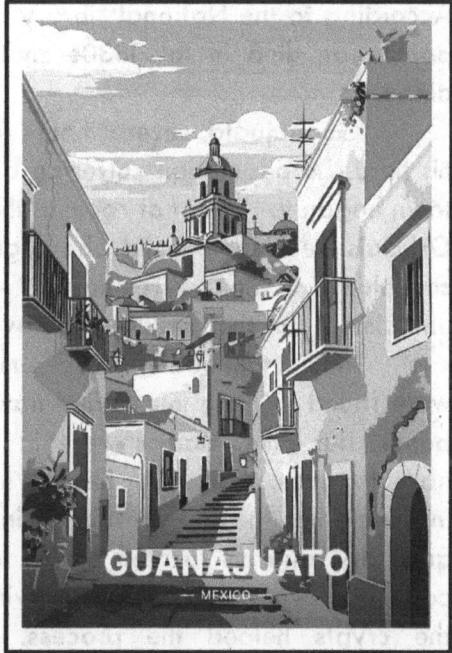

According to the National Library of Medicine, at least 5% of the population died in the 1830s cholera outbreak in Mexico City alone.

Guanajuato, several hours north of Mexico City, was also hit hard, its population suffering a heavy death toll. In fact, the town began to run out of room in the cemeteries for all the bodies. Officials decided to build above-ground crypts for the mounting casualties. Bodies were hastily - sometimes only partially - embalmed. But then nature took over.

When the bodies were removed from their crypts, many were found to have mummified naturally. Some of them were just bones, but other bodies were in excellent condition, with hair, nails, tongues, even eyelashes still intact. Some were even dressed in the clothes they'd been buried in. The climate in Guanajuato is quite dry, and it's located 6,000 feet above sea level. The arid conditions were good for preserving corpses. The lack of air in the crypts helped the process. The bodies were buried in aboveground niches, which tended to heat up in the Mexican sun. This hastened the natural mummification process.

As the bodies mummified, fingers and arms contracted as ligaments tightened, and jaws fell open as tissues loosened and then dried out. This led to the assumption that people, especially the cholera victims, had been buried alive. But these are just normal postmortem changes. This terrifying fate was not the case - for most of the people buried here.

That being said, one unfortunate woman, Ignacia Aguilar, suffered from a heart condition that made her heartbeat slow to a point where it was nearly undetectable. When this happened, she would of course pass out. Usually, her heart would resume its normal rhythm after a few minutes, and she would come to. During one of these episodes, though, her heart appeared to have stopped for more than a day. Thinking that this was finally it for Ignacia, her family mourned her and had her buried. They apparently then fell behind on the burial tax, because poor Ignacia was later dug up and removed from her crypt. To everyone's horror, she was found face-down in her coffin. Her face was covered in scratches, her arms were bitten to shreds, and she appeared to have blood smeared around her mouth. It was obvious she'd been buried while still alive and had regained consciousness for a few agonizing hours.

When bodies were disinterred for nonpayment, the authorities didn't just get rid of them. They weren't *monsters*. Instead, cemetery employees put the bodies, whether mummified or skeletonized, in a warehouse for storage. The corpses began to stack up, and by the 1900s, some enterprising cemetery workers started charging people a few pesos to tour the building where the bones and bodies were kept. The law requiring the burial tax was repealed in 1958, but the mummies still brought in some cash for the local economy. In 1969, the city opened the Mummy Museum and put the bodies on full display instead of hiding them in a creepy underground crypt.

Today, there are 59 bodies available for viewing, out of a collection of 120. As you might expect, the museum has had its share of controversy, apart from the sheer ick factor of having human remains on public display. The local government of Guanajuato is nominally in charge of the mummies, and to be fair, the museum does generate quite a lot of income for the town. It's a source of civic pride, too. Guanajuato has been on the UNESCO World Heritage list since 1988. It's one of Mexico's most beautiful cities. And hey, it's got an incredibly intriguing tourist attraction, if you're into that sort of thing.

But even with the naturally arid climate, the corpses are not in the best shape. Many of the bodies were displayed for years standing up, propped up against the gallery wall and held in place with rope. Most artifact conservators will agree that this is detrimental to their preservation. There's not much weight to these bodies, but still, it's not great to have that weight settled on fragile feet all the time. The Instituto Nacional de Antropologia e Historia accused local authorities of not taking care of the old bodies properly after an arm fell off a mummy during renovations at the museum. Also, before the bodies were put into airtight glass cases, some tourists would break off fingers and toes as souvenirs. Honestly, you can't take some people anywhere ...

Some of the mummies have been part of a traveling exhibit, and the INAH has taken issue with this as well. Scientists warned that the bodies could pose a public health risk after one of the corpses appeared to be infected with some sort of fungus.

But the corpses do have a certain eerie cachet. According to Juan Manuel Arguelles San Millan, a Mexican anthropologist, "The mummies of Guanajuato bring the biggest income to the municipality after property tax." People stand in line for hours to get into the museum. As they wait, they can buy refreshments from street vendors, including a local treat called *charamusca*, which is cinnamon-dusted sugar candy in the shape of - wait for it - little mummies.

And having the old bodies on display can be inspirational, in a weird sort of way. When the traveling exhibit came to Dallas, Texas, the exhibit designers called on nature to draw a connection between death and new life. A sign at the display read, "Death is simply a shedding of the physical body, like the butterfly shedding its cocoon. It is a transition to a higher state of consciousness where you continue to perceive, to understand, to laugh, and to be able to grow."

Many of these mummies were discovered still wearing the clothes they'd been buried in: suit jackets, elegant dresses, boots or high-button shoes. One baby boy is dressed as a saint, in colorful vestments - a common practice for infant burials in Central and South America. Some were even found labeled with tags that gave their name and the dates of their birth and death.

These were real people, who once walked the streets of Guanajuato. Sadly, just as with the tourists who broke bits off the bodies for mementos (seriously, who does that?), most of these tags have been stolen over the years, leaving the bodies anonymous.

But all is not lost. The INAH has begun research that includes genealogy studies and DNA testing of the mummies, in the hopes of identifying the bodies and giving them back their names and family relations. The study is meant to bring new respect to the old corpses, using 19th and 20th century death certificates, church documents, and newspaper archives to identify the bodies. Forensic analysis, like the aforementioned DNA studies, could link the remains to people living in present-day Guanajuato.

"These are just regular people who are repositories of information about the period they lived in," says Gerald Conlogue, a diagnostic imaging professor emeritus with Quinnipac University, who has studied the mummies extensively. "They walked these streets, they went to the old market. They shouldn't be a freak show."

Conlogue's use of the term "freak show" is intentional. The town sometimes gets a little ... too enthusiastic when celebrating its famous former residents. The Mexican holiday Dia de los Muertos (Day of the Dead) speaks to that culture's familiarity with mortality. With the mummies of Guanajuato, that familiarity is sometimes carried a bit too far. According to a National Geographic article, "They become cultural ambassadors for the city, both real-life attractions and fictional muses. The momias battled masked, caped *luchadores* (Mexican wrestlers) in a pair of 1970s horror movies." (I swear I'm not making this up. There was indeed a horror flick released in 1972 called "Las Momias de Guanajuato." It starred three famous wrestlers of the era - Blue Demon, Mil Mascaras, and Santo, the Silver Masked Man, if you're interested. The three heroes save the town from a fellow wrestler named Satan, who is actually a resurrected sorcerer leading an army of undead mummies. And for those who like their mummy-inspired entertainment with a little more class, Ray Bradbury wrote a short story in 1945 called "The Next In Line", which appeared in his collection *October Country*.)

You would think that with the corpses being on display for well over a hundred years, the Museum of the Mummies might just be haunted. And you would be right. There is a room in the museum where the bodies of five children are on display. Visitors have reported hearing a small child screaming in the room, even when there are no kids in the building. People say they can hear voices whispering to them when they are alone in the exhibit.

The museum is also said to have a ghost that staff have named "the Tall Lady." This spirit wanders around the museum, going pretty much anywhere she wants to. Sometimes, she'll join a tour. Museum guests will notice a tall woman in their tour group, hanging back and remaining absolutely silent. This creeps museum visitors out, but really, she's just one of the many people whose earthly bodies are here on display.

A CREEP FACTOR
TURNED UP TO ELEVEN
(Vent Haven Museum, Fort Mitchell, KY)

Some people get creeped out by dolls. It's the whole "uncanny valley" thing - here's something that looks like a miniature version of us but is manifestly *not* a living breathing thinking feeling human. I'm no big fan of dolls myself, but in my book, there's something creepier than dolls - ventriloquist dummies.

I mean, dolls just *sit* there.

Dummies actually *talk*.

I know, I know, it's all done for entertainment. And there are ventriloquists that are very, very good at their jobs. It's impressive, quite honestly. But when the performer takes their hand away from the dummy's back, and sets it on a chair, and walks away ... you can't help but look at it and think to yourself, *what would I do if that dummy turned its head and looked at me with those glassy eyes? And what if its mouth* started to move *without its master's hand pulling the string?* Dummies are just plain creepy.

Luckily for us, there was a man dedicated to collecting memorabilia of this entertainment niche. The Vent Haven Museum is the only place in the world where you can go and see more than 1,200 dummies housed all together, in one nightmare-inducing gathering.

This unique museum all started with the passion of one man, the impressively named William Shakespeare Berger. (His

friends called him W.S., so we'll do the same.) W.S. hailed from Cincinnati, Ohio. He wasn't a professional ventriloquist, but he caught the bug in 1910 when he bought a dummy and named it Tommy Baloney. (I know.) He kept Tommy Baloney for twenty years, then in the 1930s and 1940s, he began adding to his treasure trove. One dummy turned into a whole collection of them. By 1947, W.S. had enough figures gathered that he renovated his garage to display the dummies. In 1962, he added a second building.

W.S. didn't just collect these props. He walked the walk. From the late 1940s until 1960, W.S. was the president of the International Brotherhood of Ventriloquists. With W.S. at the helm, the organization grew from just 300 members to over 1,000. W.S. also published a magazine called *The Oracle*. The monthly newsletter provided performers with news of current events in the "vent" community. W.S. was also a prolific letter writer, corresponding with ventriloquists all over the world.

Sadly, W.S. outlived his family. His wife, his son, even his grandson passed before he did, and he had no other heirs. This got him to thinking - what would happen to his collection when he himself died? W.S. consulted his lawyer, who helped him set up the Vent Haven Museum. This saved the collection from being broken up and sold off piecemeal after his death. W.S. passed away in 1972, and in 1973, the museum opened to the public.

By the time of his death, W.S. had collected about 500 figures. The museum is now home to more than 1,200 dummies used by ventriloquists from the 19th, 20th, and 21st centuries. The collection includes replicas of dummies used by such luminaries as Edgar Bergen and Shari Lewis, and memorabilia from folks like Jeff Dunham.

Besides the general creep factor of two buildings packed full of glassy-eyed, exaggerated caricatures of humans, the museum also has four dummies that have a rather eerie backstory. William B. Wood was a ventriloquist who performed in the later years of the 19th century. He began his career in 1886, touring with his wife - they were both members of a stage company, then branched out to perform on their own. They were both illusionists, with his wife performing as "Edna." Wood was granted a patent in 1889 for his levitation illusion, in which Edna was lifted up in the air, doing pirouettes and flips while levitating.

Wood and his wife performed their stage show all over the world for several years. By 1895, they had performed in twenty countries, and they toured America from October 1901 to January 1902. Beginning in 1903, they embarked on a three-year tour through South America. Their travels together ended in 1906, when Edna had to retire due to failing health.

Here comes the weird part. In January 1908, Wood and his daughter were on a tugboat going from Tabasco, Mexico, to Yucatan. On the night of January 20, the boat was caught in a tropical storm. The tugboat was towing a schooner, and the captain decided to cut the other ship loose and try to ride out the storm. The tugboat ended up sinking anyway. The captain and crew made it to safety, but Wood and his daughter - the only passengers on board - were lost.

Reports of their demise were sketchy, to say the least. One newspaper said the two had been killed by pirates. Another story had it that they had been robbed by the tugboat's crew, then "abandoned to the sharks."

Whatever fate was in store for Wood and his daughter, their bodies were never found. However, their luggage later washed up on shore. One of Wood's trunks survived - the one containing his ventriloquist dummies. Those figures ended up at the Vent Haven Museum.

As far as anyone can tell, none of those four dummies, whose owner was lost so tragically, is haunted. The museum itself doesn't seem to be the site of any paranormal activity either. It's just deeply, deliciously creepy.

ONE MAN'S DREAM
(Historic Auto Attractions, Roscoe, IL)

Let's see a show of hands. How many of you reading this collect stuff? Beatles memorabilia, rock concert t-shirts, ceramic pumpkins, matchbooks, mugs with funny sayings on them ... the list of things that folks collect is as varied as the folks who collect them. (Me, I'm a sucker for frogs and cute socks.) But some lucky people get to take their passion for collecting things to a whole new level.

Wayne Lensing is one of those people. He's the owner of Historic Auto Attractions. With a firm handshake and an easy smile, he's always ready to talk about his acquisitions. And there is a *lot* to talk about.

When you drive through the little town of Roscoe, Illinois, and find your way through the cornfields to the long, low building that houses Historic Auto Attractions, nothing - and I mean nothing - can prepare you for what waits inside. The double doors at the entrance lead into the gift shop. Further down, past the magnets and the books and the posters and the t-shirts (a picture of Lincoln's face, underneath it a one-star review of Ford's Theater, "Would not go there again"), there is a meeting room for events. My partner James and I were there for the Dead Guy Festival, put on by Kathi Kresol and Haunted Rockford.

"Thanks so much for coming to speak at the event," Kathi said. "Did I tell you the museum is haunted?"

I was stoked to hear it, and I couldn't wait to wander through and investigate. I had already heard a couple of intriguing stories from museum employees in the gift shop. Melissa was manning the cash register when I came up with a pair of Ghostbuster socks in hand. (I told you.) She told me that she was standing at the Miss Belvidere exhibit, looking up the long corridor of the building, when she watched an apparition walk through a wall into the Lincoln room. She thought at first that she had seen a member of a news crew or a reporter, as the press has access to the museum in the mornings. She turned to Alex Merry, the museum director, who was with her. "Who's that?" Melissa asked.

That's when she found out that she and Alex were the only two people in the building at the time.

"It's not like when people say they see a ghost, they say it's a white misty figure. This was gray, and staticky-looking. See-through, kinda." She said the quick experience wasn't scary at all. "It was just like, who's that? Alex said, there's nobody in here. Then it was over with. Within two seconds, just nothing. Over and done."

Alex was standing nearby, listening to us chat. "We hear noises and crashes from the museum all the time. All the time. The first time I heard one, I was with the owner's son. We both looked at each other, and he's like, 'GO - investigate it now!' So I turned to run, and it sounded like it was in the Lincoln exhibit. I'm looking around, and there's people in there walking around, and they're looking at me like I'm crazy, and I go back to him and I'm like, 'Nothing fell.'"

By now I was fairly panting to get into the museum and experience it for myself. The museum is housed in a long warehouse; the exhibits line both sides of two corridors that run the length of the building, so you can walk down one hallway, then come back up the other. And oh, the treasures that await!

"I build racecars across the street," Wayne Lensing told me. Every year, he would attend a big show in Las Vegas - "all about high-performance stuff." While there, he regularly stayed at the Imperial Palace, a hotel and casino. The hotel's claim to fame was its collection of classic cars. The casino's owner, Ralph Engelstad, would send buyers all over the world to get the finest and best cars for the museum.

"I'd go through that museum every year," Wayne said. "All I could do was just ..." He sighed. "I wish it was me."

In 1998, Englestad became terminally ill. He made the decision to sell off the casino, the classic car collection, everything. "I flew down there, and I talked to him about it, and he gave me a price on twelve cars." Those twelve cars included vehicles belonging to Mussolini, Hitler, FDR, Truman, Eisenhower, the King of Siam, and other luminaries.

Wayne had the land already. All he needed was a place to display these rolling pieces of history. "So I got the price of putting up the building, the price of the cars, went to the bank ... and they accepted and made the loan." Wayne now had fifteen years to make good on the bank's faith in his project.

"In 2001, I opened up the museum. At first it was quite slow, but I managed to make the payment." Every year that followed, things got a little better. People heard about Wayne's museum and began donating items to him. A fellow named Robert White had a private museum in Florida; he loved President Kennedy, and his collection reflected that. When he passed away, the items came up for sale. Wayne already had the following car from JFK's motorcade, so he bought the contents of White's museum.

Another presidential aficionado, a Dr. Lattimore, collected nothing but Abraham Lincoln. His collection formed the basis of this museum's stunning Lincoln room. Lattimore "just got the special stuff - 3-D stuff, not paperwork," Wayne gushed. "I like 3-D items. I don't like a wall of just pictures, like a lot of presidential libraries are - you get yourself all daydreaming and not stay focused. When you see an item right there, and you read about it and you look at it, and it draws you into it ... I like 3-D."

The museum was gaining momentum. "Gosh, I was on my way, I was starting to get some neat stuff." Money was still an issue: "I sometimes had to sell things that I loved, if I wanted to buy something I loved better." But the sacrifices were worth it. In 2016, Wayne paid off the bank loan, right on schedule. Donations continued to find their way to him. And he kept getting ... well, "neat stuff." The Pate Museum in Dallas, Texas, closed down, and auctioned off their holdings. They had the taxicab that Lee Harvey Oswald used when he left Dealey Plaza; that joined the collection of Kennedy memorabilia. Just around the corner from it is a display of fashion icon Jackie Kennedy's dresses - outfits fit for the First Lady who turned the White House into the museum of the American people.

In 2022, Wayne took out another loan, and built an addition, extending the museum's square footage and providing room for even more wonders. And most of these wonders are, as Wayne prefers, 3-D.

"One of the neatest things I got that I do love is that Conestoga wagon. It's from 1798, unrestored, like it was - it tells a story. You look at it, it's there. You get the feel of the people riding in it."

The excitement of sharing history is evident in Wayne's voice as he talks. "Oh," he sighs, "it's just coming together finally after all these years of ditching out a lot of money. So what is it doing? It's carrying its own now." There's a warm note of satisfaction in his voice as he says this.

"Boy, I'm just enjoying the heck out of it."

James and I wandered slowly through the museum, soaking up the history that surrounded us. Now, sure, I've been in plenty of museums before, and I've been moved by exhibits before. But good lord, the sheer variety of stuff in this unassuming building is just staggering.

We paused at a wide spot in the corridor. We were surrounded by legends: to our left was the Elvis exhibit, including the King's white 1972 Lincoln Mark IV. In front of us was James Dean, while Buddy Holly flanked him on our right. A little farther down, Marilyn Monroe flashed her dazzling smile. (And in her exhibit was, among other things, the cake topper from the famous Madison Square Garden gala in 1962 at which she crooned birthday wishes to JFK. The pink sugar paste roses have faded over the decades to a dusty mauve, but a faint hint of celebration still clings to the decoration. It was donated by the wife of one of the Secret Service agents who attended the gala, and snuck his then-girlfriend into the kitchen to get a behind-the-scenes peek at the party prep.)

In the middle of the walkway was a freestanding glass case. And in that case was the only known piece of James Dean's Porsche 550 Spyder, the car he called "Little Bastard" with rough affection. The car that he was driving to the Salinas racetrack when he crashed it at 85 mph on September 30, 1955. Dean was killed instantly.

The car was declared a total loss by the insurance company but was stripped for parts. The engine was installed in a Lotus IX race car, which crashed at the Pomona race in 1956. The transmission and suspension went into another car, which plowed into a tree in the same race, killing the driver. Two of the tires from the 550, which had been put onto a third car, both blew at the same time, causing yet another accident. The car was loaned to the Los Angeles chapter of the National Safety Council and toured the West from 1957 to 1959 in a gruesome object lesson on the dangers of reckless driving. In Sacramento, the Spyder fell off its display stand and broke a bystander's hip. The car claimed another victim, George Barkus, when Barkus was transporting it to a road safety convention. The Spyder rolled off the transport vehicle and crushed Barkus, killing him.

After that, the Porsche 550 Spyder disappeared from history. The lore says that it vanished from a sealed boxcar while en route from Miami to LA in 1960. But no one knows for sure. Porsche has offered a $1 million reward for information as to the whereabouts of any part of the car. The only known part of James Dean's 550 that has survived - and has been verified by Porsche as being genuine - is the 3-inch-square chunk of silver metal that sits on a folded piece of red fabric in a glass case in the corridor of Historic Auto Attractions.

James turned on his EMF meter and put it on top of the glass case, almost directly over the silver piece of metal. Then he raised his camera and started to take a couple of pictures. I looked over at the case.

"Is that your camera doing that?" I asked.

"Doing what?"

I pointed. "Making the meter peg up into the red."

It was a valid question, and an interesting one. A meter can register electrical activity nearby, like cell phones or other devices. But if it's picking something up, but there aren't any gadgets around to make it go off, then we start to get excited. And both of our phones were in airplane mode.

"Hmm." James moved his camera up to the meter, which had moved back down to base-level green. No reaction: it stayed in the green. We looked at each other. Had the meter picked up on some kind of paranormal energy coming from the artifact?

Tony Farrell, the Chief Historian for the museum, had some interesting information about the small piece of metal. He told us that a fellow named Harry Camby picked up the silver shard on the day of the accident. He was so haunted by it that he gave it to Dean's family, who kept it in a museum they'd cobbled together in the actor's memory. "When they sold the museum, we bought everything you see here," he said.

Then he told a story that really got our attention. Since Historic Auto Attractions is so very haunted, several television shows have filmed episodes there. Christopher Garetano, filming for the Travel Channel's show *Strange World*, decided to put a meter on the case, just as James had done. The meter gave a readout of 10.2 mG (milliGauss). He explained to Tony that any reading under 20 mG with that meter is considered "normal." Then he carefully took the piece of metal out and placed it on top of the case.

The meter jumped to 272 mG.

"He would not drive the rental car back to Chicago," Tony told us. "He rode in the back seat of someone else's car, and somebody else drove his car back. He even waited until the next day before he flew back to New York. He was that shook by it."

James and I continued to wander the museum. We kept stopping to gawk at the exhibits that caught our eyes. (Which, really, is the joy of visiting a museum.) In the War Room, we ran into a friend of mine, Sara Bowker, who was hanging out to represent Haunted Rockford. I can listen to Sara tell stories for *hours.*

The War Room focuses on World War II, so Sara loves to do spirit box sessions there, along with Samantha Hochmann, another member of Haunted Rockford. Nino Pasquali, of Midwest Ghost Investigators, sits in on these sessions too. They like to use several different versions: SB7, Ghost Tube, just switch things up a little. Sara took me through one of these experiments in communicating with the dead.

"We'll start by playing the national anthem. Then we'll go through and do each of the service branches, play their theme songs. Then we'll pause and then start the ghost boxes. It will round-robin, and it'll give you the craziest information. One of us will stand there, and there --" she pointed to a couple of the dioramas - "we call it triangulating. I started to ask questions, like 'what theater were you in? Did you serve in the Pacific? Did you serve in Europe?' And, all of a sudden, one came across and said 'Okinawa.' Then boom, another ghost box said, 'There were so many bodies.' And the next one said, 'I shouldn't have died,' and just boom boom boom around and around and around. It's just wild. Then when we go to leave, we'll play 'Taps.' We'll say thank you for reaching out, thank you for speaking with us."

Sara's ghost box luck held - sort of - when the trio took the SB7 ghost box to the Nazi area of the museum. "They were giving us responses in German." This is a conundrum. As an investigator, what do you do when the responses to your questions come back in a foreign language? That's when the Internet comes to the rescue ... they used Google Translator to ask their questions. "Samantha would ask the question, then hit Google Translator, then we'd get a response back from the ghost box in German."

Sara admitted that doing investigations in the Nazi area is a bit problematic. "We try to be respectful, but with those guys it's like ..." Her eyes narrowed, and a clipped tone slipped into her voice. "You know what you did."

She pointed out that the lights and music in each exhibit are on motion sensors. She and her team have been in the museum when no one is anywhere near the Gangster Land area - but the music swells and the lights flicker on. Laughing, she admitted to being a bit conflicted when that happens. "Should we go that way? Or do we back up, give them space? 'Cause there are all kinds of serial killers ... I'm gonna stay here, where it's a little bit less murdery."

Sara, like so many others, is entranced by the museum

Wayne has created. "I can't help but wonder - what eBay are you on? What does your search history look like?" The massive museum boasts 90,000 square feet of exhibit space, and the artifacts on display represent only about half of what Wayne has collected. "I know he said he had the most-used guillotine in France during the French Revolution. What did you *search*?"

Regardless of the dark recesses of Wayne's search history, Sara remains a fan. "It's crazy to me, but I love it. It's so well preserved, and it's here for the next generation, so you can come and appreciate the history. I love it. I love that he has done so much to save all this from going to private collectors."

James and I told Sara about how the meter seemed to react to the bit of metal from the cursed Porsche. She said they don't usually get anything from James Dean, but that Samantha has good luck talking with Buddy Holly. Sam is sensitive, and she shared a few stories with me, to my intense delight.

"I love that Buddy Holly is here," she gushed. "It was so funny - the first time Kathi [Kresol] and I came through here, we were gathered around the Spyder piece. Kathi's like, 'Are you picking up on James Dean?' And I'm like, 'Uh … no? But, uh, I got Buddy Holly here. *Everybody comes to see James. Nobody comes to see me. What about me? It's always about James.'*" I had to laugh along with Sam - I could just hear Holly's frustration in the indignant tone in her voice.

Samantha also mentioned the motion-activated lights and music in the Gangster Land room. For the record, she's in favor of rushing over there to see what's going on, not hanging back in case of murdery-ness.

I listened, entranced, as Samantha shared an utterly fascinating tale of spirit communication. The Lincoln room is one of the most amazing exhibits in the museum. In keeping with Wayne's passion for 3-D artifacts, the room is vibrant with history. One of Lincoln's chairs is there - along with a replica of the chair in which he was sitting when he was assassinated. A scrap of fabric from the actual chair is also in that display, and the way the upholstery craftsman matched the color and design of the fabric is uncanny.

There is a daguerrotype photograph of Lewis Powell, one of the conspirators who worked with John Wilkes Booth. A handsome young bull of a man, he stares grimly into the camera. His manacled hands rest in his lap ... and those very manacles are displayed below the photograph. In this room, history is very nearly close enough to touch.

In one somber display is one of the coins placed on the dead president's eyes, a nod to the ancient Greek custom of paying the ferryman Charon his fee to get across the River Styx. Close by is a folded handkerchief. A placard explained that the piece of fabric was tied around Lincoln's head, to hold his jaw closed until rigor mortis set in.

With all these artifacts, some of them celebrating Lincoln's life, some of them inextricably connected with his death, it's no wonder that the Lincoln room is also one of the most paranormally active displays at the museum. Samantha and Kathi spent an extraordinary evening in there, getting amazing evidence from the ghost boxes.

"There was a man in there," Sam told me. "I knew he was upset about something. The moment I walked in, he's like, '*I didn't do it, I didn't do it, I didn't do it!*' I said, 'I don't know what this is, but this is what I'm getting - there's a man, he says he didn't do it.' Then on the ghost boxes, one said '*knife*,' and another one said '*hanging*.'

"Kathi said, 'Well, that's really interesting. George Atzerodt was hanged because he was one of the Lincoln conspirators. He had a knife, and he was supposed to kill the vice president. He didn't actually have the guts to do it.'"

Kathi told me her perspective of that evening as well. "He

mentioned that he was supposed to attack someone but couldn't go through with it when the time came. He said he got drunk instead. I knew the story, so I could ask a couple of questions that he confirmed." She began to go through the names of the Lincoln conspirators. "I was going to say 'George,' but it came through by itself."

George Atzerodt was indeed another one of the conspirators. He booked a room at Kirkwood House, a hotel in Washington DC, because Andrew Johnson was staying there. Booth had tapped Atzerodt to kill the vice president; he was supposed to do the deed at 10:15 pm on the night of April 14, 1865, while Lewis Powell attacked Secretary of State William Seward ... and when Booth aimed a derringer at the back of Lincoln's head and pulled the trigger. Atzerodt lost his nerve and got sloshed in the hotel bar. He spent the rest of the night wandering the streets of the capital in a drunken haze. He dropped his knife in a nearby gutter. A woman saw this and reported it to the police. Atzerodt was hanged with the others - Lewis Powell, David Herold, and Mary Surratt - on July 7, 1865, at Arsenal Penitentiary in Washington.

George told Samantha that he wanted to cross over, so she helped him to do that. But the story wasn't over yet.

"Today, when I was sitting in there, I felt someone behind me - there was a warm embrace on my shoulders. I got out my ghost box, and I got the name George. I thought, did it not work last time? And he said, 'No, *it did, it did! I just came back to say thank you.*'"

As I was writing this chapter, and revisiting the amazing experiences of this museum, I realized something interesting. I spent as much time as I could manage in the Lincoln room, but I felt like I just couldn't settle. The artifacts were truly fascinating, and as big of a Lincoln dork that I am, I really should have walked through the room quite slowly, savoring the stories told by these intensely personal items. But as I look back, I realize that I was wired and fidgety, unable to focus on any one artifact for more than a few moments at a time. I didn't have this reaction to any other display. I wonder now if I was picking up on the energy in that room, and if my psyche found it a little overwhelming.

My good friend Liz Nygard has had a couple of experiences at the museum, and she kindly shared them with me. I'm always interested to hear what she has to say - you'll recall, if you've read the first volume in this series, that Liz is a powerful psychic medium, and often picks up on strangeness in the most ordinary places.

Liz was in the gift shop at the museum, getting ready to walk out the door. "I whirled around because I heard a woman say 'hi' in a raspy voice." Liz is naturally polite, so of course she said "hi" back. She also added, "I'm sorry." See, Liz is functionally blind, and she was worried she'd nearly crashed into the woman on her way out the doors. Liz's husband, Karl, came back into the store to find her. Puzzled, he asked, "Who are you talking to?"

"I said hi to the woman that just said hi to me," Liz explained.

"Liz, there's no one there," Karl sighed in exasperation. (But really, he should be used to that by now. Liz has a long-standing history of conversing with people that most of us can't see.)

Liz had another very strange experience at the museum, one which was a great deal more unsettling than nearly bumping into a stranger in a gift shop. She was recently at the museum and kept asking about "the room with the cobblestones." The first time she'd gone to the museum, she'd been in an area that she perceived as being a recreation of a Berlin street in the thick of World War II, with buildings hung with swastika flags. "I remember my cane just going across the cobblestones and making that bumping sound everywhere I went, like a speed bump."

After much discussion, and questioning several docents, Liz finally established that she was looking for the War Room, with its dioramas of World War II. But, she was told, there's just a regular floor in there. No one could explain why she felt cobblestones under the tip of her cane, or why she sensed a heaviness in the atmosphere.

"I was having an experience on the streets of Berlin," Liz told me in a text later. "It was bizarre and so real. Now I know it was a true experience, World War II and Berlin. Terrifying."

If you are ever in Rockford, or the Chicago area, or southern Wisconsin, do make the time to visit Historic Auto Attractions. One of the marvelous things about this museum is that it is centrally located in northern Illinois, within an easy drive of Chicago, Peoria, Madison, Dubuque, or any point nearby.

And of course, the other marvelous things about this museum are its extraordinary collections of artifacts ... and its equally amazing ghosts.

THANK YOU FOR YOUR SERVICE
(Wisconsin Maritime Museum, Manitowoc, WI)

When the United States entered World War II, the Navy had a pressing need for ships. Many shipyards were tasked with building boats, including submarines, for the war effort.

One of these boatyards was located on the Great Lakes in Manitowoc, Wisconsin, where the Manitowoc River empties into Lake Michigan. During the war years, a labor force of 7,000 men and women employed by the Manitowoc Shipbuilding Company worked around the clock, 365 days a year, to build boats. They produced 28 submarines, sending them from Lake Michigan to Lockport, down the Illinois River to the Mississippi, and from there to the Gulf of Mexico. This was also the leading shipyard for building LCTs (Landing Craft Tanks). Some of the 1,465 LCTs produced there played a huge role in D-Day and other amphibious assaults.

The mouth of the Manitowoc River would later become home to the Wisconsin Maritime Museum. Here, visitors can experience interactive exhibits about the history of shipbuilding in the area over the span of 150 years, see a display of model ships, including a diorama of the wreck of the *Edmund Fitzgerald* as it currently looks resting on the floor of Lake Superior, and even see a tank of live sea lampreys, an invasive species that slithered into the Great Lakes from the Atlantic Ocean through shipping canals.

One of the many fascinating exhibits at the museum is the *USS Cobia*, a decommissioned United States submarine that served her country during World War II. Her history is illustrious and inspiring - let's take a look.

The *Cobia* was not built at the Manitowoc shipyard; she was built by the Electric Boat Company at Groton, Connecticut. She was launched on November 28, 1943, and commissioned March 29, 1944, under the command of Lieutenant Commander Albert L. Becker.

She was sent to Pearl Harbor, arriving in port June 3. Later

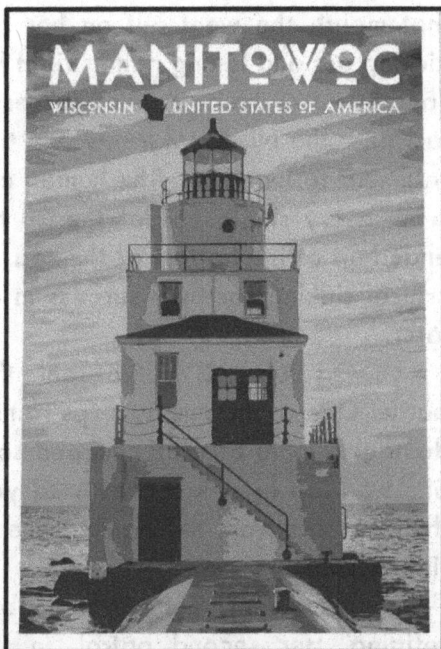

that month she went out on her first war patrol. *Cobia* started kicking ass and taking names right from the jump. She sank several Japanese freighters in quick succession, on July 13, 17, and 18. The last one, the *Nisshu Maru*, was a troop transport carrying a tank regiment to Iwo Jima. The human casualties were not too terrible - but every single one of the 28 tanks aboard the *Nisshu Maru* ended up at the bottom of the sea. The Marines later credited this critical sinking for their success in capturing Iwo Jima six months later.

On July 20, *Cobia* sank three more ships in a running battle. One of the enemy ships rammed her but caused only minor damage. *Cobia* basically rubbed some dirt in it and walked it off. She went on to sink a converted yacht on August 5. She rescued the survivors from the drink; these sailors would become *Cobia's* first prisoners of war.

After that, *Cobia* took a breather for several weeks for refitting. Her second patrol, in Luzon Strait, was marked by frequent encounters with Japanese aircraft. (It wasn't all fighting, though. She also rescued two survivors from a Japanese ship that had been sunk by another American sub.) On January 14, 1945, during her third patrol, she sank the minelayer *Yurishima*. When she surfaced to photograph her victim as it sank, *Cobia* was driven into a deep dive, menaced by a Japanese bomber. The next day, she rescued two Japanese sailors from a raft on which they had been adrift for forty days.

Cobia's fourth patrol took her to the Java Sea. On February 26, she engaged two ships in a vicious, two-hour surface battle. One of the ships shot back. The machine gun barrage damaged *Cobia's* radar equipment. *Cobia* managed to sink both targets, but this time, her victory came at a cost. The machine gun fire also killed Ralph Clark Huston Jr., who was on deck loading the 20 mm gun. He was the sub's only casualty of the war.

Cobia limped to port at Fremantle, Australia, for repairs, which took from March 4 to March 8. Then she went back out into the Java Sea and went right back to work. On April 8, she rescued seven surviving crew members of a downed Army bomber.

Her fifth patrol found her in the Gulf of Siam. On May 14, she attacked a cargo ship but was driven under the surface by depth charges from the minelayer *Hatsutaka*. She had to dive deep to escape the attack. She took her revenge, though; on June 8, she attacked a tanker convoy, sinking a tanker and the landing craft *Hakusa*.

Cobia earned four battle stars for her service during the war. She was credited with having sunk thirteen vessels, amounting to a total of 16,385 tons of shipping. She was decommissioned in May 1946. By 1959, the Navy judged her to be obsolete. She served as a training ship at the Milwaukee Wisconsin Naval Reserve Center for eleven years.

At last, though, her years of service came to an end. On July 1, 1970, the *USS Cobia* was removed from the Naval Register. She was towed to Manitowoc, WI, to begin a new era of service, as an international memorial to submariners. In 1986, she was designated a National Historic Landmark, listed on the National Register of Historic Places, and given pride of place at the Wisconsin Maritime Museum. The submarine is open to the public, with several levels of tours - general tours daily, plus a "nooks and crannies" experience where visitors can learn about daily life on the sub. This tour even simulates the terror and uncertainty of a depth charge attack, taking as its script a journal entry from the *Cobia's* logbooks.

You can even - and I am not making this up - stay overnight on the *Cobia*. The Sub B&B includes a private tour of the boat, and exclusive access for up to 65 people at a time. You can range all over the boat to your heart's content and hang out in the museum after hours too. (You can even watch a private screening of one of the museum's many maritime- or submarine-themed movies in the theater, to get yourself in the mood.) Then at midnight, you can snuggle down in one of the bunks in the Forward Torpedo Room, the Aft Torpedo Room, the Crew's Quarters, or the Officer's Quarters. They even feed you breakfast the next morning.

And while you're wandering the submarine, or catching some sack time, maybe you'll have an encounter with *Cobia's* resident ghost.

In the museum stands a life-sized poster of a heartbreakingly handsome young sailor, standing at parade rest. The poster bears the request, "He gave his life to save a nation. Help save his submarine."

This good-looking kid, so like so many other young men captured in black and white in the prime of their youth, is Ralph Huston Jr. Another photo of him shows a strong jaw, dark wavy hair tousled just enough, full lips, and serious eyes that gaze into the camera. A more candid picture, taken on *Cobia's* deck, shows a smiling Ralph with his shirt off, the waves behind him gently lapping at *Cobia's* hull. He is a teenager, only months out of high school. And in that picture, he has no idea that he will not live to celebrate his 20th birthday.

Ralph Clark Huston Jr. was born on December 27, 1925, in West Virginia. He enlisted in the Naval Reserve on September 9, 1943, just months after graduating high school. He was sent to the Great Lakes Naval Training Center and graduated three months later. He worked his way through more training, eventually picking up a promotion to Seaman First Class.

He reported for duty on *Cobia* on February 12, 1944. On February 18, 1945, *Cobia* sailed from Fremantle for her fourth war patrol, in the Java Sea. Just over a week later, on February 26, *Cobia* locked horns with two ships. The surface battle lasted for two grueling hours. Ralph was manning the 20 mm cannon on deck, loading rounds the size of a man's thumb into the chamber.

At 6:15 pm, two machine gun bullets tore into Ralph's body. Ralph was shot in the left shoulder - that bullet shattered the bone in his upper arm. The other bullet hit him in the upper left side of his ribcage, exiting his lower back on the right side.

Ralph was taken belowdecks to the mess for treatment. The medic on duty, Dr. Herbert L. Starmer, tried to control the blood loss by amputating Ralph's ruined arm. He treated Ralph for shock, but there was nothing he could do to stop the internal bleeding. He told the sub's captain that if they could get Ralph to a hospital, they might just be able to save his life.

Captain Albert Becker made the decision to head back to Fremantle for better medical treatment for his sailor. Sadly, though, Ralph lost his battle at 5:43 am the next morning.

Dr. Starmer wrapped the young man's body in mattress covers and placed some fire bricks from the crew's mess inside to weigh it down. Then he sewed the sad bundle closed. Ralph was wrapped in an American flag, and at 6 pm that night, he was laid on a door that had been removed from the sub's bathroom. Four of his shipmates acted as pallbearers, carrying the impromptu bier up to the deck. Captain Becker led a Protestant service, as another four sailors stood at attention as a Guard of Honor. They played a recording of "Taps," then fired off a ceremonial rifle salute. Ralph Huston Jr. was committed to the deep in the Java Sea with full military honors. His sacrifice is commemorated by a bronze plaque on *Cobia's* sail (what civilians usually call the conning tower), next to the 20 mm gun Ralph was serving when he caught two bullets. He was posthumously awarded a Purple Heart.

Losing his life so young and so violently, a victim of war, Ralph does seem to still be tied to the submarine on which he died. Tour guides report hearing strange noises on the boat, and curtains moving without any rational explanation. Ralph does seem to be one of the helpful spirits we hear about sometimes. Occasionally - these things happen - a guide will accidentally drop their keys, and they'll fall with a clatter through the gate to land on the floor of the hull. Later, the keys will be found hanging on their proper hook.

The museum hosts an event called Sub Fest. Reenactors volunteer to teach visitors about life aboard a submarine, and in thanks for their time and expertise, they are invited to sleep aboard *Cobia* for the night. (There are some volunteers that refuse this perk. They complain of odd feelings, or the sense of being watched.) One year, two reenactors had a strange experience as they slept.

They both had the exact same dream: that they were chasing ghosts through the boat.

One of them doesn't claim to be sensitive to paranormal energy. They just said that the distinctive smell of the sub reached them even in the dream. The other one has a family history of encounters with the supernatural. Unsurprisingly, their experience was more intense. They woke up unable to move, locked in sleep paralysis. They felt something hit the side of their bunk, as if trying to wake them up or get their attention. This barrage went on for about 15 or 20 seconds, then stopped. The reenactor rolled over, able to move again, and went back to sleep.

The reenactors slept on the submarine the next night too. They spoke out loud to Ralph, thanking him for letting them sleep on his boat. They explained that they really did need to get a good night's sleep. That night, they both slept soundly, and the one witness who complained about the smell of the boat infiltrating their dream smelled nothing all night long. They only smelled the boat once they were fully awake and took a deep breath. There were no more experiences.

Lest you think that *Cobia* is the only exhibit at the Wisconsin Maritime Museum that's haunted, let me assure you that the 60,000 square foot museum building proper also has activity. Lights go off with no explanation, and museum guides hear footsteps in empty rooms. Submarine Curator Karen Duvalle shares the fact that sometimes, doors in the museum will open on their own … doors that are kept locked, and which require a special code to open.

Maintenance man Dale Hornburg had an experience in the museum that went well past a spookily opening door. He was cleaning in one of the exhibits one morning and saw a woman standing near one of the displays. He strolled over to tell her good morning … and she was gone. He knew she hadn't gone past him to get to the only door leading out of the room.

Dale walked to the corner where he'd seen the woman, wondering what was over there that might interest a spirit. He peered at the display - and what he saw "made the hair stand up on my arms."

It was a display on signal flares. Ever since the 19th century, the United States Navy has used colored flares to send coded messages at night. Flares are also used to warn sailors of dangerous conditions, and of course, used by ships in trouble to summon help. What caught Dale's attention was the signage for the display … that informed visitors that a woman named Martha Coston patented the first practical maritime flare and code system in 1859.

Maybe that spirit was Martha, enjoying the recognition of her accomplishments. No one knows. But just as with Ralph Huston, she is a friendly spirit. Karen Duvalle adds that people aren't terrified of the ghosts at the museum. "It's just a part of the building. You just learn to live with it."

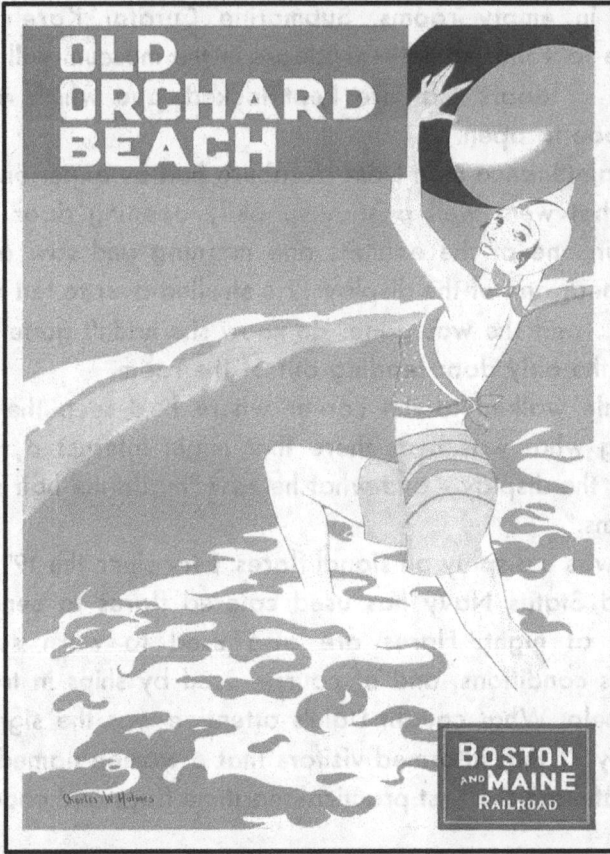

WHERE THE RESIDENTS HAVEN'T LEFT

Haunted Historic Villages

It's interesting to wander the streets and buildings of historic villages, to walk on the same paths that the folks that lived there in other centuries walked, to realize that this place was home to them. We look at a general store, or a schoolhouse, or a church, and see a tourist attraction. But for the people who once lived in that town, these were places where they went about their days. Even now, their spirits still inhabit these places, and as far as they're concerned, it's business as usual.

HAUNTINGS THROUGH THE AGES
(Colonial Williamsburg, Virginia)

Even before the Pilgrims arrived on New England's shores in 1620, there was a European presence here. The first permanent English-speaking settlement in the New World was at Jamestown, founded in 1607. By virtue of this longevity, Jamestown was considered the original capital of Virginia.

But Jamestown had its issues. Its physical location was not ideal. The original settlers slapped together a settlement, trying desperately to survive their first few years in an unknown, often hostile world. Other towns eventually gained a foothold in the area; the settlement that would later become Williamsburg was established in 1638.

By 1699, a petition reached the House of Burgesses to move the capital from Jamestown to Middle Plantation, five miles inland

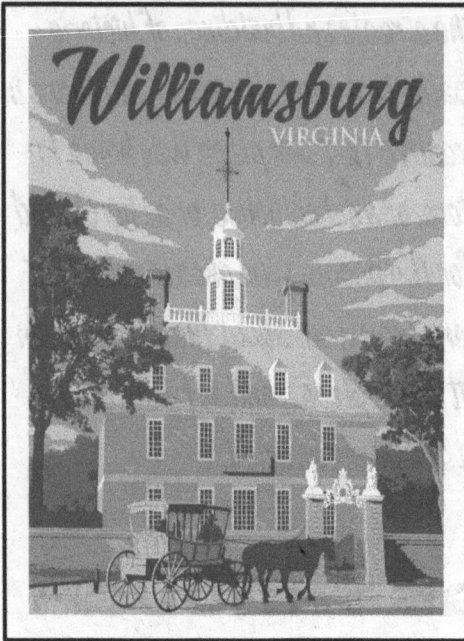

between the James and York Rivers. This would put the capital on higher ground, and even a five-mile move inland meant a cooler climate and much less discomfort than the mosquito-infested low marshes of Jamestown. Also, the State House in Jamestown had been severely damaged in a fire in 1698 - for the third time. It was time for a change. The new city was renamed Williamsburg in honor of the English monarch at the time, William III.

Virginia was the largest and most populous of the British colonies in America. Therefore, it needed an impressive capital. Williamsburg quickly and gracefully rose to the challenge. The town was laid out in 1699 under the supervision of Governor Francis Nicholson. Beautiful buildings were constructed, as befitted the home of the oldest legislative assembly in the New World. Williamsburg was also a center of learning. The College of William and Mary was founded in 1693, even before Middle Plantation became the capital and changed its name. The college later counted Thomas Jefferson, James Monroe, and John Tyler among its illustrious alumni.

Williamsburg was also the site of the first hospital established in America for the care and treatment of mental illness. Built in 1773, it was originally known as the Public Hospital for Persons of Insane and Disordered Minds. We'll come back to this place later in this chapter.

Williamsburg was witness to history yet again just a few years later, in 1781. George Washington assembled the Continental Army there in preparation for the siege of Yorktown, the final battle that led to independence for the young nation.

In 1780, Governor Thomas Jefferson moved the capital up the James River to Richmond. Stripped of its legislative prominence, Williamsburg reverted to being a rural county seat and a quiet college town. This actually turned out to be a good thing, as far as preservationists are concerned. Williamsburg's loss of capital city status meant that the town fathers no longer felt compelled to modernize at every turn. Many 18th century buildings survived into the 20th century, and this was Williamsburg's salvation.

The historic village we now know as Colonial Williamsburg had its roots in one man's vision. Reverend Dr. W.A.R. Goodwin was the rector of Bruton Parish Church in the early years of the 20th century. He accepted the rectorship position in 1903 on the condition that the interior of the church be restored to its colonial appearance. Dr. Goodwin believed that the entire town of Williamsburg could be restored, and stand as a living, three-dimensional introduction to the history of colonial Virginia and North America. Visitors to the town would come away with a renewed sense of what it meant to be an American. Goodwin figured that this common background would lead to a stronger sense of national community.

Going on the principle that "shy babies don't get any sweeties," Goodwin approached the man with the deepest pockets in America. John D. Rockefeller Jr. was a philanthropist who was passionately interested in art and culture. Even though his fortune was built on industry - by 1880, his father's Standard Oil Company controlled 90% of the oil business in the US - he felt that the pre-industrial past was superior to the present day.

Rockefeller was drawn to the beauty of the past: he helped restore Louis XIV's Palace of Versailles. He was also a perfectionist. He believed that if something was worth doing, it was worth doing well. (Or, to put it another way, do it properly or not at all.)

When Dr. Goodwin approached him with the idea of returning Williamsburg to its colonial form, Rockefeller was all in. Beginning in 1926 until his death in 1960, he threw himself into the undertaking. He usually spent a month there in the spring, and another in the fall. He was passionate about the restoration and saw it as his most important project. Colonial Williamsburg was dearer to him than any of his other philanthropic works, including Rockefeller Center.

Rockefeller Center, in New York, represented John D's role as heir to one of America's great industrial fortunes, but Williamsburg spoke to his personal ideals. He wasn't interested in power. He preferred his legacy to be one of quiet cobblestone streets, quaint handicrafts, and old-fashioned manners. He knew he could create a tribute to the people, both famous and unknown, who had built a nation based on liberty, democracy, and the worth of the individual.

Colonial Williamsburg was always intended to be an educational landmark. Rockefeller and Dr. Goodwin agreed: if people could mentally transport themselves back in time to the 18th century, they could gain a better appreciation of the importance of the struggle for independence. The lesson the men hoped to impart was subtle, yet clear and effective. History was no longer a boring, dusty litany of dates and battles. On the contrary; it was now novel, immersive, and exciting.

During World War II, soldiers and sailors stationed at nearby military bases were invited to Williamsburg for day-long educational programs as guests of the Rockefellers. The purpose of these visits was twofold. Firstly, they were intended to remind the servicemen of the values that the armed forces were fighting for, in Europe and the Pacific. Secondly, and more pragmatically, they kept the tourism aspect active during years of low attendance due to wartime travel restrictions.

After the war, many service members returned to Williamsburg, bringing their families to share the experience. The postwar era also brought a change in the social climate of the town, just as it did to the nation in general. The Colonial Williamsburg adventure now included information on the historical presence of African Americans and women.

Some critics liken Colonial Williamsburg to a sort of Disneyland. But here's the thing: Disneyland was completely built on fantasy. There never was a real place called "Disneyland" that the theme park seeks to recreate. Williamsburg, on the other hand, was a real town, where real people lived and died.

And some of them are still there.

Dr. W.A.R. Goodwin once told newspaper columnist Ernie Pyle when Pyle visited Williamsburg in 1936, "I wouldn't give a hoot for anybody who doesn't believe in ghosts." Goodwin was very open to the possibility of a life beyond this one. In a letter to ten-year-old Joan Scott, he wrote that you can "shut your eyes and see the gladsome ghosts who once made these places their home. You can learn to call them back. You can train yourself to hear what they have to say."

For Goodwin, a receptiveness to the supernatural was just another facet of his restoration efforts. Pyle wrote that it was when Goodwin "was alone in the starlight, strolling in the night, talking with the ghosts, that he learned about Williamsburg." He accepted that many of the good citizens of the town were indeed still residing in their homes. But not all the spirits here are of the friendly variety.

I did tell you we'd circle back to the Public Hospital, so

that's where we'll start with the ghost stories. The 18th century attitude towards the treatment of the mentally ill was nothing short of barbaric. Psychiatric patients were confined to isolation cells for long stretches of time, their contact with the outside world limited to a single barred window. Patients were shackled to the walls and slept on the floor or on filthy sacks filled with stale musty straw. Treatment for their mental illness often consisted of beatings to drive out their infirmities, or tying a sufferer's hands and feet together and dunking them in cold water. None of these so-called "treatments" worked, of course, and most were just savagely cruel.

The vast majority of lunatic asylums continued these inhumane practices throughout the 19th century as well. But in 1841, things at the Public Hospital changed, at least for a little while. John Minson Galt II became the hospital's superintendent. He immediately set about changing the abysmal conditions there. He believed that people suffering from mental illness should be cared for with dignity and respect. He threw himself into this work, and for 21 years, he improved the lives of the patients in his care.

But in 1862, the Civil War came to the hospital's doorstep. During the Battle of Williamsburg, Union soldiers commandeered the hospital and forced Galt out. The compassionate administrator, devastated at losing the ability to protect his vulnerable charges, saw only one way out of the desperate situation. He dejectedly went home to his house on the hospital grounds and drank a massive amount of laudanum, a powerful opiate. He was found dead there a while later. The overdose of the medication caused many of the blood vessels in his brain to burst, and Galt was found lying in a large pool of his own blood, a pool that was slowly spreading across the wooden boards of the floor.

Soon after Galt's death, the Lee family moved into the house. Mrs. Lee was acutely aware of the tragedy that had taken place there. She wrote, "I could do nothing to get the blood stain out of the floorboards. No amount of scrubbing would remove it. We finally had to pull up the soiled portion and replace it with fresh wood. I was shocked to find the stain somehow made its way onto the new flooring the next morning! My children are frightened. They wake me most every night claiming a man is in the upstairs room where Doctor Galt died."

The former Galt home has since been torn down, but locals believed that Dr. Galt's spirit simply moved from his home back to the hospital where he once worked, and whose inhabitants he championed so tirelessly.

The Bruton Parish Church is the oldest surviving building in Colonial Williamsburg. Construction of the original building was completed in 1683, when the town was still known as Middle Plantation. The original brick building was soon judged to be in poor condition, and James Blair, rector from 1710 to 1743, oversaw the construction of a new church. (We've already met Reverend Blair; he was also the president of the College of William and Mary from 1693 until his death and was the leader of the group that suggested that the Virginia Assembly move the capital from Jamestown to Williamsburg.) The building project lasted from 1711 to 1715, but the thorough job was worth it. Bruton Parish Church was designated a National Historic Landmark in 1970. It's still an active house of worship today and is considered an exquisite example of colonial religious architecture.

The church is surrounded by an extensive cemetery, with burials dating back to the 17th century. All these graves have their own story to tell, but the tale contained in three graves in particular give rise to one of our ghost stories.

During the colonial era, a Reverend Jones served as the rector of Bruton Parish Church. When his wife was in labor with their first child, complications endangered her life. The doctor regretfully told Reverend Jones that his beloved wife would not survive the birth. The reverend was devastated at the news. He knelt at his wife's deathbed and wept at the impending loss. Tearfully, he begged her to wait for him so that they could be reunited in Heaven. When she passed, he buried her in the cemetery next to the church.

Mrs. Jones seemed to agree to her bereaved husband's request. Witnesses saw her roaming the cemetery and the church, even sitting in one of the pews. To all who saw her, she seemed indeed to be waiting for her husband to join her in good time.

But her steadfastness was misplaced. Three months later, Rev. Jones arrived at the church with a tombstone to mark his late wife's grave. He also brought another addition to the church - his new wife.

This betrayal broke the heart of the first wife. Her ghost still wandered the cemetery, but now people saw her wailing with grief and anger over her husband's unfaithfulness. To make things even worse, when the second Mrs. Jones passed away, Rev. Jones had her grave plot placed between him and his first wife. The first Mrs. Jones has never had the opportunity to get over her shock and betrayal.

When Williamsburg became Virginia's capital in 1699, city officials realized that the town would need a jail. They had a simple brick building constructed, intending to keep things small and uncomplicated. In the beginning, the Public Gaol had only three rooms: two for inmates, and one where the jailer lived. But human nature being what it is, the town's population of lawbreakers soon overran the facility. An exercise yard was added in 1703, and a debtors' prison was built in 1711. A separate house was built for the jailer's quarters in 1722.

In 1704, the prison played host to a celebrity. Edward Teach, better known as the pirate Blackbeard, was captured along with his crew, and locked up in Williamsburg to await trial. Out of fifteen members of the pirate crew, thirteen were hanged.

Conditions in the jail were brutal, with diseases like typhoid running rampant. The cells were freezing in winter and stiflingly hot in summer, and the food was awful and unhealthy. It's no wonder that the Public Gaol is another haunted building in Williamsburg. The spirits of inmates are still locked up in the prison. The apparitions of two women are seen on the upper floor of the jail, with their footsteps heard below. They'll also carry on heated conversations that echo hollowly through the rooms.

Visitors also report seeing eerie shadows moving around the jail. Chains on display have been seen swinging without any human hand setting them into movement. People experience an overwhelming sense of sadness or fear when entering the jail or hear unexplained banging coming from inside the cells.

The King's Arms Tavern was originally opened in 1772 by Jane Vobe. She intended her establishment to be a place, she said, "where all the best people resorted." The tavern did indeed gain acceptance and became a place where important meetings were held. George Washington was a frequent customer, which helped the tavern's reputation as a gathering place of renown.

The re-creation of the King's Arms opened in 1951. The present-day building is a faithful rendition of the original, with pewter candlesticks on the tables illuminating the period-appropriate meals. The tavern's bill of fare features recipes that would have been served in the 18th century.

For example, "An Onion Pye," a recipe from a 1767 cookbook called *The Kitchen Garden Desplay'd*, takes its description from the actual cooking directions. "Pare some potatoes ... apples ... onions and slice them ... make a good crust. Lay in a layer of potatoes, a layer of onions, a layer of apple and a layer of eggs until you have filled your pie, strewing seasoning between each layer. Close your pie and bake it an hour and a half." That doesn't sound half bad.

Stepping into the King's Arms feels like the best kind of time travel - a place where you can taste the past as well as see, hear, and feel it. Maybe that's why the tavern is so very haunted. This is the stuff of life, food and drink, and the ghosts feel right at home here.

One of the spirits is believed to be Gowan Pamphlet, a formerly enslaved man once owned by Jane Vobe. His other vocation was that of preacher; he's said to be the first Black ordained minister in America, and after his ordination in 1772, he helped to secretly found the First Baptist Church of Williamsburg in 1776. The church began with secret meetings in the woods, as the celebrants didn't want to arouse suspicions of a slave uprising. They just wanted to worship in peace. Pamphlet was freed in 1793 and led his congregation for the rest of his life. People in the tavern sometimes hear hymns being sung. They say that Pamphlet's spirit has a calming presence.

Interestingly, the most frequently spotted ghost at the King's Arms is not a ghost from the colonial era. The restaurant's manager in 1951 was a woman named Irna, who lived upstairs at the tavern and died in her rooms. Staff members report seeing a candle burning in Irna's room when no one has lit one and seeing her face in mirrors. At the end of a shift, it's common for a server to blow out the candles in the tables, only to turn around and see them relit.

The George Wythe House was built in 1753, another fine example of colonial opulence. The brick mansion was a wedding present from Wythe's father-in-law. The house was designed for the newlyweds, George and Elizabeth, by her father, the renowned architect Richard Taliaferro. George Wythe was one of the elites of Williamsburg. He was America's first law professor, teaching at the distinguished College of William and Mary, and taught law to Thomas Jefferson. Wythe was also one of the signers of the Declaration of Independence. He offered his beautiful home as headquarters for George Washington and the Marquis de Lafayette before the Battle of Yorktown.

The hauntings here began very early in Williamsburg's history. The story involves Lady Ann Skipwith and her husband, Sir Peyton Skipwith. The two were friends of the Wythes and spent much time at the house in the late 1770s. In fact, the house is where Ann Skipwith died in 1779. The circumstances surrounding her death were murky even back then. She ostensibly died following a miscarriage, but wagging tongues claimed she committed suicide after discovering that her husband was having an affair with her sister. (Sir Peyton did indeed marry the sister shortly after Lady Ann's death.)

The most detailed story also explains one physical aspect of the haunting. In this version, Sir Peyton and Lady Ann were attending a ball at the Governor's Palace, where Peyton was shamelessly flirting with other women. Ann angrily confronted Peyton about the affair, then stormed out of the palace. Her husband, meanwhile, stayed at the ball, leaving her to make her own way home. Ann was in such a hurry to clamber into her carriage that she lost one of her shoes. She got home and ran up the stairs, slamming the door in her fury.

The ghost lore of the Wythe House now holds that you can hear a woman running up the stairs, with a very distinctive noise: the sharp clack of a heeled dancing shoe followed by the dull thud of a bare foot.

Ann's ghost is also still seen at the Wythe House and in the gardens, appearing as a full-bodied apparition in colonial dress. One visitor to the home claims to have seen Lady Skipwith's wardrobe door open on its own.

Another sense that is involved in the hauntings at the Wythe House is the sense of smell. Specifically, the scent of perfume. Sometime around 1986, an employee whose job it was to keep track of visiting groups was sitting on a chair in a hallway when she smelled perfume. At first, she assumed that someone in a recent tour group had been wearing it. But when she checked her clipboard, she realized that the last group had left the house twenty minutes earlier, and that any smell with them had long since faded into the air. It was, she said, as if someone wearing strong perfume had leaned over her shoulder to read from her clipboard.

In March 1999, an evening tour guide smelled perfume as she stood alone in the open front doorway. At the same time, she also heard chairs being dragged across the floor in the empty parlor.

One of the most interesting reports from the Wythe House again involved one of the interpreters on staff. A young woman opened the door that led to the basement when she suddenly felt pressure against the back of her knees that gently forced her to sit down on the top step. She said she didn't feel weak or faint, she just felt compelled to sit on the bare wooden step.

She ended up sitting and turned slightly to her left. Oddly, she saw what she described as a mirror that reflected both herself and another woman. Like her, the figure had red hair. Feeling no fear or surprise, the interpreter turned to her right and found the red-haired lady sitting beside her on the step. The ghostly figure smiled at her, then faded into the white-painted brick wall.

The Ware House (now the Kimball Theatre) was owned by a widow named Mrs. Ware during the Civil War. The Battle of Williamsburg resulted in appalling loss of life, with combined casualties on both sides of more than 4,000 men. The quiet streets of the colonial city were littered with the dead and wounded, both Federal and Rebel. Mrs. Ware found a wounded Confederate in the street outside her home. She took him in and made him as comfortable as she could manage, but he later died of his injuries.

Mrs. Ware covered the soldier's body respectfully. Soon afterward, Union troops knocked on her door. They were there to commandeer her home for use as a field hospital. Mrs. Ware invited the men into her home and informed the commanding officer that a Confederate soldier had just died, and was laid out awaiting burial.

The Union officer inspected the casualty. Slowly he drew back the blanket that covered the enemy soldier's face. Then he dropped the blanket in shock - the body was that of his younger brother. The two Virginia men had both joined the army when the war began, but one had chosen to fight for the Union, the other for the Confederacy. The officer was devastated to learn of his brother's death. He himself was later killed in battle. To this day, two spirits dressed in Civil War uniforms can be seen roaming the Ware House.

Confederate ghosts also haunt the Fort Magruder Hotel and Conference Center. Tourists say that soldiers in gray uniforms wander through their hotel rooms. One woman woke up in the middle of the night to find a Confederate soldier with red hair sitting on the edge of her bed - and she's not the only one who's seen him. He shows up with some regularity.

The hotel was the site of three paranormal investigations led by three different teams during a science fiction convention. Pamela Kinney was a member of one of those teams. She is a seasoned investigator, and it takes a lot to rattle her: she leads a group in North Carolina and has written a book about the ghosts of that state. But one experience during this investigation, by her own admission, creeped her out.

"Someone took a picture at the one on Friday night and in the photo, the lead investigator had a figure behind her. It wore a hat and its hand rested on her shoulder."

Kinney also spent some time alone, exploring the Civil War

earthworks on the grounds of the hotel. An unexplained mist appeared in several of the pictures she took. "That day, I swore I felt as if a crowd of people surrounded me," she said.

Civil War soldiers on both sides of the conflict are not the only dead folks that hang out at the hotel. "We heard from a British person from 1644 that night ... and I was told of a modern child that died in the hotel after we got a child that night communicating by my EMF meter."

Constructed in 1695 on the campus of the College of William and Mary, the Wren Building is the oldest college building in continuous use in the United States. It's built in kind of a weird place - directly over a crypt. The crypt is the burial site of many of Williamsburg's prominent residents ... and during the Civil War, it was looted by Union soldiers. (It's always bad news when human remains are disturbed. That just never ends well.)

Even worse, the college was used for a while as a "re-education" center for Native American boys who were taken from their families and forced into the white man's culture. Many of these kids tried to escape. Most of them were unsuccessful in the attempt.

Apparitions of young Native American boys have been seen running through the Wren Building's courtyard, still seeking desperately to return to the loving embrace of their families. Ghostly soldiers patrol the building's hallways. And that disturbed crypt? People have heard unexplained noises and screams coming from its depths.

I've saved the best - or at least the most notorious - for last. The Peyton Randolph House is a large two-story mansion on Nicholson Street. Its reddish-brown brick and lack of architectural ornamentation make it look like a grade school rather than a house. But this building's imposing appearance hides a dark secret.

Freak accidents, mysterious illnesses, and even a murder or three have claimed about thirty lives here over the centuries. It's known not only as the most haunted place in Williamsburg, but also the most haunted home on the East Coast.

It was built in 1715, and was originally owned by Sir John Randolph, a wealthy colonist who'd been knighted by King George II. Ownership passed to his son, Peyton Randolph. Peyton was a cousin of Thomas Jefferson and an ardent patriot. He served as the president of the First and Second Continental Congress.

The house, it's said, has been haunted ever since one of the Randolph family's slaves cursed it in 1782. (Who knows how some houses get haunted, but a good juicy curse by an enslaved person is always a great place to start.) It was used as a military command headquarters during the Revolutionary War and was one of the fifteen private homes in Williamsburg that were pressed into service as field hospitals during the Civil War. The hauntings here are aggressive. Visitors have been touched, even pushed. People have witnessed violent shaking of furniture and walls. Objects move on their own, and voices are heard coming from thin air.

The paranormal activity at the Peyton Randolph House has been going on for two hundred years. In 1824, Revolutionary War hero, the Marquis de Lafayette, returned to Williamsburg for a visit. He'd spent time here during the war and came back to the place he'd made so many memories.

"I considered myself fortunate to lodge in the home of a great man, Peyton Randolph." Lafayette later wrote. "Upon my arrival, as I entered through the foyer, I felt a hand on my shoulder. It nudged me as if intending to keep me from entering. I quickly turned but found no one there. The nights were not restful as the sounds of voices kept me awake for most of my stay."

Colonial Williamsburg is the granddaddy of all historic

villages. It's been going strong for over a century, giving visitors a taste of what life was like in the colonial era, and inspiring generations with the spirit of independence. It's a place where the past comes to life ... and a place where the dead still walk.

GHOSTS OF THE BLACK COUNTRY
(Avoncroft Museum of Historic Buildings, Stoke Heath, Worcestershire, England, and Black Country Living Museum, Dudley, England)

Not quite two hundred years ago, someone discovered that the West Midlands region of England was incredibly rich in natural resources, and that those resources could be used in manufacturing goods at a rate never before seen, in England or anywhere else. The area was home to deposits of coal and limestone, so it made sense to put factories there. A *lot* of factories. By the 1830s, the region had gotten a new nickname.

People were calling it the Black Country.

The Black Country encompassed about twenty towns that are located in four boroughs: Dudley, Sandwell, Walsall, and Wolverhampton. This region was one of the most industrialized parts of the United Kingdom, home to enterprises like iron foundries, brick and glass factories, and loads of coal mines. This was the location of the largest seam of coal in England, and men and boys were kept busy working in the 500 to 600 mines in the area. All of this was fuel for the Industrial Revolution.

At one time, the Black Country produced 22% of Britain's entire output of iron. Technology had advanced to the point where heavy industry was possible. The factories there produced the iron columns and huge panes of glass that went into the construction of the Crystal Palace in 1851. Also - fun fact - those ironworks manufactured the anchors and anchor chains that were used in some of England's most famous ships, including *Titanic*.

All these products - the etched glass and glass panes, the anchor chains, the bricks, the textiles, the leather goods, the

WEST MIDLANDS

ENGLAND

myriad useful things crafted from iron - were shipped out of the area via a canal system dug for that purpose. And from there, they were sent all over the world. To feed the insatiable factories, there was another industry that churned out raw materials, so that production could run 24-7. The landscape was plundered for resources: coal, fire clay, and limestone. Any area of the countryside that wasn't occupied by factory buildings was scarred by the constant demand for material or cluttered with waste from the manufacturing process. There were huge mounds of coal slag and dust, bits too small for fuel that simply piled up, that were just left to burn uncontrollably. All this industry, belching pollutants into the land, water, and sky, is really what gave the Black Country its name.

By the mid-20th century, manufacturing had turned to other, lighter industries. Instead of coal mines and iron foundries, the region became known for factories that produced cars and motorcycles. By 1968, heavy industry had dried up, and the canal system fell into disuse.

But even with the move away from grinding factory work

and coal mining, people realized the worth of remembering the importance of the Black Country. This was, after all, the cradle of the Industrial Revolution. A couple of museums dedicated to living history were formed; buildings from all over the region were rescued from demolition and moved to these villages, and slowly, they grew.

The Avoncroft Museum of Historic Buildings was the first of these. Founded in 1963, it opened in 1967. This was England's first open-air museum, and the second in the UK. (St. Fagan's, in Cardiff, Wales, was the very first. We'll look at that in the next chapter.)

The buildings at Avoncroft, in Stoke Heath, span several hundred years of history. The museum began with the rescue of a 15th century timber-framed merchant's house that was moved from Bromsgrove. This medieval home was the first in a collection that has grown to over thirty buildings.

One of these is a chain shop from nearby Cradley. Built in the mid-19th century, it produced handmade chains until 1969. The craft of making nails by hand declined in the early 19th century, so nail shops pivoted and adapted their forges to produce chain instead.

There's also a cell block at Avoncroft, which was built in the 1870s. It was attached to the Magistrates Court in Church Street, in Ledbury, Herefordshire. The cells housed people who were charged with various crimes such as vagrancy, arson, burglary, petty theft, begging, and poaching. It was a place of quiet misery, where prisoners were kept as they awaited trial.

Other buildings at Avoncroft include several private houses, a church, and other shops. In one of these, witnesses saw a couple of men dressed in 18th-century clothing walking past an old forge. At the same time the ghosts were seen, the experiencers realized they could hear the unmistakable sharp *"ting"* of a hammer striking an anvil. Was this a time slip? Or just a couple of ghosts going about their day? Could be a little of both. There's also been poltergeist activity reported at Avoncroft, and a visitor was smacked on the back with an unseen hand.

The most reliable and detailed account of a ghost sighting at Avoncroft happened over a decade ago. On March 31, 2013, a visitor saw a boy standing by a fireplace in the medieval Merchant's House. The boy looked about 13 years old, with wavy hair that fell to his shoulders. He was dressed in a red tunic cinched with a brown leather belt. As the visitor came close to the hearth, the boy disappeared.

Another historic village in the area is the Black Country Living Museum in Dudley. Dudley is considered "the birthplace of the Industrial Revolution," so when the museum opened in 1976, it quickly gained recognition for its preservation of the area's history. Like Avoncroft, Black Country Living Museum is made up of buildings that have been relocated to the site. Costumed demonstrators move through the restored buildings, giving visitors an idea of what life was like. They portray life in the Black Country spanning two hundred years of history, with a focus on 1850 to 1950.

The Black Country Living Museum sits on 26 acres of what used to be waste land, pocked with coal pits and lime works. Now, sixty donated buildings make up the historic village. In 1990, the museum opened an underground exhibit depicting life and labor in a coal mine.

Life wasn't all just dreary, back-breaking labor, though. Behind the school sits a 1930s fairground, fitted out with historic rides. It represents the traveling fairs that would bring entertainment to people in the early part of the century.

One of the first structures added to the museum was the Canal Street Bridge. From 1879 to 1976, it sat over the Birmingham Canal. When it was moved, it would seem that a ghost came with it. The figure of a man has been seen falling from the bridge into the canal below. Historians have no idea who this man was. The question that makes people wonder is this: did he jump, or was he pushed?

The Toll House dates to 1843. Very often, visitors will get a spooky vibe from the bedroom on the right. There's a fun story from this building. A woman was taking a tour and asked if she could look inside the room. The door was closed, and she didn't feel right just walking in without at least asking permission. The tour guide said sure, go on in. The woman opened the door to the bedroom, peeked inside, then quietly closed the door without going in. When the tour guide asked why the woman hadn't gone in after all, she replied that she hadn't wanted to disturb the little girl who was sound asleep on the bed.

The kicker? The room was empty.

Some of the buildings in the historic village are only partially original. Take the shop in the village that bears the name "H. Emile Doo - Chemist & Druggist." The chemist shop was founded in 1886 by the eponymous Mr. Doo. He passed the business down to his son Harold, who ran it until his death in 1968. The shop sat empty for a few years, and in 1973, the shop and its contents were donated to the museum. The shell of the building was purpose-built as sort of a frame for the exhibit; the storefront and the contents of the building are original. Everything in the shop was actually used back in the day.

Early one morning, before the museum opened to the public, a staff member was walking past the chemist shop. Costumed interpreters would come to work in their street clothes, change into their garb, then make their way to the building where they'd been assigned. The guide glanced into the shop as she passed, and through the plate glass window, she saw three old ladies in authentic Victorian dresses chatting inside. She assumed that they, like her, were costumed staff. She looked away for a moment, then looked back - she hadn't really clocked them as co-workers, so she took a second look.

All three ladies had vanished.

Even though the shop is filled with items that were in use when the place was a going concern, it's doubtful that even one of these spirits, much less all three of them, attached themselves to anything in the store. Whoever heard of a haunted packet of cough drops, or an ear swab jar with a spirit attachment? No, it's more likely that this is a residual haunting, or that the three ladies regularly met at the chemist's in the morning as part of their normal day. They must have enjoyed those catch-up sessions so much that they've decided to continue them in the afterlife.

A YouTuber who goes by the name of Don't Scare Claire did an episode on the Black Country Living Museum. A commenter, @chriseccles6342, posted on the video about their experience. They said that in 2016, they were an extra in a film shot on location at the historic village. The director was filming a night shot on the high street, and the poster claims that they saw "echoes" in the shops. Yes, of course there were lots of living people in costume wandering around, but "some could just disappear in front of your eyes." The commenter saw flower sellers that were offering their wares on the cobblestone street. They asked one of the production crew if there were, in fact, any flower sellers in the scene.

There were not.

One of the most haunted buildings at the Black Country Living Museum is the Bottle and Glass Inn. This pub began life as The Bush in the 1770s. At that time, it was in Brockmoor, where it sat with its back to the Star Bridge Canal. Management changed the name of the pub to the Bottle and Glass Inn in 1840, and it closed in 1979. It was then moved to its present location at the historic village, and reconstructed as it sat in Brockmoor, next to the canal.

The hauntings here began before the pub was moved to the museum. A woman who lived at the inn with her aunt and uncle from 1914 to 1928 reported that the smallest of the three bedrooms in the living quarters of the inn was completely haunted by ... something. They couldn't put their finger on exactly what was wrong with the room, they just knew that something was off. The energy in the room just put everyone on edge. Small items would go missing for no reason, and the room gave everyone an uneasy feeling. One morning, the woman woke to find that every article of clothing and all the bedsheets had inexplicably been piled up in one corner of the room.

The piano at the pub will play when no one is around. People sometimes even see the indistinct figure of the man sitting at the piano playing it.

One of the ghosts that has been seen peeking out of the windows and moving around behind the bar at the inn is a man with round glasses and a pudgy round face. This description actually fits a fellow named William Mollett, who was the landlord of the pub in the 1860s and 1870s. He appears in the historical record - he was fined in 1871 for "allowing drunkenness in his pub." (Oops.) Pub staff regularly hear someone moving around in the back room, even when they know there's no one in there. Staff members have also experienced someone tapping them on the shoulder - someone who isn't there when they turn around.

Female staff in costume sometimes feel their long skirts being pulled, as if a young child is trying to get their attention. This last manifestation has a deeply tragic backstory. This is one of the most famous ghost stories associated with the Black Country Living Museum, and it involves a ghost who is intimately connected to the Bottle and Glass Inn.

The young spirit who seeks the comfort of a motherly figure might very well be the ghost of a ten-year-old boy named Isaac Male. Unfortunately, his tale is a tragic part of local history.

I mentioned the network of canals that served as a watery highway to move raw materials and finished goods around the Black Country. This transportation system was busy with barges, which were powered by horses harnessed to the barge. The horse would plod along the bank, pulling the barge as it went. Because the Black Country was a great source of employment (and because this story comes from a time well before child labor laws), both men and boys worked, in the coal mines, the factories, and on the canals.

Young Isaac worked for a boatman named James Haines. One very foggy night, Haines and two of his men had released their horse from its barge harness and were leading it along the Star Bridge Canal back to the stable. Isaac was riding the horse - it may have been a few stolen moments of simple pleasure for the child. But in the dense, soupy fog, the horse lost its footing, stumbled, and fell into the canal, with Isaac clinging desperately to its broad back.

Haines and his men barely noticed the human element to this tragedy. The only thing they cared about was rescuing their valuable horse. It took them about twenty minutes to get the horse out of the canal. It was only then that they realized that Isaac needed to be rescued, too. But when they finally began their search for the boy, it was far too late. Isaac had already drowned.

The boy's limp body was taken to the Bottle and Glass Inn, right next to the canal, and an inquest was held. The verdict was delivered: Isaac's death was ruled accidental. However, Haines and his men were severely criticized for allowing a ten-year-old boy to drown that dark night.

Even though the pub is now in the historic village, and not in Brockmoor, young Isaac's spirit is still attached to the place where he - sort of - got a little bit of justice.

THE LEGACY OF CIVIL WAR

(St. Fagan's National History Museum, Cardiff, Wales)

So, I mentioned that Avoncroft is the oldest living history village in England and promised to tell you about the oldest in the UK as well. That would be St. Fagan's National History Museum, in Wales. And it is thoroughly, sometimes delightfully, often terrifyingly haunted. As a matter of fact, it does hold the title of the most haunted museum in Wales.

Let's take a stroll around the grounds, shall we?

St. Fagan's Castle is a 16th century manor house, built on foundations that date back to the 13th century. This was at one time the summer home of the 3rd Earl of Plymouth, who graciously donated the castle and grounds to the people of Wales in 1946. The museum opened in 1948. Now there are over forty reconstructed and refurnished buildings on the 100-acre site. Again, most of the buildings were rescued from demolition and brought to the museum for future generations to enjoy.

And many of them are quite haunted indeed.

Even the grounds are haunted. The English Civil War, fought from August 1642 to September 1651 between the Royalists who backed King Charles I and the supporters of Parliament led by Oliver Cromwell, spilled over into Wales. The bloody Battle of St. Fagan's, fought here in 1648, was a critical engagement of the war. Thousands of men fought, over two hundred men lost their lives, and the battle ended in a catastrophic defeat for the Royalists.

Security guards patrolling the grounds at night report hearing horses at full gallop getting closer and closer, but they never see the pounding steeds. Sounds of pitched battle are heard in the distance - gunfire, the clash of steel on steel, and the screams of wounded men. Horses have also been heard and even seen running in a panicked frenzy through the trees, as if fleeing wild from the terror of the battle.

At the Cilewent Farmhouse, a ghostly boy has been seen around the building in the trees, but also in the entrance courtyard. He's seen inside the farmhouse too, coming up from the stone floor in the main living room. This is thought to be the spirit of a boy who was accidentally killed in the confusion of the battle. His body lay forgotten where it fell in the chaos. The house was later built right over that spot.

A tour guide was leading a group through the farmhouse one night. The room next to the group was pitch black; beyond the open door, nothing could be seen. The entire group heard a loud "snap" from the blackness. The sound had no explanation. Seconds later, the sharp odor of spent gunpowder filled the room, then quickly faded.

In 2016, a mother who'd brought her kids to St. Fagan's Museum for a pleasant day out got a nasty shock. She took a picture of her two boys playing on the grass - not realizing that in the tall brush just a few yards from the kids, two men in Parliamentary blue uniforms were watching.

And those are just some of the earliest ghosts at the museum. There are buildings here from centuries of Welsh history:

an Iron Age farmstead, the 16ᵗʰ century manor house, a medieval prince's court from the 13ᵗʰ century, a Tudor merchant's house, even a postwar bungalow. They each have attachments, spirits that refuse to move on.

Capel Penrhiw (Penrhiw Chapel), which translates to "Hilltop Chapel," was established in 1770 to serve a tiny town in the west part of Wales called Drefach Velindre. The walls of this humble church saw centuries of emotion, both happy and sad, and the chapel echoed through time with the sound of hymns solemn and joyful and heartfelt prayers of the faithful. All of this seeped into the stone and was brought here with the building.

Visitors sometimes say that when they enter Penrhiw Chapel, they get overcome with emotion, as if they'd walked in while a service was going on. They experience an overwhelming feeling of sadness as if they were interrupting a funeral or are suffused with joy at a wedding or baptism. Some visitors report a feeling of being watched. They can even pinpoint the place in the chapel where that creepy feeling seems to originate - they point to the balcony, right above the front door. Unexplained lights have been seen moving around in the darkness of the balcony. Witnesses have claimed to see a little boy crouched in the balcony, peering down between the bars of the railing. This makes sense, as the chapel also served as the village school.

In fact, many of the ghost stories at St. Fagan's feature children. This could be due to the high juvenile death rates in the poor communities from which the buildings came. Or, it could have nothing to do with the buildings. All of this area was farmland for centuries. Children played in the great outdoors and helped their families work the fields here for generations.

Two of the buildings that are home to child ghosts are small white cottages, called Nant Wallter and Llainfadyn. They share similar hauntings, but that's really where the similarities end. Let's explore them both.

Nant Wallter was built around 1785. Interestingly, it originally stood in rural Carmarthenshire in west Wales, not far from Penrhiw Chapel. This is a very basic home, just a rudimentary shelter. The walls are made from a material called "clom," a mixture of mud, clay, gravel, and twigs. This compound hardens into walls that provide very good protection against cold, rain, and wind.

But it's no luxury accommodation, that's for sure. There is a single room; the bedroom is at the back, with a curtain for a bit of privacy. There's more sleeping space on a platform overhead. Families would rent the cottage from the landowner, staying only for a year or two.

This arrangement changed in 1871, when Evan and Mary Thomas bought the cottage to live in with their eight children. The Thomas family would occupy the cottage for the next fifty years. Tragedy struck the family in 1889. Mary Thomas died in the cottage trying to bring her ninth child into the world. The baby didn't survive birth, either.

Little points of light will appear in the cottage, like orbs, moving as if they have intelligence and purpose. This ghostly manifestation actually tracks with the Welsh folklore of "canwyll corff" or "corpse candles" - glowing lights that appear indoors or outside that warn of approaching death. Welsh legend holds that these lights will follow someone who is about to die, or someone who will soon lose a loved one to death. There are repeated reports from Nant Wallter of hearing children whispering, or of stepping into the cottage and immediately hearing a child begin to cry. The misty figure of a distraught woman is seen sitting on the bed, clutching a bundle to her chest - a bundle that looks a lot like a swaddled infant. Sometimes, a little girl will silently join a tour group and just stand there, listening to the tour guide tell their stories.

Llainfadyn, on the other hand, couldn't be more different

than Nant Wallter. Yeah, okay, it's also a small white cottage. But this house is strikingly different. For one thing, it began life - in 1762, on the coast of Wales near Caernarfon - as a quarryman's cottage. Quarrymen were well paid; they did a dangerous job, and happily for them, there was a high demand for slate. This cottage was built not from cheap clom, but from large stones, and it had a slate roof. Pretty fancy for a cottage. In the 1800s, it was purchased by Hugh and Ann Williams. They lived here with their six children, plus a maid and a lodger.

This cottage is also haunted by the spirits of children, but these are playful little ghosts, not the gloomy shades that inhabit Nant Wallter. Staff and visitors have reported seeing and hearing children playing in and around Llainfadyn. The children are heard more often than they are seen.

One former staff member had an unforgettable experience at the cottage one morning. It was a gloomy, wet morning, with few visitors. The guide was sitting by the cheerfully crackling fire, reading a book to pass the time, ready to greet anyone who came in. She heard a gaggle of children coming towards the cottage, chattering with excitement as they got closer. She stood, preparing to greet the kids and start her talk.

No one came in, and the chatter stopped suddenly. The guide figured the group had just gone on without stopping at the cottage, but she opened the door anyway. She looked up and down the path, but there was no one in sight. She shrugged, went back to her seat, and picked up her book. A few moments later, she again heard children's voices talking excitedly right outside the door ... and again, no one came into the cottage.

This time, the guide opened the door and went outside. There was still no one on the path in either direction. She walked all the way around the cottage and found no one.

Shaking her head in puzzlement, she went back to her post. She sat down, and immediately the voices started up again. This time, they were inside the cottage. She could hear the faint voices of several children around her, talking, giggling, just having a great time.

But she couldn't see the kids at all.

She wasn't scared by this. She just sat by the fire, stunned into silence by the paranormal experience. In less than a minute, the sounds faded. Soon they had stopped altogether.

Another building at the museum that holds the echoes of history is St. Teilo's Church. Teilo lived in the 500s and became the patron saint of Cardiff. One of his tombs is in Llandaff Cathedral in Cardiff. (Yes, I said one of his tombs. After he died, three different places wanted the honor of burying him. So, his body miraculously divided into three bodies, to accommodate the wishes of each of the three churches.)

St. Teilo's Church was built around the 1300s, which makes it one of the oldest buildings at the museum. It originally stood about 46 miles to the west, near the city of Swansea. It closed in 1970 and fell into ruin. While it was being dismantled in preparation for relocation to St. Fagan's Museum, murals from the 1400s were discovered under layers of plaster and whitewash. The original murals were stabilized and preserved, then the artwork was recreated in the church, to show how it might have looked in the early 1500s, before religious reforms led to church interiors becoming much simpler.

The church still seems to be alive with ghostly activity. Faint chanting or singing can sometimes be heard in the church. Shadowy figures of priests are seen still going about their pastoral duties. One of these is a man dressed in vestments, who appears to be confused, with a troubled look on his face. This fellow could be a priest who is thrown off by the appearance of the church, now that it is back to the cheerful colors of its pre-Reformation décor.

So, you ask, which is the most haunted building in the most

haunted museum in Wales? That would be Cilewent Farmhouse. This structure dates from the 1400s and was extensively rebuilt in the 1700s. It's a prime example of a Welsh "long house." People lived in one end of the house, and cows lived in the other end, with a hallway in between to separate the two areas. Residents of this house lived in one main downstairs room. A smaller back room was added later and used as a dairy. A small upstairs room was originally used to store hay but was later converted into another bedroom.

There seems to be a very dark, angry energy here. It is human, but resentful and aggressive towards the living who visit the house. A tour guide noticed that people in his tour groups gathered in the main room of the house would stare into the pitch blackness of the dairy with nervous dread. People claimed to see a stocky male shadow figure moving around in the near-total blackness of the dairy. The figure would sometimes approach the group, and sometimes do it quite quickly and aggressively. Members of the tour group would feel as though something pushed them or grabbed their arm. Even more terrifyingly, the figure would sometimes lunge at the group from a dark corner before vanishing.

On one warm spring evening in 2015, something very strange and unnerving happened to one lucky (or unlucky) tour group. The group was standing inside the farmhouse as the guide spun his tales. Suddenly, there was an almighty crash from the empty room above them, and something seemed to roll loudly across the floor. This was followed by a blast of icy cold air that enveloped everyone in the room, even though the weather outside the farmhouse was pleasantly warm and still.

There is one more spirit at St. Fagan's who deserves a mention. This is because he can be seen anywhere on the museum grounds, and there's a very good reason for this. He manifests as an elderly man, seen at night by the security guards or by staff members who are working late. This gentle spirit is a kind-looking man, who is sometimes seen smoking a pipe or walking a dog. He appears quite often near Penrhiw Chapel, and his pipe tobacco can be smelled there too.

This is the ghost of Iorwerth Peate, who was the founder of St. Fagan's Museum, and its first curator. He served from the museum's opening in 1948 until his death in 1971. It makes sense that he has the run of the place, appearing all over the grounds, sitting on benches or walking the paths. And the reason he hangs out near Penrhiw Chapel is because his ashes are buried right outside.

TERROR IN TAILEM
(Old Tailem Town Pioneer Village, South Australia)

"If you've got a ghost in the house, and you pull that house away on the back of a truck, does the ghost just stand there and go, 'Where did my home go?' Or does it come with the walls?"

That is the excellent rhetorical question posed by Alison Oborn, of Adelaide's Haunted Horizons. You met her and her team back in England, at the Ragged School Museum. But in this chapter, they are on their own turf, in southern Australia. Adelaide's Haunted Horizons ghost tour company does tours of several fascinating sites. One of the most viscerally terrifying of these places is Old Tailem Town.

Alison's take on the village is that the hauntings there are mostly connected to the land rather than the buildings - but the buildings are pretty darned active in their own right. There are about 115 of them, on fifteen streets. It's quite a collection.

Peter Squires, the owner of the place, inherited the land from his grandparents. They had run a cattle farm, but Peter wasn't

SOUTH AUSTRALIA

MORIALTA

8 MILES *from* ADELAIDE

interested in keeping cows. He had his own ideas about what to do with all those acres.

Peter had recently visited a pioneer village at Swan Hill, and was intrigued by this hands-on way of experiencing history. He decided to set up his own pioneer village, as a way of teaching visitors about the history of southern Australia. He began purchasing buildings and moving them to the site.

But something strange began to happen when he did. Visitors realized that the village was alive with eerie, unexplained noises, both day and night. Guests would catch movement out of the corner of an eye. When they'd turn to look, nothing was out of place … but a lingering feeling of unease remained.

And that was during the day. At night, the buildings of Old Tailem Town took on a creepy malevolence. Some buildings were more paranormally active than others, but a feeling of dread permeated the entire site.

Many groups have investigated the splendidly haunted village, but it is Adelaide's Haunted Horizons that leads the tours for people who are not necessarily paranormal investigators, but who just want to experience the history and hauntings of these buildings for themselves. Alison and her team are capable, thoughtful guides, giving good history to round out the tour experience.

And sometimes they get to have their own encounters with the supernatural.

Alison shared a deliciously creepy story on her Ghostcast podcast (it's the 2023 Year in Review Christmas episode, if you're wondering). This story originated in Bells Emporium, a dry goods store in the village. This is an intriguing building: it actually used to be three houses, which were put end to end when they arrived at the site. At some point, the interior walls were knocked down to form one big long building, which became the store.

Bells Emporium is, Alison says, the building that makes her the most uncomfortable - and that's saying something. "I'd rather be in the church at the end of the night packing up on my own, than in here." (We'll get to the church in a bit, don't you worry.) Alison's nervousness is well-founded. The dry goods store is chock-full of mannequins ... creepy antique mannequins. Some are fairly normal-looking, but others are much the worse for wear. Several are cracked and battered by years of use, staring blankly at visitors with empty eye sockets.

Several years ago, Alison was in the store alone, tearing down the equipment the team had used for a ghost hunt. She deftly unplugged the IR (infrared) light, then some instinct made her shine her flashlight around the room. She knew the layout well ... which meant that she got a nasty shock when she realized that the mannequin that usually sat at the end of the counter was now suddenly next to the door.

In 2023, Alison was leading a tour at Old Tailem Town. When her group got to the dry goods store, Alison had to share her story, to let the guests know what ghostly shenanigans went on there. She was reenacting the tale as she told it, and shone her flashlight on the same mannequin, now back in its accustomed place.

"I was undoing the light when this manneq--"
She stopped, flummoxed.

In the flashlight's beam, the mannequin was slowly turning.

A man spoke up, his voice wary, almost accusatory. "That MOVED."

Another voice rang out. "That just turned, didn't it?"

Every single person in the group saw the mannequin slowly pivot in the beam of Alison's flashlight. Then shrieks and f-bombs filled the air as the mannequin toppled towards the group.

The history of the buildings that make up Bells Emporium is spotty, but as I mentioned, researchers do know that the store is formed from three houses put together end-to-end. Alison theorizes that one of the houses may have been home to a family that suffered through an abusive relationship. There's something in that building that just doesn't seem to like women.

As active as the dry goods store is, there is another building that has the reputation of being one of the most haunted places in Old Tailem Town. Wolseley Church is solemnly creepy during the day, but at night, it fairly hums with disturbing energy.

During one of the group's first investigations there, Alison says, she had been sitting in the church for much of the night, asking questions, waiting for something - anything - to happen. She and a couple of other women sat in the darkness of the church from 1 am until half past 3, with absolutely no activity at all. Feeling a bit let down, the women went outside for a break.

While outside the church, reviving themselves with snacks and caffeine, the group looked at the old building. They were surprised, and a little creeped out, to see mysterious blue lights playing over the church. When they realized that the eerie blue lights were actually *inside* the building, where they had just been sitting, their nervous energy kicked up a few notches.

Alison had left a voice recorder running inside the church. Upon playing the recording back, the group heard a massive "BANG" in the empty building, followed by shuffling footsteps. Then, she said, it sounded like someone had leaned over the mic and given several deep, heavy, weary sighs.

Alison, like many other investigators, can point to a "defining moment" that really solidified her belief in the paranormal, the moment when you say to yourself, okay, I cannot explain away what just happened, maybe there's something to this ghost business after all. For her, that moment came when she was leading a tour in the church. Eight people in the group got poked, or had their clothing tugged by invisible hands. Two teens wearing hoodies put the hoods up over their heads and tightened the drawstrings, saying that the feeling of someone playing with their hair was weirding them out. A man in the group decided to go with the energy in the church, and he sang a hymn, hoping to encourage the religious vibes. As he finished the song, Alison noticed the dark silhouette of a man standing in the shadows beyond the reach of the flashlight. He seemed to be listening to the music, standing silently without comment.

Old Tailem Town is, without a doubt, one of the most hair-raisingly active places in Australia. The continent is full of terrifying things - and Old Tailem Town Pioneer Village is one of them.

A GOOD LITTLE GIRL
(Historic Cold Spring Village, Cape May, NJ)

In the beginning of the 17th century, exploration of the New World was in full swing. The English explorer Henry Hudson landed in North America in 1609 and made the region around what is now New York City his stomping grounds for a while. His voyages opened up the region for the Dutch East India Company, and helped establish European contact with the natives, leading to trade and a foothold for commerce.

Hudson had done a lot of trading with the tribes of the area, getting quite a lot of furs from them. The fur trade later thrived, and a trading post was established at Albany in 1614. This laid the groundwork for a Dutch presence in the region, with the Dutch acquiring Manhattan. New Amsterdam - later to be renamed New York - was designated the capital of the province in 1625. In 1630, the Dutch East India Company bought even more land from the native tribes and began to colonize the region in earnest. They were all about the money - their aim was to develop strong trade relations with the native population. They wanted this new land to be commercially viable, and the beaver pelts that the natives were trading made this a very appealing proposition. (The Pilgrims, seeking religious freedom, intended to colonize the area around Albany in 1620, but after reaching Cape Cod and running low on supplies, they settled in Massachusetts instead of going on to the Hudson River.)

Decades later, in Cape May, New Jersey, the Cold Spring Presbyterian Church was founded in 1714. It got off to a bit of a rocky start; the second pastor, Hughston Hughes, only lasted a year before being sacked in 1727 for his "too free use of intoxicating drinks." But the church eventually thrived. (Fun fact: the graveyard surrounding the church holds the burials of more Mayflower descendants than anywhere else outside

Massachusetts.) A community soon sprang up around the church, which would also become known as Cold Spring.

This town still exists, as Cold Spring Village. Here's what happened: in 1973, Dr. Joseph Salvatore, along with his wife Patricia Ann, bought the Cold Spring Grange Hall. The building had been constructed in 1912, and it was to be the first building of a historic village. Joseph and Patricia Ann's kids, Rick and Kate, opened Cold Spring Village in 1981, and in 1984, they donated it to the public. The village is made up of 27 structures, some of which, like Cox Hall Cottage, date as far back as 1691. (Not surprisingly, this is one of the buildings where most of the paranormal activity is reported. Other active buildings include the Spicer-Leaming House, the Dennisville Inn, and the Corson-Hand House). Visiting the 30-acre site is like stepping back in time to the early 1800s.

The time travel experience is heightened by interpreters in period dress, who demonstrate trades like bookbinding, blacksmithing, woodworking, and a myriad of other crafts that went into daily life two centuries ago. Cold Spring Village is dedicated to hands-on demonstration and education. It even has a Junior Apprentice Program, that teaches students ages 11 to 14 about life in the early to mid-1800s.

They don't let just anybody in, either. Students who apply to be a part of this program have to have maintained a B average or higher during the previous school year and have to get a letter of recommendation from a teacher. Once accepted, the kids work alongside museum artisans to learn an Early American trade or craft. The work they produce is displayed in the Welcome Center. It's a big deal.

And interestingly enough, this situation sort of set the scene for one of the village's most enduring hauntings.

Tammy Patterson works in the Spicer-Leaming House. She'd been working at Historic Cold Spring Village for about four years when she had a curious experience. She had left her post at the house briefly to go outside to get a bottle of water. As she walked back, she looked up and noticed a young girl looking out of one of the windows on the second floor. The kid was sitting there with her hands tucked under her chin, just as cute as could be. Tammy assumed that the girl was an apprentice who'd been assigned to shadow her. She smiled at the girl, and the kid smiled back.

Tammy hurried into the house, eager to meet her new young pupil. She went up to the second floor, to the room where she'd seen the girl.

There was no little girl there. As a matter of fact, there was no little girl in the entire house.

Tammy dropped her water and ran next door, seeking the comfort of a familiar - and living - coworker. "You look like you just saw a ghost," the other woman kidded. Tammy assured her that she had, indeed, seen a ghost.

She was so spooked by the experience that she thought about quitting the job. But in the end, she decided to stick it out. She hasn't seen the girl since that day, but she does feel the young spirit's presence. "She pulls on my clothes. She opens and shuts doors, and she rocks in the rocking chair." Tammy noticed that the ghostly little girl seemed to hang out mostly upstairs in that second-floor room, and that she frequently seemed to hover around a doll bed in the room.

The next season, the ghost story was making the rounds of the village. A couple heard the story, and sought out Tammy, asking her to tell them of her experience personally - they wanted to get it straight from the source. She told her tale ... and the man began to sob. With tears rolling down his cheeks, he told Tammy that he had once owned the doll bed. It had belonged to his ten-year-old daughter. In fact, it had been her favorite toy. And when she died, he donated it to Cold Spring Village as a way of keeping her memory alive.

It seems to have worked.

Just as the little girl still loves to play with her doll bed, other spirits at the site still act the way they did in life. Ghost hunters know, if someone was a jerk when they were alive, they probably won't be mellow after death.

Clare Jeuchter, the special project manager for the village, has worked there since 1998. She and a colleague were in the Village Country Store when they both heard a pounding noise coming from the porch. Someone was on the porch stomping back and forth and muttering and swearing to himself. Clare and her co-worker tried to ignore the disruption; neither of them wanted to go out and confront the rude visitor. Fifteen minutes later, the commotion started up again.

"I yelled out to them, 'Be a man. If you have something to say, come in and say it.'" The ruckus stopped ... and Clare and her friend realized there hadn't been anyone out on the porch at all. Oddly enough, there was a repeat performance of the rude, noisy, cussing ghost the next year, on the same day.

Some spirits just like to be ornery.

WHERE PAST AND PRESENT MEET
(Billie Creek Village, Rockville, IN)

People have asked me, "What's the best thing about being a paranormal investigator?" I tend to keep my answer pretty simple. The very best thing is, of course, capturing good solid evidence. I really dig a good EVP, when you feel a connection, a communication with someone who has gone on to the Other Side. But one of the *other* coolest things that gets an investigator all

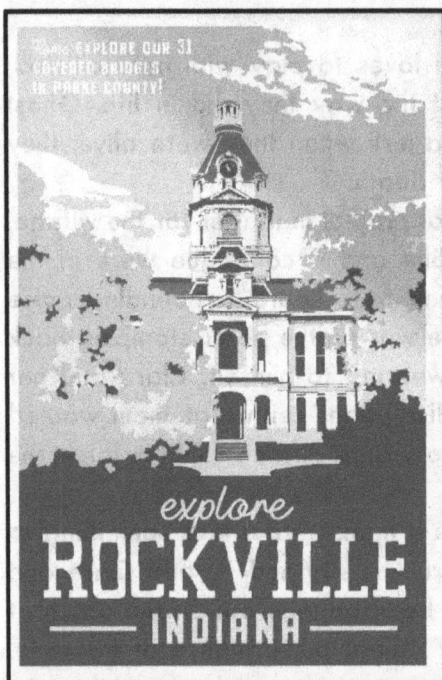

EXPLORE OUR 31
COVERED BRIDGES
IN PARKE COUNTY!

explore
ROCKVILLE
— INDIANA —

revved up is to have something paranormal happen when you're not really looking for it.

James, Roger, and I were on the road in James' truck. It's a silver-gray F150 done up to look like an Ectomobile, lovingly dubbed ECTOW I. It was a bright winter's day, and we were headed for Whispers Estate in Indiana, where we planned to meet up with another group of ghost hunters for an investigation. Since our route would basically take us right past Rockville, I suggested we stop in at Billie Creek Village for a quick visit on the way. I'd been there once already, before investigating the Roads Hotel, and I'd fallen a little in love with the tidy village. The guys were up for a side quest, so we turned down the road, rumbled across one of the site's three covered bridges, and drove into Billie Creek Village.

We were met at the General Store by Steve, the site manager. I had called Gregg Larson, the owner, to make sure we could get a visit in. (I had last visited in summer, but our Whispers trek was in early February.) Steve met us at the store and gave us a rundown of the history of Billie Creek Village.

The place was founded in the late 1960s and opened in 1961. And all the buildings originated from Parke County.

"People in the county would say, there's this great old one-room schoolhouse that someone's storing hay in, and it's falling down. The Governor's house is dilapidated. The General Store just sat empty. All these buildings are just gonna deteriorate, and we're gonna lose all this history," Steve said.

In the late 1960s, seventy or eighty people got together and got a grant from Eli Lilly for $5 million. They went out and rescued the buildings, picked them up, brought them here, and arranged them in the configuration of a little town. There are three covered bridges in town; Billie Creek Bridge is the only one of them that was built here. The other two were moved here.

Here's an example of the dedication this group showed, in their pursuit of saving history. Steve mentioned the livery barn near the General Store where we were talking. When it was purchased for the village, it was dismantled, every piece was labeled, then it was reassembled on site. "The barn was donated, but to move it here cost $800,000 in 1972. So that's like $2.5 million today. Just to move it here, to keep it intact."

Volunteers portrayed the inhabitants of Billie Creek Village: blacksmith, stable hand, preacher, schoolmarm. Their devotion to historical reenactment didn't go unnoticed. In the 1970s and 1980s, 750,000 school kids came here for field trips every year.

By the early 2000s, the volunteers were getting older, and the next generation wasn't stepping up. One volunteer's son did take over, to keep the dream alive. Eventually, though, he offered Billie Creek Village's forty buildings to Gregg Larson. Larson already owned another historic site, the Indiana State Sanitorium. "We had resources he didn't have," Steve said.

Now, Gregg and his helpers are in the process of restoring the buildings. They don't do living history, as in the past; they're not quite there yet. Instead, the village is open for events - the Covered Bridge Festival, weddings, Easter egg hunts, gatherings of medieval sword-fighting enthusiasts.

"This summer, we're doing three weekends in a row - it's kind of a Renaissance Faire, but it's a western theme. There's about eighty reenactors that come out, and they all have roles that they play. We've got the sheriff, we've got Black Bart, that kinda thing. Super excited to see that."

When Gregg bought the Indiana State Sanitorium, he knew nothing about the paranormal. "We got a call from the Discovery Channel. They said they wanted to come out and film a TV show in there. We were like, why? And they said, duh, it's haunted."

As it turned out, the Discovery Channel had been trying to get into the sanitorium for years, but the former owner wouldn't let them in. When they heard that the property was for sale, they had their lawyer keep an eye on it in the county records. When it was no longer for sale, they figured out that somebody had bought it. "So we hired a private investigator, he found your number, and that's how we got ahold of you. We said, wow, you guys *really* want to come out and film!"

A film scout did come out to the sanitorium and found it to be as impressive as she'd always heard it was. The Indiana State Sanitorium was a tuberculosis hospital from 1908 to 1968, then it served as a mental asylum from 1976 to 2001. There are twenty buildings on the property, some over 100 years old. The site has two hundred acres, miles of tunnels ... it's a ghost hunter's playground. As Gregg was talking with Addie, the scout, she mentioned that there were people who go out and investigate the paranormal as a hobby. As a matter of fact, she managed a couple of properties in Ohio that she rented out for investigations. Intrigued, Gregg asked her how much she generally charged for a night's stay. Addie told him, and he was flabbergasted. He quickly realized that this could be a potential new income stream. He hired the scout to do bookings for the sanitorium. When Billie Creek Village became available, they opened it up too.

This, naturally, led us into the ghost stories. Steve began with the Civil War house.

"When the village was open, they did chicken and

dumpling dinners. You could go down there, pay whatever, get your dinner, and they had places to sit. His staff did not want to be in the building at night." Steve said he actually met the women who ran the dinners.

"There were about six ladies who used to work here. They said, we're the chicken 'n dumpling ladies. I said, oh yeah! Tell me about the building. And one lady's like, I don't believe in ghosts, but I will not go back there because it's haunted!"

The Civil War house, Steve said, is responsible for about 70% of the stories from Billie Creek Village. Every group that comes out has experiences there. People downstairs will hear someone walking around on the second floor, but when they go upstairs, there's no one there. People will hear voices, they'll get unexplained chills, their meters will go off.

Steve told us a very intriguing story involving a group of ghost hunters who'd been at the village for an event and stayed for a few extra days to investigate the Civil War house. They ended up getting a much more personal experience than they'd bargained for.

"The entity took possession of Christopher. A different entity took possession of a girl. And those entities..." Steve paused, searching for words to convey the inexplicable. "So Christopher said, when I looked at that girl, I saw a completely different woman. And she said when she looked at him, she saw a completely different man. And they were married, pre-Civil War, these entities."

That was Monday night's investigation. On Tuesday, the group went back and got more information.

"This woman was married to another guy and murdered him so she could be with the guy who was in Christopher. And they had names! It was like Phineas and Jane, they knew their names, they knew the name of the guy that died."

Another investigator felt that she'd been possessed by the

spirit of a former slave, who knew the wife, and had helped to kill the first husband. "It became this *huge* - we called it 'Days of Our Past Lives.' They came back Wednesday night and expounded on the story even more." The group couldn't believe how active the building was. Every investigator felt like they were part of this story that was evolving, with all of them smack in the middle.

One of the men who used to work in the living history village was a potter. About thirty years ago, he was in his shop working, when a park guest came up to him.

"You work here, right?" the guest asked. The guest needed assistance; they thought there was someone in the barn who needed help. They'd heard a child or a woman up on the barn's second floor saying, "Please help me, help me."

The two of them went into the barn and climbed up to the second floor. There was no one there. The potter shrugged and dismissed the incident.

Ten or twelve years later, a completely different person stuck their head in the door of his pottery studio. "Hey, you work here, don't you? Can you help? I was just in the barn, and heard a woman or a child saying, 'help me, help me.'" Again, the potter accompanied the guest to the barn. Again, they looked around on the second floor.

Again, they saw no one.

Then, about ten years later, it happened a third time.

"I didn't tell anyone. I didn't tell any of my co-workers because I didn't want them to be weirded out by the place. I never told *anyone* about this."

After a bit of questioning, I got more details from Steve. The potter never heard the voice himself; it was just the guests who heard it. And the woman (or child) wasn't screaming, just asking quietly for help. The potter, though, flatly refused to take Steve up to the barn's second floor to show him where it had happened. "Nope, I won't go in there."

Steve also told us about a newspaper clipping that researchers into Billie Creek Village's history had found. The newspaper article mentioned that the schoolhouse was known to be haunted. A photograph accompanied the article. It showed the outline of a spectral child standing in the window of the schoolhouse.

We asked Steve which of the village's buildings was the most haunted.

"Most reports of activity? The Civil War house," he replied promptly. "Hands down. Three out of four reports are from the Civil War house. But it's a little skewed because some people come here, they just go to the Civil War house. They get tons of activity, and they're like oh my God, we had a great time! I'm like, what about the other buildings? We didn't go to any other buildings! We were here to see ghosts, and they were all over there!" Steve thinks that if a team were to come out and spend an hour in each of the buildings, the reports would be more even.

Steve left us with one last tidbit of information.

"If you look up that hill, that first house there, we just bought it, and we're turning it into an AirBnB for people that come here. And that guy told us that his grandfather was in the outhouse pooping, and had a brain aneurysm and died, and his father went down and found his grandfather dead in the outhouse. So, I know for sure one building that somebody died in." We couldn't help it - we dissolved into helpless giggles at the morbid story. Steve continued with a grin, "We were like, can we tell people that story? And he said sure, I don't care!"

With the interview at an end, Roger went outside to get some outdoor B-roll shots, while James and I stayed in the General Store to do a bit of shopping. Gregg had been kind enough to welcome us in the off-season, so we figured we'd drop some coin in return. As we wandered the store, trying to choose from the truly impressive array of goods on offer, Roger quietly came back inside. He sidled up to Steve.

"Hey," he asked quietly. "Is there anyone else here today? I mean, in any of the other buildings?"

Steve shook his head. "No, we're the only ones here." I looked around. Steve, his girlfriend Patty, Roger, James, and myself. We were all accounted for.

"Okay, that's kinda what I thought. Thanks." And Roger turned and walked back out of the store.

I just *knew* something was up. James and I made our purchases, then headed outside to find out what Roger had experienced.

Let's switch to the Roger-cam for a moment. He'd been standing in front of the store, in the town square. He was taking still shots of the surroundings and trying to get a few "glamour shots" of ECTOW in front of the store.

The schoolhouse is a wooden building, painted red, with tall windows. The windows let lots of natural light into the building; it would've been a delightful place of learning, back in the day. In fact, if you're looking at the front of the school, you can see all the way through the big classroom and glimpse the white walls of St. Joseph Church beyond. Roger panned his camera around the square, clicking off pictures, taking in the schoolhouse and other points of interest.

It was after he swept the camera past the schoolhouse that he realized that he'd seen someone standing in the window, watching him back.

He swung the camera back, but the watcher was gone. Discussing it outside, I told the guys (since I'd been in the schoolhouse on my previous visit) that according to Roger's description of where the figure had appeared in relation to the window, whoever it was had been about the height of a ten-year-old child.

Our visit to Billie Creek Village was already turning out to be pretty exciting. Since we were pressed for time, we had a quick huddle to discuss what to do next. We'd heard good things about the Civil War house, so we decided to focus our exploration there.

We drove ECTOW the short distance from the village to the outlying house. (Again, in summer, it's a pleasant walk, but this was at the beginning of February.) We got out, and James and I went in to explore the house, while Roger stayed in the yard for a quick smoke.

"You're going to love this; it's so neat inside," I gushed as I led James to the house. We wandered through the first floor, admiring the tidy parlor and front bedroom, trying to imagine cooking in the antiquated kitchen, drooling over the open hearth in the *original* kitchen.

"You gotta check out the upstairs, too!" James followed me up the stairs from the side hall. We got to the top of the steps, which opened onto the second floor.

The second floor of the Civil War house is open and airy, with a wide-open floor plan. The windows let in plenty of cheerful daylight. Very little furniture clutters the two big rooms; there are a few beds, a couple of dressers, and that's it, really. A silver bell sat on the dresser in the first room we came to. James picked it up and shook it with a playful smile.

"You rang?" came a deep, doleful query from the bottom of the stairs. It was Roger, doing his best impression of Lurch, the butler from the *Addams Family*. James laughed, and I giggled. Some people might be freaked out walking through such a haunted place, but I felt completely at ease. I was with friends, showing them a gorgeous home. We were all having fun. Everything was going great.

We worked our way slowly from one side of the second floor to the other. At the other end, we took a peek out of the window. "Hey, I can see my truck from here!" James said with a grin. We wandered back towards the stairs, stopping to comment on the picture hanging on the wall. It was an old-fashioned household scene, family members gathered around a matriarch who looked like she could have attended Washington's inauguration. It looked very archaic to modern eyes, and I'm afraid we both poked a bit of gentle fun at it.

We decided it was time to head back downstairs and find Roger. Again, I went first on the staircase. There are several steps down from the second floor, then a landing, then the staircase takes a ninety-degree turn. Halfway down the second set of steps, there is a door.

The door was now closed.

"Huh," I said. "That's odd. I wonder why Roger decided to shut the door on us? Maybe he thought it would be funny?" A few steps above me, I felt James shrug. I tented my fingers on the door and gave it a gentle push.

It wouldn't open.

"Hmm." I placed the flat of my palm on the door and shoved. The door gave a fairly loud groan of protest as it finally opened. Roger came around the corner from the parlor, camera in hand.

"Dude, what's the deal? Why'd you shut the door on us?" we demanded.

Roger looked befuddled. "There's a door?"

When the door is open, it sits flush with the wall. Roger hadn't even noticed it on his walkthrough.

The three of us spent the next ten minutes or so trying to debunk the incident. Even though there was no source of any draft whatsoever, we took turns pushing the door closed from its open position. Most of the time, its trajectory wouldn't even reach the door jamb. At most, when we really tried to slam it hard, it would bounce back from the jamb with the momentum. It just wouldn't shut properly.

I went halfway up the stairs and had the guys shut the

door, then I opened it. We repeated it until I said, "Okay, yeah, that's how much force I had to use to push it open." All of us clocked the fact that when the door was properly closed, and I pushed it open, the wood gave a loud groan as the door came away from the door jamb. We also heard the solid clunk as the door seated itself in the frame.

None of us registered that solid thunk of noise before James and I came down the stairs to find the door securely shut.

Here, too, I have to point something out. Roger had no idea the door was even there - which meant that it was open when he called out "You rang?" from the bottom of the stairwell. Therefore, the door had to have closed itself sometime after Roger wandered away from the stairs to film in the rest of the house.

Let's back up for a moment and rejoin the Roger-cam. This time, he'd decided to film in the cabin rather than just taking still photos. He walked slowly through the home, filming. While in the bedroom on the first floor, he could hear James and myself on the second floor. Roger heard a loud BANG and a click.

"Damn, those guys are loud," he muttered. He assumed he'd just heard me and James rattling around upstairs. He could hear exactly where we were above him. And when he poked his head up the stairwell in the hallway and groaned "You rang?", the door can be seen flush with the wall, in its open position. If you know it's there, you notice it ... but Roger was unaware of it.

After we came down the stairs to find the door inexplicably closed, Roger also filmed our debunking efforts. As we fussed with the door, finally getting it to meet the jamb and close, the same BANG and click can be heard.

That sound was the sound of the door closing. We heard it as we experimented with the door.

And Roger heard it as he was filming in the first-floor bedroom, all the way across the house from the hallway.

Heath, another team member, caught another important

scrap of evidence as he and Roger reviewed the footage. Another odd thing that Roger had noticed was that as he was filming, there was an unexplained gap in the video. As he walked from the parlor back into the bedroom, he heard an odd skittering noise near the bassinet in the bedroom. Just then, the timestamp on the video jumped forward 34 seconds ... but the video remained smooth, with no stutters. Roger was just in the parlor one moment, and in the bedroom the next - but the time stamp jumped from 17:12 to 17:46. By the time the counter surged 34 seconds ahead, Roger was in the other room.

As Roger and Heath pored over the footage, Heath noticed something odd. Just before the timestamp jump, Roger was standing in the parlor, filming towards the hallway where the door is. There's also a mirror there ... and Heath spotted the head of a shadowy figure lurking in the corner of the mirror. The side of a head was just visible ... and then Heath noticed the raised open hand in the mirror as well. He advanced the video frame by frame, and the hand smoothly closed, thumb to fingertips, as if making some sort of "enough" motion.

And the time stamp was suddenly 34 seconds further along.

"The best part of it is that it couldn't have been me," Roger told us. "This figure was in front of a door on the other side of a wall in a room I wasn't in yet.

"It's really interesting. It can't be me, because I'm not in the room. It can't be you or James, because you guys were upstairs. The three of us were the only living creatures in the house."

One other incident is worth mentioning. As the three of us stood in the kitchen, we all noticed a door in the corner. We opened it to peer inside but found only a boring closet. James and I shut the door and turned away - and the door opened back up about a quarter of the way. Neither of us noticed it, nor did Roger, who was still filming. It might be paranormal, or it might just be a loose door in a kitchen with uneven floors. For now, we're not prepared to say this is paranormal, but we can't wait to go back to find out more.

Had the spirits of the Civil War house at Billie Creek Village been having some fun at our expense? It's possible. I know we couldn't replicate the door-closing incident going up the stairs to the second floor. (James and I joked afterwards that someone had taken offense at our dunking on the picture upstairs.) We had an inexplicable experience at the house. It would have been exciting during a nighttime investigation, but we had this happen in broad daylight. We were elated. We left the house with a new respect for whoever remained behind.

And heck yeah, all three of us were grinning ear to ear!

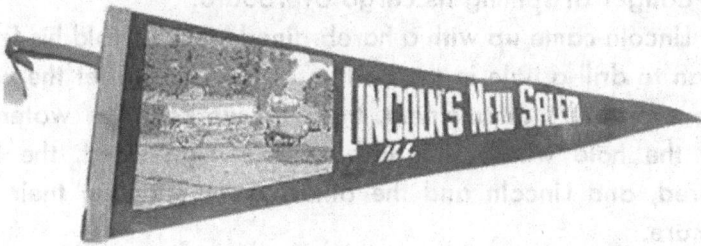

A QUIET FRONTIER VILLAGE
(Lincoln's New Salem, Petersburg, IL)

Illinois is the land of Lincoln. This is where our sixteenth President grew up, practiced law, and where he got elected to the highest office in the land. Not bad for a gawky dork from the frontier. Of course, Springfield, the state capital, is known for its Lincoln connection. But that's not where he started out. One of the places that played a big part in Lincoln's early life was a small town on the Sangamon River, called New Salem. Let's poke around this rustic collection of cabins for a bit and see what we can uncover.

New Salem was founded in 1829, when James Rutledge and John Cameron built a grist mill, using the Sangamon River to power the mill's wheel to grind the wheat into flour. The Sangamon is quite shallow, as rivers go, but it had its uses for the little settlement. There was a high spot in the riverbed, right at New Salem, and the townspeople put a dam there. In 1831, a flat boat piloted by a 22-year-old Abraham Lincoln got stuck on the dam on its way to New Orleans. The little flatboat wasn't in too much trouble; the Sangamon is not a treacherous river by any means. But the boat was well and truly beached, taking on water, and was in danger of spilling its cargo overboard.

Lincoln came up with a harebrained idea: he told his fellow boatman to drill a hole in the bottom of the boat to let the water out. To everyone's amazement, the plan worked. The water ran out of the hole where the flatboat was high sided, the boat recovered, and Lincoln and the others were soon on their way once more.

But Lincoln didn't forget the little town of New Salem. He settled there later that year and lived there from 1831 to 1837. He ran the general store, served as postmaster, and worked as a surveyor and railsplitter. It was when he lived in New Salem that Lincoln was called to serve in the Black Hawk War, although he and his company didn't see action. It was in New Salem that he was elected to the Illinois General Assembly. And it was in New Salem that Abe Lincoln fell in love with pretty Ann Rutledge.

New Salem was home to about twenty to twenty-five families. When Lincoln lived there, the village also had a blacksmith's shop, a cooper's shop where barrels were made, a tavern, two doctors' offices, a church that doubled as a schoolhouse, a grocery store, and four general stores. Craftsman in the town included a tanner, a shoemaker, and a hatmaker, and people who worked in the wool carding mill. New Salem was more than a collection of homesteaders clawing a living from the frontier. This was a place of industry and small business.

A display at the visitor's center gives an idea of the personality of the small but vital community. The population was literate. There was an active social environment, including storytelling sessions, a debate society, church functions, and gaming activities. Politics was serious business, as Illinois grew and organized itself.

New Salem existed for a little over ten years. The village began to decline when it was determined that the Sangamon River could not be navigated by steamboats. It was too shallow for any craft but flatboats. Residents began to move to nearby towns, and by the early 1840s, New Salem had ceased to exist. Despite the high hopes and diligence of its settlers, New Salem was not destined to become a thriving, lasting community. Nearby Petersburg became the county seat, while New Salem was passed over for that honor. Soon, the town was abandoned. The little village, laid out with such hopes for success, had only lasted for eleven years.

But the state of Illinois didn't forget this little settlement that played such a large role in Lincoln's life. The land was gifted to the state in 1919, and during the Depression, the CCC rebuilt the village on its original foundations. Today, the place is known as Lincoln's New Salem Historic site, complete with visitor center, theater, and gift shops. Come take a stroll through New Salem with me, and we'll get to know the place.

The home that Parthena Nance Hill shared with her husband was just across the road from the general store that Lincoln ran with his partner, William Berry. So she had a front row seat to the relaxed attitude Lincoln took to storekeeping. According to Parthena (and others), Lincoln spent most of his time sitting on the store's front porch, reading the newspaper and swapping tales with the customers.

But it wasn't all "Little House on the Prairie" and "Young Abe Lincoln" in New Salem. The settlement only existed for eleven years, but that was enough time for the town to be touched by tragedy.

Rowan Herndon was an early settler of New Salem. His cousin was William Herndon, who later became Lincoln's law partner. Rowan married Elizabeth Graham in 1827 in Kentucky. By the spring of 1831, they had moved to New Salem. Rowan and his brother James built a log home, and later in the fall, built a store. In the summer of 1832, James sold his interest in the store to William Berry and moved away. Rowan, not liking Berry for a partner, sold his interest in the store to Abe Lincoln.

On the morning of January 18, 1833, Rowan was cleaning his rifle, getting ready to go hunting. Lincoln was already at work, doing odd jobs at the Rutledge tavern. He found that he needed a specific tool for the repair work he was doing, so he sent ten-year-old Nancy Rutledge over to the Herndon cabin to fetch it.

As Nancy came into the cabin, Rowan was loading his rifle. Nancy started to tell Elizabeth what she needed, when the rifle accidentally discharged. The ball struck Elizabeth in the neck, hitting an artery. Elizabeth collapsed in front of a horrified Nancy, arterial blood spraying everywhere. The young woman was dead within moments.

Nancy fled back to the tavern to tell the tragic news. Although everyone in the village knew the shooting had been an accident, the pall of death - and suspicion - lay heavily on Rowan Herndon. He left New Salem soon afterward and moved to Island Grove Township. Even so, he was never able to escape the rumors that he had murdered his wife.

It seems that Elizabeth hasn't left the scene of her untimely death. Visitors to the park sometimes see the ghostly apparition of a woman in homespun clothing standing in the doorway of the Herndon cabin.

One family was walking along the path near the cabin when the young girl pointed at the cabin and said casually that she liked the dress the woman was wearing. Her parents, seeing no one, were understandably confused. The girl insisted that she saw a woman standing in front of the cabin. The parents walked over to the cabin, and the father even tried the door. It was closed and locked. It was only later that the parents learned the tragic history of that particular cabin.

I didn't experience any ghostly encounters on my visit to New Salem, but I have spoken to people who have had their own brushes with the spirit world there. I gave a talk at Lillie M. Evans Library, and chatted with Anita, one of the librarians there. She told me she'd gone to New Salem in grade school, on a field trip. She and a group of friends had gone up to one of the cabins. They didn't go inside, but they pressed their faces up to the window, to peer into the small room. Anita, to her delight, saw someone cooking over the fire at the cabin's hearth. The woman was wearing a gingham dress, with an apron over it to protect her skirts. And she had eyes of the most brilliant blue. She turned her head and fixed that gaze on Anita, looking straight at her. The group of girls moved on, but Anita couldn't forget that beautiful gaze. She turned to her friends, bubbling with excitement.

"Isn't it great that they have people here dressed like they would have been in olden times?" she gushed.

The two girls with her just stared blankly at her. They hadn't seen anyone in the cabin. "They had zero clue," Anita told me, a tinge of wonder in her voice, even decades later.

I spoke to one of the reenactors at New Salem. He didn't have any experiences of his own to share with me, but he did point out that ghost stories, or "haint tales," are quite popular in

Appalachia. Many of the settlers of frontier Illinois moved here from that mountain region, the hills and hollers of eastern Tennessee, Kentucky, and what is now West Virginia. In fact, one of the buildings in New Salem is a dogtrot cabin, built in a popular Appalachian style. Two small cabins are connected by a covered breezeway. This was the home of Joshua Miller, the blacksmith, and John Kelso. They married sisters in Appalachia, then moved up to Illinois. So, with the Appalachian influence, the evenings in New Salem probably echoed with people - including Lincoln - sharing haint tales to make the dark nights even more deliciously spooky.

WILD WILD WEST
(Bonnie Springs Ranch, Las Vegas, NV)

Anyone who knows me can pretty much tell that the Strip in Vegas just ... isn't my scene. I visited my sister in Las Vegas, bringing another sister with me, and two of us went on a ghost tour on the Strip. The tour was fantastic, amazing, I'm not gonna lie. But hanging around the Strip for more than a couple of hours was not going to happen.

Luckily, Las Vegas isn't just glitz and neon. The desert that surrounds Vegas is suffused with a stark, unearthly beauty. It provides a welcome break from the hectic pace of the Strip. I dragged my ever-patient sister, Miriam, with me on a short road trip outside the city. We visited the exquisitely scenic Red Rock Canyon and drove a winding road that took us through an ever-changing view of the desert.

When we were done with that, I decided that I wanted to go horseback riding. I looked at the Library of Alexandria that I keep in my pocket and discovered a place just up the road called

Bonnie Springs Ranch.

We pulled up to a touristy-looking place, a long low roofed entrance with rustic wooden walls that just oozed with the flavor of the Wild West. And the banner over the entrance proclaimed that the place had been featured on *Ghost Adventures*.

You had me at "Ghost". We paid our admission fee and went to explore this place that we'd so happily stumbled across. I guess that's a benefit of not paying too much attention to ghost hunting shows on TV. I had no idea what Bonnie Springs Ranch was. I was about to find out.

We went through the entrance and found ourselves on a wide main street lined with wooden buildings. I went in search of someone to give me some background on the place and came across "Angry Joe."

Joe moved to Nevada years ago because his grandchildren had never seen cowboys. He landed a job at the village, and a couple months later, things started happening.

"I was a disbeliever, so I became a debunker. Then I got with some investigative groups, and it just grew. We had people come from all over the world to investigate here."

The Opera House, Joe told me, has the most energy. Some mediums that have visited the Opera House have told Joe that they believe there's a vortex in there.

"That's how I do a lot of my research." Joe said. "If you tell me something happened, I'm gonna check the weather, I'm

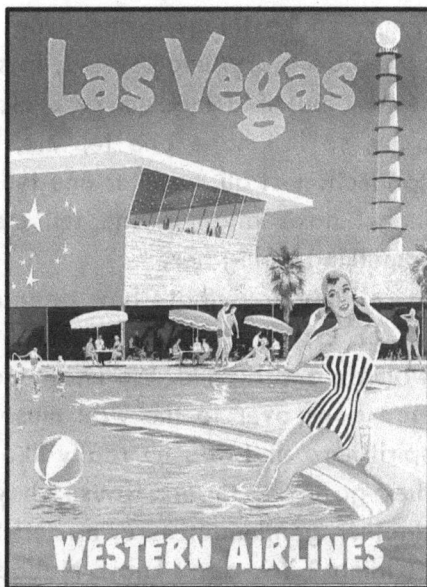

gonna shake things, rattle things, crawl on the buildings ... I'm gonna do everything there is, to see if I can debunk it.

"But if a medium or a clairvoyant tells me something ... okay, so if I have one tell me, and then like a year later, no connection at all, another one tells me almost the same thing, and then I have another one tell me again, okay, now we've got something going here."

Joe says that's how he found out the spectral background of the Opera House. "We know there's a man in there, and a woman, and a child. We know that for a fact. We know that the man goes over to the wax museum. We know there's an angry spirit here that doesn't really like women. A lot of women, when they go in the Opera House, they get a heavy feeling. We have another gentleman here, named Doc. Did they come in with the buildings? You don't know. Nobody can be very specific on that."

Joe said that the scariest thing that's ever happened to him occurred while he was using a ghost box on an investigation. They asked the angry spirit who it didn't like, and it said Joe. One of the other ghost hunters said, "Well, you always say 'Joe'. What's his last name?" The next thing they heard over the ghost box was Joe's last name, clear as a bell.

"That was the most frightening thing, because that's personal."

The schoolhouse is also very active. "The merry-go-round in front of the school? I've seen that move so many times I don't even notice it anymore. I've seen it go one way, stop, then go the other way."

I was eager to experience all that Bonnie Springs had to offer. Miriam and I went through the wax museum, and even though I had no equipment with me at all, I did a bit of impromptu ghost hunting. I had the recorder on my phone going and asked a few questions as we went along.

I didn't capture any EVPs, but something interesting did

happen while we were all in the wax museum. The inside is very rustic, with scenes from the Old West, vignettes of Native villages, cowboys leaning up against fences ... in one of the cave-like corridors I asked, "If there's anyone here, can you let us know?" Joe had joined us for this part of the walkthrough. Right after I asked the question, all three of us heard an odd noise, almost like a "clack" that echoed in the cave. Joe looked at Miriam.

"That was a pebble being thrown," he declared. He explained to us that it's very common for spirits in the wax museum to throw pebbles to make their presence known. "I've heard that noise so many times. We can replicate that by throwing a pebble against the wood and it's the same sound." That happened twice while we were in there.

The wax museum was a great experience, and we were eager for more. The Opera House was actually closed at the time, but Joe graciously unlocked the door for us and let us poke around inside for a while. I didn't experience anything negative - there was no sign of the angry spirit that hates women - but I did get a sense of a female presence. Joe told me that the spirit of a little girl named Rebecca makes her home in the Opera House, so that may have been whom I was feeling.

While I was in the Opera House doing my EVP session, Miriam, not being an investigator, got bored, and wandered outside. Interestingly enough, she got to see the merry-go-round in front of the schoolhouse spinning by itself. I found her standing there, watching it bemusedly. "It was doing this when I walked up," she said. It is quite solid, and there was no breeze to speak of that day.

The delightful little town of Bonnie Springs Ranch began life in 1843 as a watering place for wagon trains on the Old Spanish Trail, on their weary way to California. It never got very big - by 1860 there was a blacksmith shop and a one-room cabin - but the site was purchased in 1942 by Bonnie McGaugh. It was named for her and for the natural springs that provide water, an oasis in the desert.

One of Bonnie's many jobs was that of turkey farmer. She and her mother raised the birds in the 1940s, and Bonnie would deliver live turkeys to restaurants in Las Vegas.

In 1952, one of Bonnie's deliveries took her into a friend's diner. This friend also owned a ranch in nearby Red Rock Canyon. The friend showed Bonnie the ranch, and she fell in love with the rugged scenery. She bought the 115-acre ranch and started running the derelict bar that was on the property. The site grew from there, with Bonnie and her husband Al Levinson adding horseback riding, a restaurant, and a petting zoo. The zoo began when Bonnie adopted two pygmy goats from Wayne Newton in 1975. Many of the animals - sheep, deer, cats, dogs, rabbits, chickens - were former pets that were dropped off at the ranch. More exotic animals had joined the zoo by 1997, including burros, coyotes, ferrets, hedgehogs, llamas, prairie dogs, lynx, and turtles. Most of the zoo was occupied by animals who had been rescued from abusive situations.

In 1972, construction began on Old Nevada, which replicated an 1880s mining town. Al had wanted to build this recreated village for years. He and Bonnie traveled all over Nevada to do research on old buildings, and to source old wood for the structures. The town opened on May 1, 1974, with 45 buildings on five acres of land. Old Nevada featured souvenir shops that also sold artifacts and antiques, a saloon that was available to rent out for parties, a musical revue, two museums, a small schoolhouse, and a wedding chapel.

Sadly, Bonnie Springs Ranch - and Old Nevada, and the restaurant, and the petting zoo, the whole shebang - closed in March of 2019. The animals in the zoo, the horses in the riding stables, the peacocks and deer that freely roamed the grounds, were all relocated to other zoos. The structures were all demolished, and the land is now the site of The Ranch at Red Rock, a gated community of residential lots.

Such is the march of progress.

CIVIC PRIDE ... AND MORE THAN A FEW GHOSTS

(Kern County Museum, Bakersfield, California)

In 1929, the Bakersfield Lion's Club had a fantastic idea. The club wanted to preserve the history of Bakersfield and Kern County. Who better to ask for help with such a project than the people who lived there?

The Lion's Club wrote a letter and published it in the local newspaper, asking citizens of Kern County to donate historical materials - documents, photographs, any information, really, that could educate future generations about Kern County's past. The County Chamber of Commerce had opened just the year before, so the Lion's Club directed folks to bring their mementos there.

The response was gratifyingly positive. Family after family came to donate thousands of papers, records, even items of daily life. Several years later, the Chamber of Commerce had amassed enough material for a museum. In 1941, the Kern County Museum was founded, with its mission being to "collect, preserve, research, and present the history and culture of Kern County for the education and enjoyment of the public."

The Lion's Club had no idea at the time how farsighted this concept was. Oil had been discovered in Bakersfield in 1899, with rich oil fields bringing a major petroleum industry to the area.

BAKERSFIELD
CALIFORNIA

Much later, the city would become known as the birthplace of the Bakersfield Sound, with country music stars like Buck Owens and Merle Haggard contributing to this subgenre of music. Bakersfield today is often called "the country music capital of the West Coast."

But all of that was in the future in 1941. People were really stoked about the museum, but with the war on, it was hard to get the project off the ground. By 1945, though, the museum officially opened in the Kern County Chamber of Commerce building in Bakersfield.

The exhibits were originally displayed in a small corner of the basement but then expanded up to the main floor. Pretty soon, the wildly popular new museum filled the building to bursting. As a matter of fact, the museum kind of shoved the Chamber of Commerce out of its own building. They ended up moving to different digs in 1952.

The museum also spilled out of the building into the great outdoors. There was a county fairground next to the building. When the County Fair moved to another location, that land became available. The museum acquired the Barnes family log house, built in 1868, and displayed it outdoors at the fairgrounds. That became the first exhibit of the outdoor complex, called Pioneer Village. Over seventy original structures are collected on sixteen acres, focusing on life in the late nineteenth century.

There is one of almost every type of structure from the time period displayed here. There is a one-room school, a church, a photography studio, a train station, a hotel, a courthouse, and an assay office. (Bakersfield was also involved in the California Gold Rush.) A massive wooden oil derrick represents the petroleum deposits in the area: the Black Gold exhibit describes the county's oil industry.

The Beale Memorial Clock Tower was originally constructed in 1904 in Bakersfield. It stood in the center of the intersection of 17th Street and Chester Ave. It was destroyed in an earthquake in 1952 and rebuilt at the museum in 1964.

The Pioneer Village prides itself on being a destination for gatherings of all kinds - weddings, birthday parties, retirement parties, and business retreats. Not surprisingly for those of us in paranormal investigation, this has led to Pioneer Village being delightfully haunted. Spirits like to join in on joyful occasions; they are delighted to gate-crash birthday parties and wedding receptions. And business events might draw entities who once ran the shops that are now located in the village.

Golden Estate Paranormal Research Society has described Pioneer Village as being "one of the most concentrated areas of active houses and buildings ever assembled." But rather than being a place of distilled high-test nightmare fuel like Old Tailem Town, this is a place where the spirits are happily going about their afterlives, not bothering the living at all.

Take the Norris School, for example. From 1882 to 1913, this one-room schoolhouse was used to educate children in the Rosedale area. In 1914, a new school was built, so the old building was moved to the Rosedale Ranch and used for storing grain. In 1958, the structure was donated to the Kern County Museum and lovingly restored to its former appearance. A peek inside reveals a well-equipped classroom, ready to receive students once more. There are desks, books, a stove for warmth, pegs for coats, and large blackboards.

As a matter of fact, it seems that the ghost of a teacher is still hard at work forming young minds. Visitors have heard the teacher's spirit writing on the blackboard, preparing the next day's lesson. And the students are still there as well. Apparitions of children have been seen and heard playing outside in front of the schoolhouse. Guests have also heard children singing inside.

The Howell House is a gorgeous Queen Anne style home, built in Bakersfield in 1891 by William Howell. In 1902, he married Elizabeth Dugan, and they raised their two children here, a daughter (also Elizabeth) and a son (William Howell Jr). The house was donated to Pioneer Village in 1969.

Brenna Charatsaris, an employee at the Kern County Museum, was walking past the Howell House a little after dusk one night when she caught a glimpse of something out of the corner of her eye. It was a little girl standing in the second story window of the house, looking down at her.

"My brain said, don't worry - it's just a little girl. Well, it was seven o'clock-ish at night and there was a little girl just sitting, and it wasn't scary. It wasn't creepy, it was only a little terrifying once my brain kicked in to tell me we've been closed since four o'clock, and I knew there was nobody else on property."

Both of the Howells' children lived to adulthood, so no one, not historians, not paranormal investigators, can explain who this little girl might be. Maybe she's just passing through and wanted to visit this beautiful home for a while.

Alphonse Weill was a successful merchant in Bakersfield, a transplant from France. He and his San Francisco-born wife, Henrietta, raised four children in their mansion. Henrietta was very active in charity work, belonging to several civic organizations. She was dedicated to improving the lives of the poor through education and social services.

The manifestations in the Weill House are mostly

emotional. People get a feeling of being warmly welcomed when they enter the home. That probably results from Henrietta's good-hearted, charitable nature. Apparitions have been seen on the wide front porch and in the yard. Sometimes, people can hear the cheerful sounds of a birthday party in full swing emanating from the home.

One of the most active properties on the site is the Fellows Hotel. This place was hopping back in the day - it operated as a hotel, saloon, and brothel. So yeah, lots going on under that roof. The brothel was run by a madam named Ma Randall. Legend holds that one of her employees, who worked in the hotel kitchen, was murdered in a fight, and is still at the hotel, unable to move on.

Kern County Museum executive director Mike McCoy has seen some very strange things at the hotel. Museum employees will set up the dining room for a banquet the day before the event. The setup is elaborate, as befits such a grand, historic venue: full place settings, glasses, elegant napkins, salt and pepper shakers placed just so. And when the employees come in the next morning, everything is on the floor, a jumble of flatware and crockery. It's as if someone has swept everything off the tables in a fit of pique.

Kern County Museum boasts beautiful historic buildings, collected from all over the area and given new life and a permanent home. It seems that a few of those buildings are still enjoyed by their previous inhabitants.

THRILLS AND CHILLS
Haunted Amusement Parks

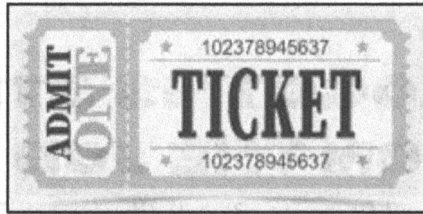

The First Law of Thermodynamics states that energy can't be created or destroyed, but it can change form or be transferred. Think of how much sheer energy is generated by a day at an amusement park. Rides whirl and spin; lights flash, drawing passengers closer with the promise of excitement; park guests stroll down wide boulevards, chatting excitedly about what to see next. A park is a great place for a first date, and many a first kiss has been shared in the gentle sway of a Ferris wheel car. People fall in love in all sorts of places. That's some powerful energy right there. And behind the scenes, park workers are busy making sure the experience is a day filled with delights.

So where does all that energy go? Is it stored up, building and building to fuel the good vibes at these places? Or maybe, is that excitement used by unseen inhabitants, former park employees who are still dedicated to thrilling their customers? Or are there invisible guests still lingering, still enjoying their experience there for eternity? In these parks, it's a little of both.

"CLOGGY" IS STILL
ON THE JOB
(Blackpool Pleasure Beach, Blackpool, England)

"If at first you don't succeed, try, try, again."

This old bit of wisdom has been a source of inspiration for countless people over the years. In one case, this encouragement led to the founding of a family business that is still going strong after well over a century. It still brings happiness to nearly six million people every year.

In 1896, William George Bean, an entrepreneur in the North of England, really wanted to build up a career as an advertising agent in the United States. He went on a pilgrimage to Madison Avenue in New York ... but instead of striking it rich, Bean struck out. Returning to England, Bean partnered with John Outhwaite to build and open two amusement parks. The park they built at Great Yarmouth turned out to be a flop, so the men concentrated on the other one -- Pleasure Beach, in Blackpool.

Pleasure Beach opened in 1903, and at first it was quite modest. The original park consisted of a few merry-go-rounds, a Bicycle Railway, and a handful of vendor stalls. Bean quickly added more rides and introduced sideshows as well. The park soon expanded to cover thirty acres and became a popular holiday destination. Pleasure Beach was an ambitious, pioneering experiment right from the jump. Bean was dedicated to offering attractions that had never before been seen in the UK.

Bean made good on this dream. Sir Hiram Maxim's Captive Flying Machine opened in August 1904. It was a swing ride, designed by a British inventor named, yes, Hiram Maxim. The very next year, in 1905, Bean opened a water ride called The River

Caves Of The World. Both rides are still going strong today, and Sir Hiram Maxim's is the oldest amusement park ride in Europe.

These two roaring successes were followed by the park's first wooden roller coaster, The Scenic Railway, in 1907. More large rides would be added in the coming years: The Velvet Coaster, The Toy Wheel, and The House of Nonsense. Quite a few of these were wooden coasters, and some even went out over the water.

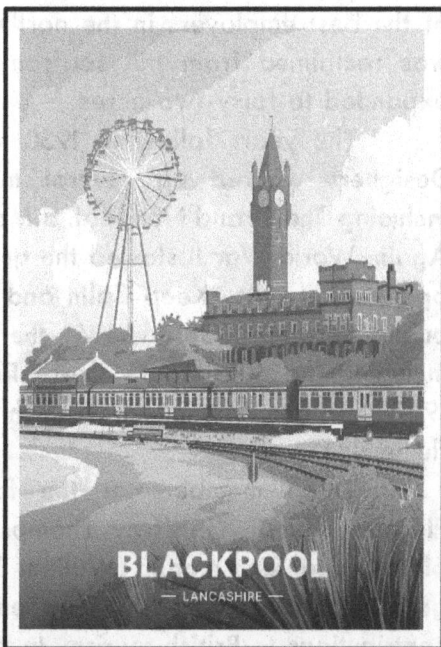

BLACKPOOL
— LANCASHIRE —

Development of the park slowed drastically after World War I, due in part to the difficulty of importing rides from the US. (The management of Blackpool Pleasure Beach has always had a great working relationship with park designers in the States. Way back at the beginning of the park, Bean and Outhwaite were inspired to grow their business by a visit to Coney Island in New York. And in the early 1960s, representatives from the Walt Disney Company visited Blackpool Pleasure Beach. It was one of the parks that served as the inspiration for Disneyland. Walt Disney became friends with Leonard Thompson, Bean's son-in-law, who ran Pleasure Beach for 47 years. Thompson and Disney would regularly riff off each other when dreaming up attractions for their respective parks.)

Development at the park picked back up in 1922, when two major rides, Noah's Ark and The Virginia Reel, opened. In spite of not having tons of rides, the park thrived. It became known as one of the best employers in the northwest of England. In 1923, land was reclaimed from the seafront at Blackpool, and the park expanded to forty-two acres.

The years following 1930 were good ones for the park. Designers worked up several more wooden roller coasters, including The Grand National, a Mobius loop coaster built in 1935. Again, World War II slowed the growth of the park, but it stayed open to help the "Keep Calm and Carry On" morale of Britain's public. Between 1958 and 1961, the park added several new rides, including The Wild Mouse, Derby Racer, and Alice in Wonderland. 1967 saw the opening of Drench Falls, the world's longest log flume ride.

Three members of the founding family of Blackpool Pleasure Beach, Geoffrey Thompson, his mother Doris, and his oldest daughter Amanda (William Bean's grandson, daughter, and great-granddaughter), have been awarded O.B.E.s for their contributions to British tourism. In 1986, Blackpool Pleasure Beach was one of the first companies in the UK to register with the Government Profit Related Pay Unit. In this profit-sharing program, once a company's profits top one million British pounds, ten percent of the extra is divvied up among full-timers according to their length of employment.

Blackpool Pleasure Beach has partnered with commercial ventures, too. In 2011, four acres inside the park, already a children's area, was set aside as Nickelodeon Land, with attractions featuring Dora the Explorer and Spongebob Squarepants, among others. And in 2013, the park worked with Aardman Studios, owners of the Wallace and Gromit and Shaun the Sheep brands, to develop Wallace and Gromit's Thrill-o-Matic dark ride.

Still, the park hasn't forgotten its roots. Several of the oldest rides in the park are still operational. The Big Dipper roller coaster was built in 1933, then extended in 1936. The Grand

National, that wooden dual-track coaster I mentioned before, is one of only five Mobius loop coasters still in existence. Sir Hiram Maxim's Flying Machine, the oldest attraction in the park, has been going strong since 1904.

Perhaps it's because of this strong link to the past that Pleasure Beach has the reputation of being one of the most haunted places in England. The gift shop at Sir Hiram Maxim's is haunted by the ghost of a nine-year-old girl. Objects mysteriously move overnight in the empty shop, appearing in different places in the morning from where they were left the night before. The Starr Pub has a resident ghost as well, a heavyset man with a full, luxuriant beard. He's been seen walking around the bar in the very early hours of the morning. There's another indistinct figure who's been seen in the pub's cellar. Is it the same guy? We're not sure. Pictures on the walls have moved, and glasses and bottles shift themselves with no explanation. Witnesses also report the eerie voice of a woman singing.

Another, creepier denizen of Pleasure Beach is the Laughing Man. This isn't a ghost per se, but the story is eerie enough that I decided to share it with you.

The Laughing Man is a statue of a clown - not a friendly one, but a clown out of a nightmare. It was added to the Fun House in 1935, and scared generations of park goers. In 1991, a massive fire swept through the Fun House, destroying much of the attraction. But when the smoke cleared, the Laughing Man was eerily unscathed.

The statue still stands at the park, with its manic laughter still ringing in the air. Some swear that the clown's maniacal voice is a recording of an actual mental patient from an asylum lost to time. The Laughing Man has become a fixture of the park, his status elevated to that of urban legend. Kids dare each other to approach it, and even adults are wary of it. The statue of the Laughing Man walks the fine line between amusement and fear.

The Arena, the park's ice-skating rink, is also haunted. There have been repeated reports of an invisible ice skater using the rink to practice long after the place has been closed to the public for the day. Staff have reported hearing the distinctive sound of skate blades carving the ice when no one is there. Padlocked doors have been found standing wide open, and windows slam shut for no reason. Staff sometimes report feelings of heaviness or dread, or the crawly sensation of being watched, especially as darkness falls. Figures have also been spotted in the Arena's dressing rooms. Are these the shades of past performers, gearing up for one more show?

The Ghost Train at Pleasure Beach is the first ride of its kind in the world. In the UK, Australia, New Zealand, and China, dark rides with a scary theme are called "ghost trains", and this is the ride that all the others are named for. (The Haunted Mansion at Disneyland is a good example of a ghost train.) It opened in 1930, and was originally called The Pretzel, partly because of the curve of the track layout. In America, rides with that design were known as pretzels - but the British public were unfamiliar with the term. So, the ride was renamed shortly thereafter. There was a play, titled *Ghost Train*, that ran for a year on the London stage. The film adaptation of the play was running in theaters in 1931, so the management of the park went with "Ghost Train" as a name for this new, innovative experience.

This particular ghost train, happily, comes with its very own resident ghost.

It's haunted by a former ride operator. This park employee passed away in the late 1970s or early 1980s after an ugly battle with illness. He'd worked at the park for many years, and after his death, he decided to stay on at the Ghost Train ride. In life, he wore work boots, so in his afterlife, he has picked up the nickname "Clogs" or "Cloggy", for his heavy footsteps.

Juliette Gregson is a historian and paranormal expert on

Blackpool. Her grandfather, Frank Gregson, used to work at Blackpool Pleasure Beach as a maintenance worker. Juliette was, of course, fascinated by her grandfather's job as a kid, and as an adult, has collected many anecdotes about the hauntings at Pleasure Beach.

About Cloggy, Juliette says, "From reports and research, I've found he was a very committed member of staff who would do anything to ensure that customer service standards were reached and that the customers got the fright of their lives when on the Ghost Train. It seems his dedication to it continued even after he had passed to the other side. Customers would say after dismounting the ride that they had been touched or grabbed by someone that they could not see but hear. Over the years the reports and stories increased when shocked members of the public found out that the extra 'sensations' were not actually part of the Ghost Train experience."

Juliette's granddad Frank also enjoyed providing a good ride encounter. When he and his apprentice were inside the ride doing maintenance work, he would stand very still and let a car approach, then lean over and say "Hello, how are you?", then laugh himself silly when the passengers screamed.

"But," Juliette pointed out, "Frank wasn't responsible for the many odd sounds, tapping, footsteps, and groaning heard echoing through the walls and reported by many staff."

Cloggy is a very active spirit: in addition to stomping around on the tracks, he's known to touch people and breathe in their faces. That would definitely be a shock!

When I was in the UK in 2023 for three solid weeks of ghost hunting, our host Paul Adams introduced us to his friends and fellow paranormal investigators, Darren W. Ritson and Drew Bartley. Darren is also a writer of true ghost stories, and he and Drew regaled us with plenty of ghost tales, including their experience at the Ghost Train ride at Pleasure Beach. The following is taken from Darren's account of their investigation, both as it was told to me and from his upcoming book, *Discovering Ghosts: Exploring the Haunted Heritage of Northern England*.

In 2002, Darren and Drew and their team were invited to go ghost hunting at the Ghost Train ride. Their investigation would be filmed for a documentary. The team split up into two groups, the Channel Four crew followed with their cameras, and the evening began.

Darren's group walked down the train tracks in the dark. Darren writes, "The ghost train is a long and winding echoic passageway and the quietest of sounds could have been amplified to a degree whereupon a false or inaccurate documentation of alleged phenomena may have been noted; we had to be extra careful not to misinterpret any normal noises for paranormal activity."

Suddenly, a very loud noise made them all jump. (Yes, even seasoned investigators jump at loud, unexpected noises.) Drew let Darren know on the walkie-talkie that his group had heard the noise too. Darren said it sounded like a pump or generator. It ran for several minutes, then shut off just as suddenly.

The group settled down in another area of the ride for what Darren called a "vigil" - American ghost hunters would call it an EVP session. A door slammed without warning. By this time, the Channel Four TV crew's nerves were wound as tight as piano strings. They had no idea what to expect; the investigators in the group were at least prepared for strange activity.

Darren admits that the team did experience "a rather harrowing series of occurrences." For us ghost hunters, that's all in a night's work; we sit in dark, spooky places so you don't have to. But the Channel Four team was properly spooked. Darren admitted that "it was quite funny watching the film crew literally trembling with fear." One of the cameramen, a big guy who looked like he took no crap from anyone, later pulled Drew to the side.

"How the hell do you people do this week after week?" he demanded. "I kid you not; I am absolutely shitting myself right now. I have been to many places in the world as a cameraman and I have seen many frightening things. I have been to war-torn countries and been caught up in crossfires and shot at multiple times; I have almost been blown up by hidden mines, bombs, and other devices, and had buildings falling down around me, and I tell you something right now, I will take that any day over this shit! I have never ... never been so fucking scared in my life, and I will never set foot in a haunted location to film ghosts ever again."

"By this time," Darren continued, "the Channel Four film crew had suddenly decided that they had all the shots and footage they required for the programme so they exited the ghost train and waited for us to finish off the investigation." Darren says it was really a shame that the TV crew bailed at that point, because some of the most interesting activity of the night was yet to come.

The group was sitting in the final location when the temperature suddenly dropped sharply.

"Cloggy, are you with us tonight?"

The area seemed to become even colder.

"Give us a sign to indicate your presence, please."

A door next to them began to shake and rattle as if someone was yanking on the handle, trying to get in. There was no one at the door - they looked.

"Thank you, can you give us another sign, please?"

Silence in the darkness.

"Come on, Cloggy, we know you're here. Give us another sign, please."

Darren felt a tap on his shoulder, and an icy chill ran down his spine.

"Let us hear your footsteps, please. That's what you're known for, isn't it? We're here with the utmost respect for you. We are just interested and want to prove you're real."

At that moment, every member of the group was astounded to hear the clump, clump, clump of footfalls echoing along the dark passageway. Cloggy was doing what he loved to do - he was making sure the people on his ride had the paste scared out of them.

"This investigation was a short but very rewarding one and it was an absolute privilege to be allowed access to the train ride to conduct it. It has been about twenty years since we carried out this investigation and I can remember it all like yesterday," Darren writes fondly.

Do you think that if the cameraman had known of Cloggy's devotion to the park and to his job, he'd have been that terrified? I like to think he'd have understood the spirit a little better.

THE JOKER GHOST AND OTHER FRIGHTS
(Luna Park, Melbourne, Australia)

In 1957, a young couple named Roy and Heather, both 19, visited Luna Park in Melbourne. Even though they were at the park on a cold, stormy Saturday, they were in good spirits - they were there to celebrate Roy getting a raise at his job. They walked through the eerily grinning mouth that formed the park's main gate, a fanciful piece of artwork called "Mister Moon", that dated back to the park's opening in 1912.

The couple started out on the tamer rides, as Heather was afraid of heights. But the excitement of the day worked to ease her nervousness, and they finally worked their way up to the Ferris wheel.

The car on this ride was enclosed, with the seats protected by a cage. Heather grabbed Roy's hand as their car rose higher into the air. The weather was really rotten by now. A flash of lightning blinded them for a moment, and a deep roll of thunder echoed around them. When their eyes adjusted, Heather gave a shriek of terror, and Roy's face went white with shock.

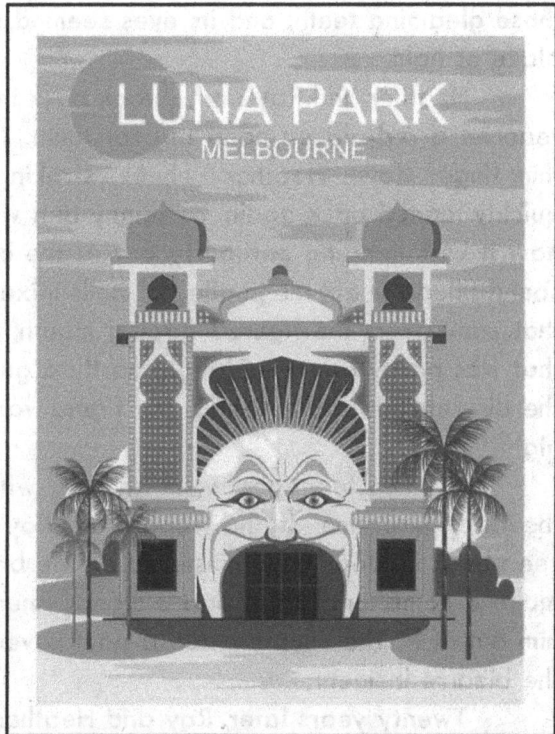

At three hundred feet in the air, they were suddenly sharing their cage with a third person.

Perched on the bar of the cage was a wiry guy, dressed in the costume of a medieval court jester. A three-pointed hat sat on his head - the couple registered that the cloth of the hat was red, yellow, and black, with a little golden bell on the tip of each point. The jester wore tights, one leg red, one leg black, with a yellow codpiece. Pointed yellow shoes, also trimmed with golden bells, rounded out his look.

This would have been quite weird enough, but the figure was also bizarrely wiry, with a threatening leer twisting its face. Its eyes smoldered with malice, and its lips were drawn back to reveal long, pointed teeth. Another flash of lightning illuminated those gleaming teeth, and its eyes seemed to glow in the sudden blaze of light.

Heather and Roy both shrank back in the seat as the jester reached a red-gloved hand out for them. The figure ran a long, thin finger down Heather's cheek, stroking it playfully. Then it quickly leaned back again. Its skinny butt was still on the bar, but now it was hanging perilously out of the cage. A cacophony of sound filled the air, the jingling of bells mixed with a terrifying cry that came from the figure's gaping mouth, a spine-tingling noise that was partly a crazed laugh, partly a guttural howl. Just when the din reached a crescendo, the figure vanished into the stormy night.

The two teenagers were shaking with cold and fear. With the disappearance of the apparition, Roy's courage started to seep back in. Soon, he'd mustered a little bravado. He swore he'd make a complaint to the park's management, but Heather talked him out of it. The couple made a pact never to tell anyone about the bizarre incident.

Twenty years later, Roy and Heather, now married, finally broke their silence. They were stunned to discover that others had seen the apparition too. In fact, it was part of the lore of Luna Park.

It was called The Joker.

The Joker showed up all over the park and took a cruel delight in causing dangerous incidents. Ten riders in a car on the Great Scenic Railway roller coaster screamed in horror as the Joker appeared on the track right in front of them. The car whizzed right through it, leaving the riders quivering with terror.

One week after that incident, a park guest filed a complaint, saying that the Joker had pushed her young daughter Betty off her horse on the Merry-Go-Round.

The patron had placed Betty, a toddler, on the horse, and shown her how to hang onto the pole. As the music began and the ride swung into motion, the Joker seemed to emerge from the machinery at the center of the carousel. Betty's mother watched in horrified disbelief as the apparition lurched over to the child and stuck his leering face within inches of hers.

Then he shoved the frightened kid right off the horse.

Betty's mother jumped onto the carousel platform and caught the girl as she fell. She glared at the Joker, who slung his skinny leg over Betty's horse as the ride picked up speed, and grinned maniacally at them as he passed.

The little girl was now hysterical with fear, but her mom was pissed. She held her daughter firmly, promising safety, but she waited for the Joker to come around again - she wanted to take a swing at him with her purse. But when the horse came into view again, the rider had vanished.

For a while, tales about the "vexatious and dangerous" Joker ghost gained traction. Luna Park management's attitude was a terse "no comment." Sightings of the Joker became less and less frequent, and no one has seen the creepy specter in decades.

The Joker isn't the only spirit that roams Luna Park Melbourne. When the park is deserted for the night, a phantom train sometimes appears. The old-fashioned steam train chugs silently along its tracks in the park for about two minutes before disappearing.

Another ghost wanders around the park's arcade games area in the dead of night. Workers hear disembodied laughter echoing along deserted corridors. The theory is that this is the spirit of some long-ago park patron who really enjoyed their time there.

As creepy as that is ... at least it's not the Joker.

NEW ENTRANCE AT CRYSTAL BEACH, ONTARIO

RIVALS
(Erie Beach, Crystal Beach, Ontario Canada)

Human beings can be remarkably stubborn creatures.

Take the story of Fort Erie, for example. The British fort was built in Ontario, Canada, in 1764. A larger fort was being built on the site during the War of 1812. American forces landed on Erie Beach in an attempt to take the fort. They did managed to capture the fort ... then they destroyed it in 1814 after a siege by the British. The British, perhaps out of spite, occupied the ruined fort until 1823. The area around Fort Erie has been a battlefield, an encampment, a field hospital, and a hastily dug graveyard.

Only about sixty years later, that area would be home to two amusement parks, Erie Beach Park and Crystal Beach Park. And just like the British and Americans earlier in that same century, the two parks were fierce rivals.

Erie Beach Park began as a picnic area called Snake Hill Grove. This park was enjoyed by both Canadians and Americans, but management realized it would be in the park's best interest to woo more Americans to the venue. In 1887, a ferry service ran from Buffalo, New York, to a train terminal, where customers could ride the train to the park.

1901 was the year of the Pan-American Exposition in Buffalo. After the expo wrapped up, the owners of the park - which had changed its name by then to Fort Erie Grove - bought the miniature train from the expo as an attraction. They added a carousel in 1904, as well as a zoo, a large aviary, and a 3,500-seat stadium.

The park grew rapidly, adding a hotel in 1905. But the expansion didn't stop there, oh no. In 1910, the park was bought by a new owner, who realized that the venue was, indeed, getting more customers from the US than from Canada. The new owner put in four ferries from Buffalo to serve the park. The 1911 season saw the addition of a restaurant, a bowling alley, a dance hall, a bathing house, and a three-story casino.

By 1915, Erie Beach Park boasted two swimming areas, one for adults and one for children, bumper cars, a swing ride, and a roller rink. 1917 brought a new carousel and a miniature railroad. There was even an airport at the park, offering flights to and from Niagara Falls. By the end of World War I, the park had a roller coaster, a Ferris wheel, and a children's play area.

But despite all this, by the beginning of the 1920's, people were staying away in droves. Management tried to save the park by adding a pony track, a Mill Chute ride, and a penny arcade in 1927, and a go-cart track and a new roller coaster called The Wildcat in 1928. But the upgrades were in vain. The park's last day of operation was Labor Day 1930.

Most of the equipment and rides at Erie Beach were purchased by the owners of Crystal Beach Park, a direct rival in the 1920s. They wanted to make sure no one could open another amusement park on the site. They later sealed the deal by buying the site outright and having it re-zoned.

The bumper cars from Erie Beach went to Springbank Park in London, Ontario. The carousel was sold to Skylon in Niagara Falls. The old train tracks were broken up for scrap metal during World War II. The hotel stayed open until 1935, when it burned to the ground. The casino held on the longest, but was abandoned in the mid-1970s, and later demolished.

Crystal Beach Park lasted quite a while longer than Erie Beach - it began in 1880, about the same time Erie Beach did, but operated until 1989. Crystal Beach started as a campground, that also had an auditorium and a picnic area. It was very popular, welcoming over 150,000 visitors every year in those very early days. Investors saw opportunity in the venue, and installed other attractions, including a hotel (which burned to the ground in 1923).

In the early years of the 1900s, a figure-eight roller coaster was constructed at the park. It was later dismantled and sold to Erie Beach Park. Crystal Beach Park experienced a huge bump in amenities in 1909 and 1910 under new ownership. Among other attractions, those heady years brought a swing ride, an athletic track and field, the Backety-Back roller coaster, swimming and boating facilities, a bowling alley, a cake walk, a dance pavilion, a theater, a penny arcade, a photography studio, a roller rink, and a shooting gallery. They were *really* trying to outdo Erie Beach Park.

Crystal Beach Park kept pushing boundaries. The Crystal Ballroom opened in 1925 - it was the largest dance hall in North America, with room for 3,000 dancers on its polished wood floors. In 1927, the park added a roller coaster called The Cyclone. The track of this coaster was made up almost entirely of curved pieces, and cars zipped around these bends at speeds of over 52 miles per hour. A full-time nurse was added to the staff, because so many passengers were passing out on the intense ride. (Although, to be fair, park guests considered Erie Beach's Wildcat coaster to be far scarier than the Cyclone.)

Even more terrifying, the Cyclone had a body count. Amos Weidrich, 23 years old, was killed on May 31, 1938, the day the park opened for the season. The safety bar was locked down, but somehow Amos found a way to stand up in the car. (He wanted to take his jacket off. I guess taking four rides on the Cyclone in a row at the end of May was hot work.) Amos fell out and landed on the track. His head and feet were sliced off by the wheels of the coaster car as it ran over him.

In 1948, the Cyclone was dismantled, and some parts from it were used to build another coaster called The Comet. The Comet ran until the park closed.

By the 1980s, Crystal Beach Park's star had dimmed. By 1983, the park was in serious financial trouble due to fading attendance resulting in bad weather, coupled with high interest loans. Attempts were made over the next six years to rejuvenate the park, but it closed permanently in 1989.

Today, the area around these two parks looks vastly different than it did in the parks' heyday. Elegant homes now stand where Crystal Beach Park once was. And what remains of Erie Beach Park is mostly in ruins. The concrete foundation of the casino litters the beach, overgrown with vegetation. The footings of the carousel are still in the woods, as well as the remnants of the Mill Chute ride.

There's been a bit of activity where Crystal Beach Park used to be, but it's fairly mild: light anomalies, a feeling of being watched, the odd disembodied voice or shadowy figure now and then.

In contrast, the ruins of Erie Beach Park are alive with paranormal activity. The full-bodied apparition of a woman in turn of the century clothing has been seen on the beach. Witnesses say she walked easily over the chunks of broken concrete without making a sound.

A paranormal investigator who goes by the name of Black

Owl has made contact with the ghost of a little boy near the ruins of the Mill Chute ride. According to the young spirit, he fell into the water and drowned when the ride ran him over. Other figures thought to be teenagers have been seen near the Mill Chute ride. They may be victims of a fire in either a hotel or a dance hall on the site. (The Erie Beach Hotel did burn down after the park closed in 1930, so maybe there's something to this theory.)

Black Owl has also captured many hours' worth of EVPs at the site - including someone screaming "Woohoo!" outside the casino. (That one makes me smile.) And apparitions of both American and British soldiers have been seen in the surrounding woods.

The ghosts of Erie Beach and Crystal Beach go way back.

THE WILD MOUSE
(Fun Fair Park, Baton Rouge, Louisiana)

Abandoned amusement parks are creepy places, no doubt about it. There's something eerie about walking through a deserted park, hearing the echo of laughter and music in your mind, and knowing that all those happy times are mere memories now.

But what if you were enjoying a day at a park, wandering around in search of your next corn dog, and came across a ride just sitting in a corner, forgotten and unloved? It's being taken over by weeds that are reaching up like skeletal fingers to caress the sides of the ride. A few patches of rust are beginning to bloom at the corners, and more rust stains weep brown tracks from the rivets. A robotic-looking rat with staring eyes waves at you, beckoning you to come closer. But it's obvious that no one has ridden on this attraction for quite some time.

Honestly? You're more than a little creeped out.

This is the Wild Mouse roller coaster at Fun Fair Park in Baton Rouge. It was shut down in the late 1980s. Rumor had it that two little girls had their ride - and their lives - abruptly cut short when they were both decapitated. Now the ride, hungry for more victims, is said to be responsible for broken bones, the death of a repair man, even the demise of Fun Fair's chimpanzee mascot.

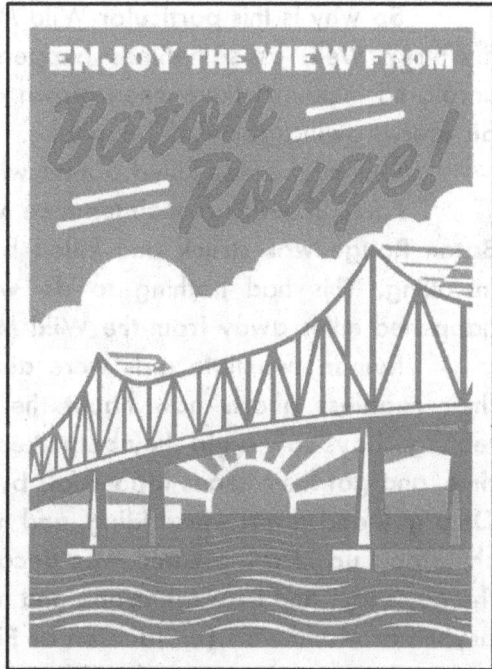

Let's unpack this and get to the truth, shall we?

The Wild Mouse (or Crazy Mouse, or Mad Mouse, take your pick) style of roller coaster was invented in Germany in the early 1960s. The signature of this design was wide cars and narrow tracks. This combination gave riders the feeling that the car was hanging dangerously off the side of the track, and gave a delicious anticipation of almost-certain doom.

Amusement park owners liked Wild Mouse rides because their compact design made them economical, and guests loved the thrill they got from the precarious feeling. But the progress of roller coaster design is always moving forward. Inventors were working with steel coasters, making them bigger, faster, with more elaborate turns and plunges. The popularity of the smaller Wild Mouse rides waned. By the 1990s, they were an endangered species.

So why is this particular Wild Mouse ride shrouded in such mystery? Well, as sometimes happens with ghost lore, a few unrelated incidents have been blown up and melded together in an ever-growing game of Telephone.

Rumor: the ride killed a man who was repairing it.

Fact: in 1985, a maintenance worker at a church fair in Baton Rouge was struck and killed by a roller coaster he was installing. This had nothing to do with Fun Fair Park, and it happened miles away from the Wild Mouse ride there.

Rumor: two little girls were decapitated on the ride, and their headless ghosts now haunt the amusement park. Or two teenage boys saw a girl they both liked, and stood up at the same time, and got their heads lopped off by the tunnel entrance beam. Or a guy and a girl were riding, and he got handsy with her, and she stood up in protest and was decapitated. The head fell into the guy's lap, and he went insane and had to be sent to the mental asylum at Mandeville (or Jackson or Pineville).

Fact: two young girls suffered minor injuries while riding on the Wild Mouse at Fun Fair Park. In the early 1980s, a boy was thrown from the Wild Mouse ride at Pontchartrain Beach in New Orleans. He fell 25 feet and ended up with a head injury. And in July 2010, Lindsay Zeno fell 30 feet from the Xtreme roller coaster at Dixie Landin'. She died from "multi-system trauma", which is about what you'd expect as a result of a three-story fall.

("But that happened at a park called Dixie Landin'!" I hear you say. "What does that have to do with Fun Fair Park?" Very good, grasshopper; you're paying attention. I'll explain that in just a second.)

Rumor: the Wild Mouse ride was, somehow, in some mysterious way, responsible for the death of Candy, the park's chimpanzee mascot.

Fact: okay guys, this is gonna suck, I'm not gonna lie. One of the attractions at Fun Fair Park was, indeed, a chimpanzee.

Candy was only six months old when she was purchased by the Haynes family of Louisiana. In her younger days, she'd had a career performing on a local children's television show. But when she got too old for that, she was essentially banished to Fun Fair Park.

She spent most of her life confined in a barren cage at the park, with no mental stimulation, and far from the company of her own kind. Occasionally, visitors would toss lit cigarettes into her cage for her to smoke. That was about the extent of her social interaction with her public.

(And here we're going to take a quick little explanatory detour. Remember how I said that Lindsay Zeno fell to her death from a roller coaster at Dixie Landin'? But somehow the Wild Mouse ride at Fun Fair Park was involved? Here's an explanation for the mix-up. Fun Fair Park actually closed in 1999 and relocated to a site next to Blue Bayou Water Park. When the park moved, Candy moved as well. With the relocation of the park came a name change, and it was renamed ... Dixie Landin'. So that explains the callback to a coaster tragedy at Fun Fair Park, even though by then, it was known as Dixie Landin'.)

The Animal Welfare Act of 1985 mandated "a physical environment adequate to promote the psychological well-being of primates." Activists worked for decades to get Candy released from her pitiful existence. They desperately wanted Candy to be able to enjoy the company of other chimps.

Finally, in 2015, a Federal law was passed that decreed that chimps in captivity are entitled to the same protection under the Endangered Species Act as wild chimpanzees. Armed with this new legislation, the Animal Legal Defense Fund sued Samuel Haynes, Jr, the park's owner.

The lawsuit asked that Candy be moved from Dixie Landin' to Chimp Haven, a sanctuary in the woods of Louisiana where she could enjoy the freedom of wide-open spaces and the company of other chimpanzees. Unfortunately, before the lawsuit was settled, Candy passed away in the summer of 2017, still in her squalid little cage. She lived to be over fifty years old, but her quality of life was severely diminished for most of that time.

The move, and rebranding as Dixie Landin', didn't do much to revitalize Fun Fair Park. Sure, the new park was in a better neighborhood. Some rides from the original park made the move to the new digs, including the Wild Mouse ride, and the park expanded with new attractions. But Dixie Landin' still suffered from low attendance. On June 2, 2025, Management announced that the park would close for good this time.

So, is the Wild Mouse roller coaster at Fun Fair Park in Baton Rouge haunted? Nope. Was it ever haunted? No, no it was not. It was all just a tangle of urban legend, spiced up with gory details, and garnished with a twist of truth.

GHOSTS ALONG THE BOARDWALK
(Santa Cruz Beach Boardwalk, Santa Cruz, California)

Okay, so you're disappointed that our previous park visit didn't turn up any ghosts. Let me make it up to you. The next place we're going is just lousy with 'em.

In 1865, John Leibrandt opened a public bath house near the mouth of the San Lorenzo River in California. He wasn't the only one with this idea: those folks who were interested in natural cures heard it was beneficial to bathe in salt water. More bath houses soon sprang up along the beach. Other attractions were added, to bring more comfort and interest to the bathers. Restaurants, souvenir shops, and photography stands joined the lineup of amenities.

Around the turn of the 20th century, an entrepreneur by the name of Fred Swanton saw this booming enterprise going on and put plans in motion for a casino and boardwalk. The casino opened on June 14, 1904. The casino building also housed an arcade, a grill, a dining room, and a theater. The boardwalk, the amusement park proper, was founded in 1907. It's the oldest surviving amusement park in California and is a California Historical Landmark.

And hoo boy, is this place ever haunted! Spirits have been seen strolling along the beach in broad daylight. Workers in the tunnels underneath the boardwalk have seen the ghost of a boy around 13 years old running through the dark hallways, only to disappear midstride.

"Oh Sylvia," I hear you say, "give us more details! We want the juicy stories!"

Ask and you shall receive, dear reader. The most prominent landmark on the Santa Cruz Boardwalk is the Giant Dipper. This is a historic wooden roller coaster that rises majestically into the air on the eastern end of the boardwalk. It was built in 1924 and has been in use ever since. It's on the United States Register of Historic Places. And there have been at least four fatal accidents on the coaster in its long, illustrious history. All four of them involved young men who stood up during the ride and were killed as a result.

The first death occurred the same year the coaster was built. On September 21, 1924, sixteen-year-old Walter Bryne was riding the Giant Dipper with his friends - over and over. The guys had gone on the ride three times already, riding in the rear car at first. On their fourth trip through, they switched to the front car. Walter, probably dizzy from the previous three rides, stood up as the car went down the first dip. He was hurled in front of the car and was crushed to death.

The second death came on March 30, 1943. At 19 years old, James Piner had been serving in the Navy for about a year and a half and had already survived several engagements in the South Pacific. He had been at the Naval convalescent hospital, waiting to be cleared to return to duty. He fell out of the car onto the roof of a tunnel that covered the start of the track, then rolled onto a lower catwalk. He suffered massive trauma and died two days later at Santa Cruz Hospital.

The third fatal accident happened on July 6, 1958. A machinist from Oakland, 22-year-old Peter Abila, had been drinking before deciding to ride the coaster. Two of his friends were in the front seat of the car, while Peter was alone in the second seat. He wriggled out from beneath the safety bar and fell 65 feet to the ground below, landing on the sand under the ride. He fell at around 11:40 pm; he was pronounced dead at the scene at 12:15 am, just over half an hour later. A detective investigating the incident personally got into one of the cars and tried to work his body under the safety bar. He said it was extremely difficult to do and involved standing up in the car.

The fourth death was that of Edward Crooks, on July 13, 1972. The 13-year-old had hitchhiked to the Boardwalk with four friends. The accident happened on a straight run of track. Edward fell from the top of the track to a lower section. He was hit by the car and dragged for some length along the track. His friends raised the alarm when their car returned to the staging area, and they realized that Edward wasn't in it. Two men saw him on the track and were about to climb up to rescue him when the car came around again and bumped him off. Edward fell onto the gravel roof of a nearby restroom. He was found dead there by police and the ambulance crew.

It seems that the Giant Dipper's first fatality gets the honor of being the ghost that haunts it. Walter is usually seen at night by ride operators, riding in the rear-most car. Riders say they've sat next to a teenage boy dressed in old-fashioned clothes, who vanishes sometime during the ride. He mostly manifests as a full-body apparition, but some ride operators have felt their sleeves being tugged or feel a ghostly tap on their shoulder.

A pizza joint near the bumper cars, Pizza One, was the site of some random weirdness in 2012. Multiple employees had the same eerie encounter with an entity they nicknamed "The Barefoot Ghost." Restaurant workers would be closing for the night, a task which included mopping the floors. They would watch, baffled, as bare footprints appeared, tracking across the freshly mopped floor.

Another haunted building on the Boardwalk is Neptune's Kingdom. Nowadays, it's a pirate-themed recreation center that houses an arcade and a miniature golf course. But from 1907 to 1963, it was a heated indoor saltwater swimming pool known as the Plunge. At least five people - again, all men, and four of them were teenagers - drowned in the pool.

In 1935, 67-year-old T. Tallaert kicked things off by dying of a heart attack while swimming. He was found floating dead in the pool.

The second death, which has never really been explained, was that of 16-year-old Richard Carona in 1937. We're not really sure of the details; we just know that he drowned.

In 1958, Raymond Johnson, 14 years old, got stuck in an underwater drain and couldn't get to the surface for air.

A year later, in 1959, two boys - 15-year-old James Hagan and 16-year-old Kenneth Matsumoto - ventured out into the deep end of the pool, in spite of not knowing how to swim. Their bravado cost them their lives.

Even though the saltwater pool is long gone, the building that used to be the Plunge is said to be haunted by the drowned victims. The activity seems to center on the mini golf course. Employees have seen dark, ominous shadow figures form on the course and wander around, giving off spooky vibes. One worker was startled and very creeped out when a translucent face appeared in one of the video monitors that were watching the golf course.

There's a restaurant at Neptune's Kingdom that's also haunted. A kitchen employee witnessed cooking utensils moving, even flying off hooks and shelves.

Next door to Neptune's Kingdom, the Casino has been standing since 1907, and spirits have made it their home too. The ghost of a tall man is said to hang out in the laser tag room. There's one employee who refuses to close the laser tag area; she's had too many sightings and experiences to be comfortable there alone after dark.

A former employee, who used to work at the old timey photo shop that was once inside the Casino, says that she would sometimes capture ghostly apparitions in her pictures.

Next to the Casino is The Cocoanut Grove, a banquet room and conference center. This building mostly just experiences poltergeist activity after hours. But there have been some reports of the ghost of a little blonde girl wearing a pink dress running through the dining room during the day. Employees claim the chairs move on their own, even stacking themselves. Security guards hear strange noises late at night - noises such as a harmonica playing.

There is no shortage of fun to be had at the Santa Cruz Boardwalk. With all its history, the tragic as well as the enjoyable, there is also no shortage of ghosts to be had there, either. The living and the dead alike have been enjoying California's oldest amusement park for well over a century.

SPIRITS OF SYLVAN BEACH

(Sylvan Beach Amusement Park, Sylvan Beach, New York)

The small town of Sylvan Beach, NY, still boasts the family-oriented park that was founded by James Spencer in 1879. The park drew visitors who arrived via the canal system, in particular the Erie Canal and the Oneida Lake Canal. Spencer envisioned a family-friendly destination, and the park has kept that vibe. It's quite small, more like a town carnival than an amusement park, but it's packed with vintage fun, offering gentle rides like teacups and a carousel. The park also has a mini golf course, arcade games, and bumper cars and boats. Sylvan Beach trades on nostalgia rather than slick modern rides.

There are four ghosts associated with this park. Just as the park is laid-back and not glitzy, the paranormal side of things is pretty chill too. The employees at the park lived on the grounds back in the day, and three of them have never left.

"Scott" was a park employee who was found dead in the Treasure Land bathroom. His ghost is quite subdued - he limits himself to making noises in the Playland attic.

"Abby" is Sylvan Beach's very own Lady in White. She is usually seen in Yesterday's Royal Hotel. The hotel burned in a fire in the 1900s, and the theory is that Abby is one of the fire victims.

Many park workers have seen Abby standing in the hotel's dining room. Two employees say they experienced cold, full-body chills as they witnessed Abby's silhouette walking in the dining room.

Abby also shows up on the rides in the park. (Although to be fair, this next story might involve the appearance of a different spirit.) A park employee told the story of how one night, three little girls got onto the Tiptop ride. The ride cycled through twice. As the ride came to a stop, the attendant only saw two girls get out of the car. Immediately, she asked the two where the other girl had gone. They swore that they were the only two on the ride.

Another ghost at the park is the spirit of "Jack," who loved to stay at Yesterday's Royal Hotel. The door to Jack's room gives employees a clue to his whereabouts. If the door is closed, that means he's in there, and you'd better leave him alone. But if the door is open, Jack is out and about, and it's cool to go into the room. He's been spotted in the dining room of the hotel on occasion.

Sylvan Beach Park actually hosts paranormal investigations. The group Casper Cops leads ghost tours in their attraction Park After Dark. The tours run in the summer months, on Friday and Saturday nights, from mid-June to the beginning of September.

The arcade at the park was particularly active during the summer of 2023. On four different nights, investigators saw coins and pieces of wood fly through the air or heard coins hitting the floor.

One investigator saw a dark object fall from an air hockey table. It looked like a bag of coins, but when it hit the floor, the investigator only heard the clink of one coin.

The next day, the investigator hunted up some old-timers on the park staff and did some research. They explained that years ago, Bill, the owner of the arcade, would go around to collect the coins from the machines as part of his duties. He used a canvas bag, with the top of the bag fitted with a metal ring to hold it open. One of the employees got an old bag out of storage. The investigator realized it was exactly what they'd seen fall from the air hockey table the night before.

The investigator followed up this research with another conversation, with a former owner of the park. Pat said that the arcade was one of the oldest buildings at Sylvan Beach. Pat bought the arcade from the widow of its former owner, Bill. Bill had grown up in the arcade and had inherited the business from his father.

Pat said that Bill was very particular about money and took the duty of collecting coins from the machines very seriously. Yes, he did use canvas bags, held open by a metal ring at the top, to collect the coins.

Bill is the fourth spirit that haunts Sylvan Beach Park. Upon reflection, the investigator noticed an interesting correlation: on the four nights that the sound of coins was heard, the park was very busy during the day. It seems Bill is active when he feels there's a need to go around to collect the coins from the day's take.

A LABOR OF LOVE
(Enchanted Forest, Turner, OR)

Roger Tofte had a dream.

The Wisconsin native had moved to Salem, Oregon in the late 1960s. To provide a living for his wife and four kids, he had taken a job with the Oregon State Highway Department. But he was itching to do something creative with his life.

In the early 1960s, Roger and his wife Mavis bought twenty acres of land for $4,000, making monthly payments of $50. Roger had the idea of building an amusement park, with the first attraction being a winding path through the woods called Storybook Lane. He began building it in 1964, working on it mostly by himself after work and on the weekends. He thought it might take him two years to build Storybook Lane.

It ended up taking seven years. And boy, did Roger take a bunch of crap about his project. He had loads of trouble finding a bank willing to lend him the last $2,000 needed to finish the park. Finally, a bank did cave and lent him the money. To add insult to injury, Roger's friends thought he was nuts to do this. They scathingly referred to Enchanted Forest as "Idiot Hill."

At last, the first attraction was finished. On August 8, 1971, the Tofts simply put up a sign at the side of the road saying that the park was open. Seventy-five folks came to check it out the first weekend. Roger figured he was doing pretty well - but he didn't realize just how powerful a marketing tool word of mouth can be. By the second weekend, a thousand tourists were waiting in line to visit Enchanted Forest. Adult admission was $1, and kids got in for fifty cents.

Like Sylvan Beach, Enchanted Forest has a laid-back vibe, for an amusement park. It's a quirky little tourist destination ... but that's where the similarities end. The energy at Enchanted Forest is dark, nearly foreboding. There are no industrious arcade coin collectors or gentle Ladies in White here.

Roger Tofte himself felt that the hauntings at his park had to do with the land on which it was built. In 1846, native American tribes from the Willamette Valley fought a violent, bloody battle with Oregon settlers, in the Conflict of Battle Creek. Tofte believed that the land held a residual energy that contributed to the park's unique atmosphere.

Visitors have seen full-bodied apparitions of both Native Americans and settlers. They've heard voices too, of adults and children.

There is paranormal activity all over the park. Many visitors report being touched by unseen hands. It's downright creepy, being touched by something you can't see.

Park employees will arrive for work in the morning to find that rides have already been set up and turned on. Visitors have claimed that items in their pockets suddenly appear ... on display in the European Village exhibit.

There's even more weirdness that stalks the wooded trails of the park. There have been reports of encounters with non-human entities, like fae. Children have insisted that they were transported to some sort of parallel dimension.

Let's leave the fairy folk alone - trust me, you do *not* want to mess with the fae - and return to the ghosts. In 1974, the Haunted House attraction was built. The latex props that provide the creep are eerily lifelike, and many guests are truly overwhelmed with the negativity they feel walking through the house. Even some staff members are scared of the attraction.

Enchanted Forest does boast a few rides, in addition to its walk-through experiences. One of these is the Challenge of Mondor ride, and the stories from this attraction were intriguing enough to attract the attention of *Ghost Adventures*.

In 2016, ride operator Chris Dunn was preparing the ride for the day. As he was doing his routine checks, he began to hear footsteps behind him. He turned around quickly, but no one was there. Still, the creepy feeling continued.

Five seconds later, Chris was caught off guard as a blast of energy ran right through him. He felt a rush of dizziness, and his body shook with chills. And as if having such a strange experience once wasn't bad enough, the whole thing - the unexplained footsteps, the rush of energy, the vertigo - happened to him again, later in the day.

When *Ghost Adventures* visited Enchanted Forest, the crew focused on the Challenge of Mondor ride. They caught some pretty good evidence, including some intriguing EVPs in a female voice, saying things like "*hello*," "*this is my house*," "*come to Mom*," and "*goodbye*." Zak Bagans encountered a female spirit: he felt a cold spot on his back, and when he asked her where she was touching him, she confirmed she was touching his back.

Enchanted Forest is full of intriguing energies, and very few of them seem to be friendly. Ghost hunters in search of the unknown would do well to experience the park ... just watch who you talk to.

THE LONELIEST RIDE
(Jantzen Beach Mall carousel, Portland, OR)

For some horse-crazy kids (and more than a few grownups), the carousel is a big draw. Sure, it doesn't have the dangerous thrill of a roller coaster's dips and loops, or the slightly illicit-feeling fun of bouncing off a friend's bumper car. But there's something about the graceful steeds, with their bright colors, flowing manes and tails, and noble faces, that takes riders back to a simpler time.

In the early part of the 20th century, amusement parks were big business. One of the heavy hitters in the industry was a guy named Charles Wallace Parker. His empire of amusement park rides and games made him very wealthy indeed. His friends called him "the amusement king," not only for his massive enterprise, but also for the high quality and extraordinary craftsmanship that went into his carousels. In 1904, Parker designed an exquisite carousel that was manufactured in Abilene, Kansas.

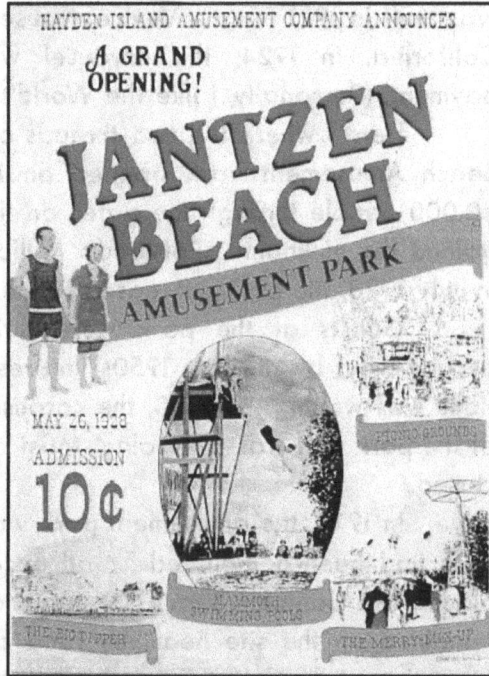

Parker's horses were hand-carved in dynamic, fluid poses, making them seem almost alive. In a nod to the fantasy that these steeds could nearly leap off the platform and take a rider on a gallop through pure imagination, each wooden horse was fitted with real steel horseshoes.

When the carousel was finished, it was a true work of art. The ride was over 66 feet in diameter and stood nearly three stories high, with 72 horses and two chariots ready to whisk riders into fantasy. Parker transported the carousel to Missouri for the 1904 St. Louis World's Fair. His ride was an immediate hit with the guests.

This is the romantic lore of the carousel, but according to the Oregon Historical Society, it's not quite that old. They say it was built in 1921 for the Venice Amusement Pier in Venice Beach, California. In 1924, the carousel was repossessed for non-payment. (Personally, I like the World's Fair origin story better.)

Here's where the two threads combine. Portland's Jantzen Beach Amusement Park opened on May 26, 1928, welcoming 40,000 people through the gates on the first weekend. It quickly gained the nickname "Portland's Million-Dollar Playground," and in July 1928, the park purchased Parker's magnificent carousel.

Guests at the park were thrilled by the carousel for decades. But by the late 1950s, interest in tame amusement park rides was waning. By 1960, the carousel was about the only ride at the park that was still going. Most of the other rides had been closed.

In 1970, the amusement park was closed, and by 1972, the park had been demolished ... all except for the carousel. In its place rose Jantzen Beach Center shopping mall. The carousel remained on the site near the food court, becoming a beloved attraction at the mall for another generation of kids.

Again, tastes changed. In 2012, the mall was renovated to the tune of $50 million. Parker's beautiful carousel was put in storage in 2011. For a few years, no one knew what had become of it. It was finally rediscovered at Restore Oregon, where it had been donated in spring 2017. In September 2023, Restore Oregon's executive director, Nicole Posser, made an announcement.

"Restore Oregon has selected the National Neon Sign Museum to be the next stewards of the carousel." The museum has dedicated lots of resources to the restoration of the carousel, to bring it back to its original appearance using replicas of colors from the 1920s.

The carousel may harbor a couple of ghosts from that era as well.

As early as the 1950s, there have been reports of two ghostly children that play on the carousel. They are usually seen by kids, although adults have seen them too. They usually run around and play in the middle of the ride, in the machinery room. A common thread runs through these reports: the children are a girl and boy, appearing about eight and ten years old, wearing clothing from the 1920s. Witnesses describe the children in detail. The younger child, the girl, has long brown hair, perhaps held back with a big white bow. The boy is dressed in knickers with suspenders, a white shirt, and a flat hat, like a straw boater.

Many times, the children are just seen playing in the machinery room, but at other times, they seem to gaze sadly at the living riders. Some witnesses report feeling as though the lonely little ghosts want company, that they want other kids to join them in the depths of the ride's machinery. Needless to say, this gives many children the creeps.

No one knows who these spectral children are. It goes without saying that there are no deaths associated with the carousel. However, when the ride was located at the Venice Beach Pier from 1921 to 1924, it was set up next to the roller coaster. And yes, there were several fatal accidents on the coaster during that time. None of them involved children that young, though.

As with so many other ghost tales, the background of the two young spirits on the Jantzen Beach carousel may forever remain a mystery. Only time will tell, after the carousel is restored, whether the little ghosts will also come out of storage.

LADY RIDER
(Cedar Point Amusement Park, Sandusky, OH)

The Kiddie Kingdom Carousel, an antique ride at Cedar Point, is considered to be the designer's masterpiece. It was built in 1924 by the Dentzel Carousel Company, with the founder's son,

CEDAR POINT
CEDAR POINT
CEDAR POINT

SANDUSKY, OHIO

William H. Dentzel, at the helm. For a while after it was built, Dentzel used the carousel as a display model to show potential clients the craftsmanship that went into his rides. The display model was purchased by the Philadelphia Toboggan Company in 1928, and for forty years, it traveled from park to park. It was bought by Cedar Point Amusement Park in 1968.

This ride is another work of art. Rather than simply a stable of horses, it features a menagerie of creatures, 52 in all. There are horses, naturally, but they are joined on the platform by bears, ostriches, and rabbits. A lion, a tiger, and a donkey round out the varied collection of mounts.

But it is one of the horses that is the subject of this story. It's not one of the flashier steeds. In fact, this is a plain brown horse, carved by Carl Muller in 1924. Perhaps during the day, it got passed over by young riders in search of a mount with more pizzazz, maybe the lion or the panda bear. But after Cedar Point closed for the evening, and lights were winking out all over the park, and workers swept up the day's litter, and the rides went silent for the night, there was one ride that still continued to run.

Witnesses swore that a woman in a long white 1920s-style dress mounted that ordinary-looking horse. She rode it around, a dreamy look on her glowing face, while the carousel took a few more spins before slowing to a stop. Her identity has never been discovered, although people have theorized that she may be the wife of Carl Muller, the artist who created the horse.

The haunted horse now resides at the Merry Go Round Museum in Sandusky. No one has yet reported seeing the ghost of a young woman in a white dress at the museum, but maybe she still shows up once in a while, to stroke the wooden nose of her favorite steed.

GET YOUR **NEW**

DARK RIDE

WITH A MINIMUM INVESTMENT

All you need are these NEW dark ride ROTATING CARS .... they fit your present Pretzel Ride!!!!!

MORE FUN!   MORE PROFIT!

Pretzel's "New" Dark Ride embodies all the features that have made the Pretzel Ride an outstanding success throughout the country and abroad the past 25 years, plus new thrills of illusions and the sensational new action of the car itself.

The "New" Dark Ride Car is constructed to rotate in either direction—sideways, backward, forward—in an unpredictable manner as it follows the crazy pattern of the track through the illusion-filled darkness. Slow turns, fast turns, whipping turns soon befuddle you completely. Add to this the funny scarey illusions sprinkled with weird noises of all description, and you have a general idea of the confusion created in the "New" Dark Ride.

Keep your present Pretzel track, point on a new front, add these "New" Dark Ride Cars and illusions and have a brand new ride. We will make a liberal trade-in allowance on your old Pretzel cars.

**SLOW TURNS — FAST TURNS
WHIP TURNS**

"Most meritorious new riding device" award to Pretzel Amusement Co. for "New" Dark Ride exhibited at 1954 convention of National Association of Amusement Parks, Sherman Hotel, Chicago, Nov. 29 to Dec. 7, 1953.

WHERE THE SCARES ARE REAL

Haunted Haunted House Attractions

Haunts are a staple of the spooky season. Volunteers spend much of the summer hammering, painting, and decorating. Set designers put their imaginations to work devising scenes and props to scare the paste out of their audience. By the time the calendar pages turn to October, all is ready. Fallen leaves crunch underfoot, and the chill of coming winter thins the autumn sunlight. Scare actors put on gory makeup, celebrating Halloween all month long. Line actors keep haunt audiences entertained as they wait their turn to stumble through the darkness.

But the actors are not the only ones haunting the darkened hallways of these attractions. Some of the inhabitants of these haunted houses are made of more ephemeral stuff than latex and greasepaint.

There are some people who seek out the adrenaline rush of a haunted house attraction. It's a great way to get your blood pumping, to experience excitement and a dash of terror. For all the gory props, gruesome effects, eerie noises in the dark, and jump scares, it's a controlled environment. The creepy hallways or trails through the spooky woods aren't really populated by chainsaw-wielding maniacs or deranged doctors or brain-eating zombies.

But sometimes, there's more lurking in the dark. We're going to take a look at several haunted attractions, places where the frights have a solid basis in reality, where history provides the undercurrent of dread beneath the screams.

Old Whitley County Jail

One of the popular haunted house tropes is the haunted prison. Locked up for eternity ... what a terrifying thought. The Haunted Jail is an attraction in Columbia City, Indiana, that is set up in the old Whitley County Jail. The building was constructed in 1875 and was considered one of the best jails in Indiana when it was open. Spirits do still wander its halls. Paul Harrington, who runs the attraction, assured a reporter that The Haunted Jail is a no-touch haunt, where the actors don't reach out and grab the guests for an extra scare. Then he walked back his statement.

"Things will touch you, but nothing alive will touch you."

That's an inelegant way of saying there are a couple of spirits at the attraction that still make their presence known.

Charles Butler decided he really didn't want to be married anymore. He had already been arrested 27 times between 1877 and 1883, and was always threatening to kill his wife, Abbigael Sheehan Butler. Abbie ran away and took their son, four-year-old Henry, to find safety with Charles' aunt and uncle. Charles heard this news while he was in jail. When he was released, he went in search of Abbie and Henry. Abbie wanted nothing to do with him and refused to let him see their son. Enraged, Charles shot her twice. She died hours later. He was found guilty and hanged at Whitley County Jail on October 10, 1884. He died hard - he intentionally stood too close to the hinges of the trap door, and when the door was released, he slid off. Instead of breaking his neck in a clean drop, he struggled for several minutes.

Butler's ghost is said to walk the halls of the jail, forever searching for the sheriff who hanged him. In a macabre twist, Sheriff Frank Allwein was so affected by having to pull the lever to hang Butler that he never really got over it; he ruminated on it for the rest of his life. Local lore holds that the sheriff, too, wanders the halls, looking for Butler.

Old Joliet Penitentiary

Old Joliet Prison is famously haunted. It was built in 1858, out of local limestone quarried by the men who would live in the prison they were building. The first ghost story to come out of Joliet made the rounds way back in 1932, when spectral singing was heard coming from the prison cemetery. Officials tried to convince people that the eerie voice belonged to a live convict, who was in the habit of singing to himself as he went about his job manning the pumps at a nearby quarry. Setting aside the fact that there's no way a convict would have been allowed out at night alone, ghost hunters went out to the quarry while the singing was going on and found no one.

The prison is a magnet for paranormal investigators. Spirits show up in photos taken at the prison, and pictures also capture strange mists and shadow figures. It seems that the singing ghost has long since vanished, but the cell blocks are still noisy with spirit activity. Ghostly crying and wailing are heard, and some visitors are even whistled at as they walk past. Guests also experience the angry emotions of vanished prisoners. The residual violent rage still permeates Old Joliet Prison. The energy given off by haunted house visitors feeds these entities, and the attraction is considered to be the scariest haunt in Illinois.

Old Lake County Jail

John Dillinger may have escaped from the Old Lake County Jail in Crown Point, Indiana, but many spirits are still trapped there. The jail plays host to the Criminally Insane haunted attraction every October. But the activity here, including photographic anomalies, unsettling EVPs of spirit voices, cell doors that open and close with no explanation, and mysterious footsteps that echo down the cell block hallway, goes on all year round.

The jail was built in 1878, and in 1934, it received a celebrity guest: John Dillinger, who was sent there to await trial for the murder of a Chicago police officer. Authorities bragged that the jail was escape proof, but on March 3, Dillinger bluffed his way out of his cell with a wooden gun he'd carved himself. He snagged a couple of machine guns, locked up the guards and several trustees, and went on his merry way.

Paranormal activity at the Old Sheriff's House and Jail includes a lot of physicality, with people getting pushed or yanked in cells. The cell where Dillinger was locked up is reported to be particularly active. A blue light is said to appear in the cell, and people have heard the lonesome sounds of a harmonica playing - the same simple instrument Dillinger played when he was kept here.

Eastern State Penitentiary

Another prison that trades on its unsavory history during the spooky season is Eastern State Penitentiary in Philadelphia. It was built in 1829 and boasted walls thirty feet high. Prisoners who arrived here in the early days were placed in extreme solitary confinement. The theory was that this would encourage the wrongdoers to ponder their misdeeds and learn from them. In practice, though, it was a truly diabolical exercise in vicious psychological abuse.

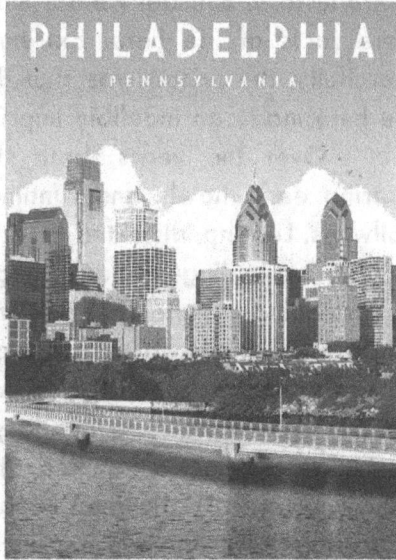

Inmates were on 23-hour lockdown. They were forced to wear hoods, preventing them from even seeing their fellow prisoners, much less communicating with them. In a sadistic display of cruelty, guards covered their shoes with cloth, so that prisoners couldn't hear their footsteps in the halls. Any attempt to communicate by tapping out messages on cell bars or pipes was immediately and severely punished.

One prisoner who had it better than most was Al Capone, who spent seven months here. It was Capone's first prison sentence. Here's what happened: on May 17, 1929, Capone was arrested outside a Philadelphia movie theater for carrying a concealed, unlicensed .38 caliber revolver. He was sentenced to one year but was released on March 17, 1930, for good behavior.

Some cynically said he'd gotten arrested on purpose, so he could hide out safely in prison while the heat from the St. Valentine's Day massacre cooled.

Conditions at Eastern State Penitentiary were brutal for its entire history. Suicide, mental illness, murder, torture, and disease were facts of life here. Extreme cruelty was the daily reality. Mercifully, the prison was shut down in 1971, but the brutality of life here made an indelible imprint on the building.

Over the years, both staff and visitors have reported hearing eerie howls and running footsteps in the prison's dark hallways. Leering, distorted faces appear on the walls, then vanish. Oppressive feelings of heavy negativity are a constant, with some visitors being affected not just emotionally, but physically as well. One staff member was paralyzed where he stood, unable to move as something beckoned him to come deeper into the cell.

Eastern State Penitentiary is either the worst place or the best place to host a haunted attraction - I haven't made up my mind which it is. Halloween Nights at ESP is ten acres of haunted attractions. Five haunted houses are set up to scare the paste out of haunt goers: Delirium, Big Top Terror, Machine Shop, Nightmares, and The Crypt. For those who want a little more thrill in their experience, the haunt offers an "opt in" choice. You're given a glowstick necklace. If you wear it, that tells the scare actors that it's open season. They are then allowed to touch you, separate you from your group, and generally make your trip through their haunt a whole lot scarier.

But of course, it's not *their* haunt. The true scares at ESP belong to the ghostly inmates who left their agony imprinted on these walls.

Ohio State Reformatory

Ohio State Reformatory, in Mansfield, Ohio, is well-known

as the set for Stephen King's *The Shawshank Redemption* and other films. But the actors in these movies could go home at the end of the day. For the prisoners who lived here, this was home, and there was no escape.

It was also home to the prison wardens. Tragedy struck an innocent at the prison in November 1950. Helen Glattke, wife of Chief Arthur Glattke, was getting dressed in their quarters on a quiet Sunday morning when she reached up to a high shelf to get her jewelry box. Her seeking fingers found her husband's .32 caliber pistol. As she moved it out of her way, the pistol discharged, and the round struck her, piercing her left upper lung. The 41-year-old mother of two died three days later at General Hospital.

Helen's flowery perfume is smelled in the administration building, a gentle reminder of her continued presence there. Sometimes, she even touches visitors in welcome. Witnesses also smell Arthur's cigar smoke. Other manifestations include furniture being moved and the sound of a piano playing in the empty rooms of the warden's quarters. Helen will sometimes appear as a full-bodied, intelligent apparition, telling people that she's not dead.

Other spirits there are not as friendly. Ohio State Reformatory was designed as a place for first-time male offenders who were too old for juvenile detention. These young men were encouraged to learn a trade and given the opportunity to gain a

high school education if they needed it. For many years, this system worked very well. The reformatory was so effective that former inmates often returned to thank the staff for giving them a second chance at life.

This changed dramatically in 1930. There was a massive fire at the Ohio State Penitentiary in Columbus. The disaster killed 320 inmates, and hundreds more were left homeless. They were relocated to other prisons, including the reformatory. This meant that suddenly, the non-violent offenders were living with hardened criminals.

Things went downhill very quickly from there. In 1960, the reformatory was changed to a maximum-security prison. Guards began inflicting harsh punishments, and inmates turned on each other, fighting and killing with frightening regularity. Disease became rampant, and rat infestations were common. Many prisoners sought escape through suicide.

The Hole was one of the grisliest parts of the prison. This was the solitary confinement area. The unlighted cells were kept at a temperature of 95 degrees, and prisoners were sometimes confined here for three days. Many inmates were driven insane by the punishment, and visitors can still hear the ghostly ramblings of the tortured souls. Another spirit trapped in the Hole is said to be that of a guard named Frank Hangar, who was murdered by an inmate in 1932. The inmate broke out of his cell and used a piece of pipe to beat Hangar to death so he could steal his keys. Frank's spirit is still furious at being dead, and he often strikes people with his police baton, as if he is still fighting off the prisoner who killed him. Other spirits, including the terrified ghost of a 14-year-old boy, haunt the basement of the prison.

All this negative energy fuels Blood Prison, the haunted attraction at Ohio State. Guests at the haunt can experience terror that goes well past the efforts of the scare actors. These actors portray twisted inmates and violent guards, and they play their parts well. And sometimes, the screams that echo off the peeling walls of the prison have a more ethereal source.

West Virginia Penitentiary

West Virginia Penitentiary, in Moundsville, is home to the Dungeon of Horrors haunted house. This tour takes guests through the basement of the prison, and there are plenty of jump scares to be had. For those who want a more historically focused experience, the penitentiary also offers the North Walk. This is not a haunt - there are no scare actors in this area - but rather a tour through the oldest and most paranormally active part of the facility. The tour guide shares real stories from over 100 years of history and violence, plus paranormal accounts from after the facility's closing.

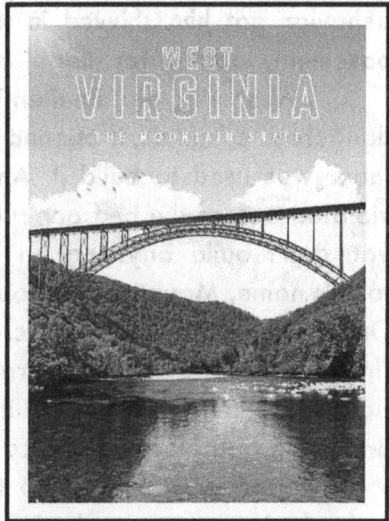

North Hall was where the worst offenders were housed; not the ones who were the baddest guys on the outside, but the nastiest characters on the inside. This was a place of 23-hour lockdown, but two inmates still managed to get themselves murdered there. One was a biker named Danny, who was fatally stabbed in the eye by another inmate. The other was William "Red" Snyder. He was in for murdering his parents and hacking their corpses into pieces. Everyone hated Red, and he was always getting into fights. One of those fights ended with him being stabbed 37 times right in front of his cell.

Another incredibly haunted part of the prison is the

recreation room in the basement, which the prisoners nicknamed "The Sugar Shack." This place is vibrating with activity, with disembodied voices arguing, random cold spots, and unexplained voices. The entire basement is the stomping grounds of a maintenance man who once worked here. He was a rat, and often spied on the inmates to curry favor with the guards. This sneaky behavior got him shivved in the bathroom. He still wanders the basement, looking for illegal activity.

West Virginia Penitentiary was built to house the most dangerous criminals. It opened in 1876, and just as at Joliet, inmate labor was used to build it. And in doing so, the powers that be violated one of the bedrock rules of the paranormal, which is that you don't build anything on top of Indian burial grounds. The town's name, Moundsville, should have been a clue. (So should the Grave Creek Mound, right across the street from the prison.) The first prisoners to be incarcerated there reported seeing shadow figures in their cells. Modern investigators have captured EVPs of drumming and Native American chanting.

Natives would not be the only folks buried on the prison grounds. Inmates were buried there, too. From 1899 to 1959, 94 men were executed at the penitentiary, most of them by hanging. These executions were open to the public in the first few decades of the 20th century. (What did people do before the internet? This. They watched public executions.) This all came to an end after a hanging on June 19, 1931, when Frank Hyer was executed for murdering his wife. You know how they say that it's not the fall that kills you, it's the sudden stop at the end? Well, Frank took this a step farther. The executioner misjudged the length of rope it would take to hang Frank. When the trap door opened, Frank fell through, and the weight of his body not only snapped his neck, it popped his head clean off. One of the ghosts that roams the prison grounds is headless, leading people to theorize that it is Frank, still decapitated, still searching for his head.

In 1949, electrocution replaced hanging as a method of execution. Nine men met their ends in Old Sparky before West Virginia outlawed capital punishment in 1965. These executions were carried out in a building called the Death House. The building no longer stands, but strange light anomalies are often seen in the area at night. These look eerily like sparks of static electricity. Maybe this is a chilling reminder of the way those nine men were ushered out of the world of the living.

Old Tooele Hospital

Wanna make a horror movie ten times more terrifying? Set it in a hospital. Double bonus points if it's in a mental asylum. Here are a few super-haunted haunted attractions at hospitals.

Old Tooele Hospital has an interesting origin story. It was originally the home of a fellow named Samuel F. Lee, who built it in 1873 for his family. The Lees moved out in 1913, and the county turned it into a makeshift rest home for the elderly. In 1953, a new hospital was built. Now, half of the building is a senior living facility.

The other half is a haunted attraction known as Asylum 49.

Ghosts abound here, and I'm not talking just about the actors who wander the halls every October. Asylum 49 has been investigated by enough paranormal groups that several distinct spirits have been identified, each with their own personality.

Robert is the ghost of a large man who haunts the main

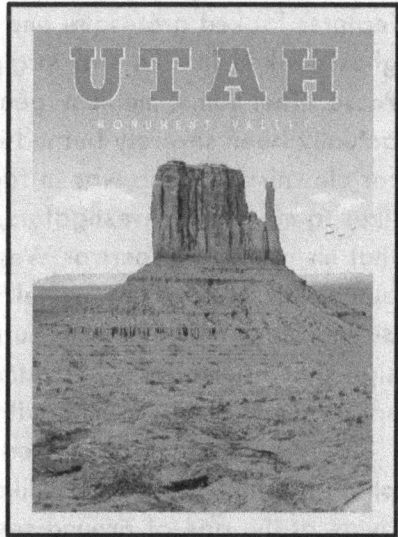

hallway of the old hospital. He walks down the hallway using a cane, peering into rooms as he goes. He seems to have a great sense of humor - he likes to crack jokes during EVP sessions, and he loves to jump-scare people. He's been spotted doing an army crawl on his belly into the conference room, as if he's hoping to sneak in unseen. He seems to be a kind-hearted soul, and a medium has discerned that he watches over the child spirits who haunt the chapel.

Another ghost who haunts the hallway is Jeremy, but he also seems to have the run of the place, appearing anywhere in the building. The owner of Asylum 49, Kimm Andersen, saw a picture taken by a guest that had captured Jeremy on film. His features looked grotesque and distorted, and Kimm joked that the ghost looked like he was straight out of the band Insane Clown Posse. The same medium gently pointed out that Jeremy had actually been severely burned in a fire in life. What Kimm mistook for clownish makeup was in fact disfiguring burn trauma. Jeremy likes to mess with investigators, telling them through the spirit box that his name is Robert or Wes or any of the other ghosts of the place. But Jeremy has a "tell": when he manifests, there is the distinct stench of something burning. He can't help it. That's a clear sign that no matter what name ghost hunters hear through the spirit box, they are talking with Jeremy.

A young boy named Thomas often lets himself be photographed. This is most likely Samuel Lee's son, who passed away at the age of around seven.

Wes is another spirit of the hospital. It's said that he was a patient who suffered from Alzheimer's and died confused and scared at the elder care facility. A medium felt sorry for Wes and tried to help him cross over into the light. She soon realized that this was not going to happen: for some unknown reason, Wes is shadowed by an extremely dark entity that follows him closely.

Paranormal investigator Richard Estep of Boulder County

Paranormal Research Society has done extensive research at the Old Tooele Hospital and was invited to participate in the haunt at Asylum 49 one year. He had an absolute blast - Asylum 49 is a full-contact haunt, which means the scare actors can do whatever they like to make you scream like a little girl. Visitors have to sign a waiver to go through the haunt, and seal it with a thumbprint before being allowed inside. This extra step ramps up the anticipation. And any actor who causes a Code Y (for yellow, when a guest pees themself in fright) or a Code B (for brown, and I'll just let you figure that one out on your own) gets a $50 cash prize from Kimm on the spot. These folks do not mess around.

After playing in the haunt all night, Richard decided to experience the haunt from the other side. He went through, looking at it as a customer rather than a scare actor.

About 45 minutes in, he was making his way through the haunt when he got jump-scared by an actor, who raised a shotgun and fired a bang of compressed air. As he was recovering from the sudden fright, he barely noticed two other haunt customers who came into the room as he was leaving. The girl was young, maybe 7 or 10 years old, wearing an old-fashioned white lace dress. She was tugging on the shirt of a woman in contemporary clothing, urging her into the room.

Richard made his way out of the haunt, and complimented Kimm on how good the scare actors were. The little girl in the lace dress, he said, was particularly creepy. That's when Kimm said, "We don't have a little girl in a lace dress."

Pennhurst Asylum

One of the granddaddies of all haunted hospitals is Pennhurst Asylum in Spring City, Pennsylvania. In 1903, the Pennsylvania legislature approved the building of a facility to house and care for people with physical and mental disabilities.

Pennhurst was a small city all on its own, with over thirty buildings on the campus. Even so, the hospital was soon grievously overcrowded. To make matters even worse, the hospital was also forced to take in immigrants, orphans, and criminals.

When patients arrived, they were classed as "imbecile or insane" (there really were no other choices) and further separated into physically healthy or not. The able-bodied were assigned jobs to help keep the hospital running. The patients were treated with heartbreaking callousness. The scandal broke in 1968 when a local news station aired a five-part report on the asylum. Still, conditions didn't get any better. In 1983, nine employees were indicted on charges of beating patients, including those in wheelchairs, and forcing patients to fight each other.

Conditions at Pennhurst, even in 1968, were appalling, with naked, emaciated patients tied to beds and left to sit in their own filth for days at a time. This abuse led to Pennhurst practically thrumming with the negative energy imprinted in its buildings. The campus is a study in urban decay, with vegetation growing rampant up the sides of the buildings. Inside, tortured spirits are still trapped in the psychic hellhole that is Pennhurst. Reports of disembodied voices abound, and investigators have heard crying and vomiting emanating from empty rooms. It truly is a haunted, desolate place.

It would seem the height of callous disrespect to set up a haunted attraction on these grounds. And when that attraction uses the hospital's history as the groundwork for its story, that disrespect becomes intolerable. But the haunt at Pennhurst has a deeper, more complex backstory that is well worth exploring.

Pennhurst closed in 1987, and the buildings and grounds were abandoned. It was purchased in 2008 by a group calling itself Pennhurst LLC. This group created the Pennhurst Asylum Haunted House, and at first it was just as atrocious as you'd imagine. A fictional doctor and his sadistic staff were shown experimenting on helpless patients. The haunted attraction opened in 2010 and for a while, was grossing $2 million a year.

A group was formed to counter this betrayal of history, called the Pennhurst Memorial and Preservation Alliance (PMPA). They tried to block the opening of that first haunt but were unsuccessful.

But in 2017, Pennhurst was sold to new owners. These folks were much more sympathetic to conserving history, and they have personal ties to the disabled community. They completely revamped the haunted attraction, with astounding results.

More than half of the actors at the redesigned haunt identify as disabled. Some of them even have personal histories of institutionalization. The narrative of the haunt has taken a 180-degree turn: in this new version, the (fictional) inmates have taken over the asylum, and it's the doctors and nurses (and the haunt customers) who are now the inmates. The Pennhurst Museum exists side by side with the haunt. One preserves history, the other reinterprets it, but in a way that empowers the patients and gives them back their agency.

Nathan Stenberg, who himself is a person with a disability, has his doctorate in theater and performance. He writes that the haunt attraction "does not simply commodify atrocity but offers a space where dis/abled people use performance as both self-expression and knowledge-making in a site once designed for their segregation and slow death."

The haunt at Pennhurst now not only shows respect for the unfortunate souls who lived and died there. It has also given the power of expression to the disabled community, which has sparked a new interpretation of the terrors of the asylum. The haunters have made the choice to tell this story. They work as tour guides, and yes, as haunt performers. Some might say this is disrespectful. But disability advocate David Hingsburger pointed out, "We take choice away from people with disabilities all the time."

They should be able to tell the story of the people who lived here ... and in doing so, tell a little of their own truth as well.

Peoria State Hospital

Another asylum that hosts a haunt is the Peoria State Hospital, in Bartonville, Illinois. This facility was about as far from Pennhurst as it's possible to get. People still gripe about the questionable taste of setting a haunt at an asylum. But the historians of the hilltop disagree. Christina Morris, who presides over the hospital, has a favorite saying: "Haunts save history." The money raised in October helps to keep the lights on at the asylum museum during the rest of the year. Plus, the patients at Bartonville celebrated holidays, including Halloween - maybe especially Halloween. A chance to dress up and pretend you're someone else for the evening? You bet! And for the spirits that are still there, the energy from the haunt is a powerful boost.

The Haunted Infirmary is a staple of the Halloween season in central Illinois. In an area full of weekend scares, this was consistently a fan favorite. The energy stirred up by hundreds of visitors over the weekends of October really brought out the spirits of the Pollak, and if you were lucky enough to go on a ghost hunt during November, the activity was off the charts as a result. And it started in October. There have been plenty of haunt volunteers who've had paranormal encounters in the halls and rooms of the Pollak.

Kristin Vogel tells one such story. "It was the start of the final weekend of the Infirmary, 2016. I was going over the final details of my scene as the hall lights went out, signaling that the first group would be coming soon. Everyone began scurrying back to their scenes excited to start the night. I distinctly remember there being a strong positive energy there.

"As I approached my doorway and took in the mixed murmur of the haunt ambiance, I was interrupted by a man behind me saying, quite nonchalantly, 'Hey, turn around.' Naturally, I spun around expecting to see Tal, Draven, or Jeff. There was no one there and I instantly froze in place and raised my hands up as a reflex. I tried to rapidly analyze and rationalize the situation. I quickly also remembered that the scenes before *and* after mine were empty. Nobody was close enough to have spoken at that volume and distance. It sounded like they were just a few feet behind me, as if they had walked up and said it.

"I admit I was a little nervous to be in my scene, but as I fell into character, I was able to let it slip my mind. Groups came through one after the other. To this day there has been no natural explanation, and I consider it my first paranormal experience."

One of the volunteers that's been at the haunt the longest is "Weapons" Spears. For real, that's his name. He got his nickname for his talent at making some of the gruesome props that make the Haunted Infirmary such a howling success. It's just a happy accident that his last name fits the theme as well. Weapons is a big guy, one of those gentle giant types. And he doesn't scare easily.

It was Weapons' first year at the haunt, which had only been in operation for two years at that time. He had just stripped off the Tyvek suit he'd worn as a crazed patient for his haunt character, and he was standing next to a gurney that was against the wall in the hallway. He'd piled the suit in a messy wad on the gurney and set his giant can of soda next to it, leaning the can against the bunched fabric.

As Weapons slouched against the wall, he heard the indistinct murmur of a little girl's voice. Moments later, the can of soda stood upright ("against gravity," Weapons told me), then fell over in the opposite direction.

"If I'd just heard the girl's voice, fine. If I'd just put the can down, fine - I'd have convinced myself it just fell." But both things happening at once? That was just a bit too much.

Weapons refused to be the last one out of the building for months afterward.

Another haunt volunteer, Cory Hill, had a role as a 1950s nurse. Cory says that on the nights she worked the haunt, she would see the locked door in her scene come open, as if someone had slowly turned the knob, then pushed it open. Another thing she noticed is that even though the other actors would work up a sweat during the haunt from all the exertion, she always felt cold. She will admit that freaked her out just a little. She also mentioned that as part of her scene, there was a television set that was tuned between channels, to put out just static. There was no remote to the set, but sometimes it would turn itself off without any help.

Christina has a theory: she thinks the spirits were drawn to Cory because she was dressed as a nurse from the 1950s. "I think they used to swarm her so badly because of the costume," Christina says. "She was always surrounded by people. I just didn't tell her that at the time, because I want her to come back someday!"

The Haunted Infirmary was such an elaborate production

that some of the elements of the haunt stayed up for a while. When you went to the Pollak for an investigation, you were quite likely to run into a bloody pile of fake guts on a cafeteria counter, or a group of sullenly brooding monks in a corner. That's all part of the haunt, of course. October has a long shelf life in the Pollak.

All these reminders of Halloween seemed to stir up the spirits in the building. Maybe they remember, throughout the year, how much fun it is to have people streaming through the halls and rooms every Friday and Saturday night in October, shrieking with delighted fear in the darkness. That really pumped the spirits full of energy, much more than the quiet respect of the paranormal investigators who file in and sit in subdued silence, listening for ghost voices.

At any rate, the spirits aren't shy about creating their own scares when they can. The volunteers are sometimes spooked when a light comes on by itself.

And when that light is intended to remind you of scary clowns, it's even creepier. One of the haunt rooms is - you guessed it - based on many people's bone-deep fear of clowns. It's one of the exam rooms off the hallway, an oxygen therapy room to be precise. When the light switch is pushed - and you do have to push it, it won't go off if someone just brushes up against it - a spinning ball starts up, throwing splashes of colored light all over the room and out into the hallway. Tinny music starts to play too - *deetdeet deedle-eedee deetdeet deedee*, that old familiar circus tune.

Brian, a staff member, walked into the building late one night. The building was dark, but Brian could hear faint music coming from his left. He looked down the hallway, and brightly colored light was cascading into the hallway from the oxygen therapy room, and circus music spilled its cheer into the air.

Brian was not cheered.

And the spirits learn, too. "It was one thing when they used to turn the hallway and room lights on and off. That at least makes sense, because those lights were here when they were living here. But now they've figured out *our* lights. That has become really interesting. Some of our prop lights are very creepy, they're red bulbs, they're under something, they cast weird shadows - you walk into that building in the dark, expecting darkness, and there are lights on that aren't supposed to be on ... it'll creep you out," Christina says.

"Or - my favorite - you'll turn all the lights off, and you'll go into the hallway and look both ways down the hall to make sure all the lights are out. You'll look this way, then that way, then this way ... and a light will be on. It was bad enough when it was just the white room lights, but now they've figured out the prop lights. So, you'll be like, nothing, nothing, *spooky-ass freaking red glowy light*! I had to unplug it!

"The worst part is, you'll go all the way down the hallway in the dark, turn the light off, then start hauling ass back up the dark hallway to the front of the building. And while you're doing that, *another* light will come on, so you have to go back and turn *that* one off too. You tell me they're not doing that on purpose and getting a charge out of your fear."

Many volunteers have balked at going down the dark hallway to turn off lights that have suddenly come back on, with no human hand on the switch. (I must admit here that even as much as I love the Pollak and her ghosts, that would be a big "nope" moment for me too.)

"That shows intelligence, that they've learned how to turn on our prop lights. It shows that they're smart," Christina told me. "I think they see us horsing around, playing tricks on each other, and they're mimicking us, how we interact with each other. Like the '*hey there*'s in the dark, when you know you're alone. My favorite is when we're all working on something, and I'll hear someone yell, "Hey!' I'll yell back, 'I'm down here!' and everyone will turn to look at me like, who are you talking to?"

History gives us a clue as to who might be playfully cutting the lights or turning them on after they've been turned off. At the end of the Pollak's working life, the building housed geriatric patients, including elderly women who suffered from dementia.

This playing with the lights business is trickster behavior. And locking people in the bathroom? Yeah, that totally happens. Tell me that's not a grade school prank. There's nothing evil going on here, the spirits aren't trying to entrap anyone. They're just trying to get a rise out of the volunteers, spooking them as they walk down the hall. These spirits have likely reverted to childlike behavior, just as they did near the end of their lives here. They've regressed, because in their minds, they see themselves as little girls. The giggling we hear in the hallways and in the Women's Ward comes from these harmless old ladies.

Let's face it, it's just fun to scare people.

The haunt has moved several times - from the Pollak Hospital to a trail through the woods, and then to the wooded area between Cemetery 1 and Cemetery 2. But with all the moves and relocations and redesigns, one thing remains the same. The spirits of former patients are still interacting with the haunt. And these friendly shades don't mean any harm.

The Queen Mary

It's not just prisons and hospitals that play host to spooky spectacles in the month of October. There are several well-known historic venues that play on their notoriety to draw customers in.

The Queen Mary is a retired ocean liner of the Cunard Line, that sailed from 1936 to 1967. There's a funny story about how she got her name. Cunard had a company tradition of giving their ocean liners names that ended in "ia" - think Lusitania and Mauretania. They wanted to name their newest ship Victoria, so

company representatives asked King George V for permission to name her after "England's greatest queen." The king delightedly said that his wife, Queen Mary of Teck, would be thrilled with the idea. How do you say no to that?

Queen Mary was originally a luxury liner, but during World War II, she was pressed into service as a troop ship. Her opulent furniture and decoration were removed and replaced with utilitarian bunks. On one voyage in 1943, she carried 16,683 passengers. This is still the record for the most people on one vessel at the same time. (Although, truth be told, they cheated a bit. The record-setting crossing was at the end of July, so passengers could sleep on deck under the stars.) By the end of the war, she had carried over 800,000 troops and had traveled over 600,000 miles.

Her trips across the Atlantic weren't without incident. During one crossing, Queen Mary accidentally sliced through one of her escort ships, the Curacoa. Hundreds were lost in the accident.

Other ghosts from different eras also haunt the ship. A young girl supposedly drowned in the second-class swimming pool. Visitors often see wet footprints forming on the concrete at the empty pool's edge. And in 1966, 18-year-old engineer John Pedder was crushed by a water-tight door during a fire drill. His spirit, manifesting as a young man dressed in coveralls, haunts the engine room where he died. Other paranormal activity includes severe temperature drops, slamming doors, and unearthly screams.

There's plenty of screaming going on during the month of October, too, and it spills over into September as well. Queen Mary's Dark Harbor is a joyous celebration of Halloween, a festival with live entertainment, haunted mazes aboard the ship, monsters galore, carnival rides, and all the fair food you could possibly want. It's an immersive experience, a heady gala of all kinds of spooky attractions.

The haunters here are dedicated, as befits such an impressive venue. The festival is open from mid-September into the first weekend of November. Halfway through October, things really ramp up, with the haunt open every night except Mondays. The riotous fun of Queen Mary's Dark Harbor is a fitting return to the opulence of the ship's original persona, the elegant British ocean liner, the pride of the Cunard Line.

The Lemp Mansion & Brewery

There are some families that seem to be mired in tragedy. Death claims family members young, in questionable circumstances. This was the unhappy fate of the Lemp family of St. Louis, Missouri.

The Lemps seemed to have the world at their feet. They lived in a magnificent mansion which happened to be right next to the family business, the Lemp Brewery. By 1870, William J. Lemp Brewing Company had grown to be the largest brewery in St. Louis. Its Falstaff brand dominated the beer industry until 1919, when Prohibition knocked the feet out from under all forms of alcohol production.

Even back then, the family was no stranger to tragedy. William Lemp's fourth son, Frederick, was born in 1873, and William hoped that Frederick would someday take over the

brewing empire. But Frederick died at the age of 28 from an undiagnosed heart ailment. William Lemp was devastated at the loss of his son and presumptive heir. On the morning of February 13, 1904, he shot himself.

William "Billy" Lemp Jr. took over the business. He and his wife Lillian were married about nine years before she filed for divorce and custody of their only child. Life's troubles, including Prohibition, broke Billy, and he died in his office of a self-inflicted gunshot wound on December 29, 1922.

Elsa, Billy's sister, fared no better. She married Thomas Wright in 1910. They separated in 1918, and in February 1919, Elsa filed for divorce. The couple reconciled and remarried in March 1920, but only a few days later, Elsa too shot herself. (Maybe. She died of a gunshot wound, but there are those who suspect her death to be a murder dressed up as a suicide.)

Charles, brother to Elsa and Billy, lived in the Lemp mansion from 1929 until 1949 ... when he shot himself in the head after shooting his dog in the basement. None of the other Lemps had left a suicide note, but Charles took the time to write: "In case I am found dead blame it on no one but me."

Edwin Lemp, the last surviving son of William Sr., lived to the age of 90, possibly by not living at the mansion. He had sold it after his brother's death, and it was used as a boardinghouse.

So, was it the mansion that caused all these deaths, or was it the failed business? We can never know what was in these people's hearts. We only know that the Lemp Mansion is quite haunted indeed.

The Lemp beer empire was helped along by the physical site of the business. The brewery was connected to the mansion by a system of underground tunnels and caverns called The Caves of St. Louis. The spacious rooms, with their stone arches and cool walls, naturally stayed at the perfect temperature for aging beer.

The underground tunnels are also, it would seem, the perfect place for a haunted house attraction. The Lemp Brewery Haunted House is widely considered one of the best in the country. The cool stone caverns give it a creep factor that is off the charts. And the ghosts of the Lemp Mansion are not shy about making their presence known.

Years ago, I talked with a couple of friends of mine who worked at the haunt. (The haunt has been going for over thirty years, so it was well-established by the time I chatted with these guys in 2015.) Mike worked at the brewery warehouse where the haunt was set up, and he admitted that it was really creepy to work there late at night, especially since the light switch panel was at the other end of the warehouse from his office. With all the props and scenes from the haunt set up, he'd get freaked out even walking through the building with a flashlight. Mike said the latest he worked in his office was 2 am. "It got so freaky just sitting in my office, I had to leave. I left all the lights on, my boss yelled at me the next day, but there was no way I was walking across the whole warehouse with the lights off. We're in the haunted house industry, so there's zombies and monsters everywhere, so walking around there with a flashlight just scares the shit out of you anyway."

Mike and another guy were working at the warehouse one

weekend and were tangentially involved in a deeply disturbing incident. There were two elevators in the warehouse next to Mike's office, one for people, and one for freight. "We heard all this screaming coming from the freight elevator. It freaked us out - we didn't even want to go look. What had happened was, a guy who was working for AT&T was working on the roof. He went to take the elevator down, and the elevator had moved six floors inexplicably. He fell like six stories into the subbasement, and broke lots of bones. Luckily, we were there, we called Emergency Services and they came and got him out."

The man survived, but it was not lost on anyone that Charles Lemp had shot his dog in that basement before taking his own life. "We went and saw the guy in the hospital, really nice guy, and he was telling us the story. He was like, I had that elevator not only left on that floor that I was working on, but I turned the power key off and made sure that it wouldn't go anywhere while I was working. When he went to step back on the elevator, it wasn't there, and he just went."

Mike went on to say that weird things were always happening in the haunt. "You walk into a room, and it was inexplicably freezing cold. All the videos we ever took in there had tons of orbs in it, I mean all over the place. It was a really super spooky place to work. I liked it a lot."

Another friend told me of his experiences in the Lemp Mansion. One night, he decided to sleep there, "just for shits and gigglery," as he puts it.

"At about 3 o'clock in the morning, I heard ballroom dancing. All of a sudden, I just heard this old ragtimey music, and then a bunch of footsteps, like people are dancing on a hardwood floor. I didn't sleep through any of it; I just laid there."

He and some friends went out for breakfast the next day, at about 7 am. A crew came into the mansion at 6:30 to start setting up for a wedding.

"We came back, and the lady was like, oh you're the guys from the haunted house! I heard you guys playing around this morning. We were like, what do you mean? Oh, you know, all the effects, and the sounds, and all that stuff going ... I said, the house is shut down; what are you talking about? She said, no, you guys were in there! We heard you! I was like, no. We have the keys. We weren't in there. There's nobody in there. She just looked at us, frowned, and went on her merry little way. She didn't believe us."

The Slaughter House

When a historic building like the Lemp warehouse is repurposed into a haunted attraction, it just stands to reason that the backstory is going to intrigue people too. The Slaughter House, in Tucson, Arizona, is a great example of this. This was an actual slaughterhouse in the 20th century, a huge meatpacking plant used by the Farmer John's corporation. And if the urban legends are to be believed, something horrific happened there in October 1964.

The story goes that the owner's two young children, Sarah and Nelson, were reported missing. Sarah was eight years old, and Nelson was six. The owner of the plant was Warren James, and he and the nanny both confirmed that the kids had last been seen at the factory. The nanny, Miss Stiles, had brought the kids in for a quick visit. She had brought the kids into Warren's office and told them to wait there until he came and got them. She had taken a short break, and when she returned just a few minutes later, the children were nowhere to be found. Warren ordered the plant shut down and searched from top to bottom, but the kids were just gone. After a week of fruitless searching, police determined that foul play was likely.

Soon after that, police issued a warrant for the arrest of the children's uncle. He was known to be mentally unstable. The situation unfolded quickly and viciously from that point.

Investigators reported finding human remains in the factory, in the meat processing area. Two days after the warrant was issued, the plant declared a massive recall of sausage products. The official reason given was "meat contaminants, human in nature," and consumers were strongly urged not to eat meat from that particular batch.

The stress of losing Nelson and Sarah, seeing his brother arrested, and having to issue a recall of meat from his factory - meat that may have contained the remains of his children - was too much for Warren, and he hanged himself in the boiler room. Sarah and Nelson were officially declared dead. Their complete bodies were never found.

Ten years after these grisly events, the new owners of the meat packing plant called police to report trespassers. They claimed they'd seen two children, a boy and a girl, running through the factory. As if that wasn't eerie enough, two employees came forward with separate accounts. They each said they had seen the apparition of a man throw two children into the meat grinder, then vanish as the witnesses watched.

The legend further holds that in 1984, twenty years after the children went missing, the body of their uncle was found in the boiler room, hanging in the exact spot where their father had killed himself. The chilling words "I killed them" were carved into his chest.

It's said that during the month of October, the ghosts of the children can still be seen running around in the factory. The anniversary of their disappearance is sometimes marked by the recurring residual scene of a man dumping two small bodies into the meat processing equipment.

Now, maybe this is just an urban legend, albeit one with incredible staying power. But with a backstory like this, the old Farmer John's meat packing plant is a grand place for a haunt attraction. The ghostly legend only adds to the thrills.

The Slaughter House is a multi-level haunt, and it is very popular. It's been named the number one rated haunted house in Tucson for five years in a row, from 2019 to 2023. In 2021, it was the top rated in the entire US. Its reputation even convinced Ghost Adventures to take a look.

It seems there may be something to the ghost stories. Teresa Hewitt, a haunt employee, went to the back to turn on the breakers one night. When she walked back into the office, she was chilled to realize that she had blood dripping down her arm. There are customers and actors alike that refuse to come back.

Becky Gydesen, owner of Tucson Ghost Company, has investigated The Slaughter House, and she is intrigued rather than terrified. She says that the spirits of this place are pranksters. "They love to get your attention, so because of that, they definitely interact with you."

That certainly sounds like the behavior of child ghosts to me.

Old Movie Theater Complex

Theaters are notorious for being susceptible to hauntings. Tucked into the back corner of Laurel Centre Mall in Laurel, Maryland, is the "Old Movie Theater" cinema complex.

Abandoned in 2009 and neglected for years, it was brought back to life by Richard Blankenship. He was an avid haunt enthusiast, and wanted to turn the theater into a haunt attraction. After experiencing paranormal activity, he asked Chesapeake Ghost Hunters to investigate the place. Other groups have spent many hours in the old theater. Zak Wenzel, of Blood Moon Paranormal says that the place is definitely haunted. It "messed me up. It's no joke."

Zak says he's never experienced anything like Laurel's House of Horrors in his long career as a ghost hunter. He's never put much stock in the demonic stuff - he says that would take a lot of convincing. But, "whatever is haunting that place does not seem human, and I don't quite understand what it is."

Zak says that the main focal point of this non-human haunting was an old cabinet, of all things. "Whatever is attached to it seems to just know things about people, like it really pulls from your inner traumas."

Investigators Evan Webb and Mandy Gibson describe this cabinet as a portal, a way for spirits to move between dimensions. They warn visitors not to touch the cabinet or close the door. They've seen firsthand how spirits can get cranky when people mess with the cabinet. Staff have reported strange happenings while working the haunt. They've seen unexplained shadows, heard strange voices. Some actors have even had things thrown at them or have been physically attacked.

Ethan, of Charm City Paranormal, calls the place "one of the most bizarre cases of a haunting I have investigated so far. There are so many variables to its activity, it's nearly impossible to narrow it down to just one or two theories."

Ethan points out that there were two mental asylums in the area, both with reputations of abuse. Laurel Sanitarium was virtually right next door to the theater. And there's a connection to Forest Haven Asylum as well. A haunt attraction in the area lasted just one season before folding. Somehow, the haunt organizers got permission to store their props in the abandoned asylum. Rich and Charlene Blankenship later bought the props from the defunct haunt and used them to improve their own attraction. Could some of those items have picked up spiritual attachments?

To add to the potential for paranormal activity, the haunt has been the site of a death. Artie's Butcher Shop, one of the scenes, pays homage to a former scare actor. Artie Staub absolutely loved his job. Towards the end of the second year of the haunt, he had a heart attack in the men's bathroom in the building. Several hours went by before he was found.

Artie has found a home in Laurel's House of Horrors. He interacts with the ghost hunters who come to investigate the theater. And it would seem that he has quite a lot of company in the afterlife.

Blood Moon Manor

Our last haunted house stands all by itself on the edge of Forest City, Illinois, surrounded by cornfields. And it is indeed a haunted house. The haunt attraction, Blood Moon Manor, has expanded in all directions out from it. The house stands battered but proud in the middle of the haunt complex.

The Skinner House was purchased in 1862 by Joel Alphonso Barnes, who lived in it with his wife Mary and their two daughters. In 1864, Joel heeded Lincoln's call and joined an infantry unit. By the time he came back, war had changed him. Mary cared for him as best she could, but combat does things to a man, and Joel was just never the same.

The family lived in the house for many years. The two daughters grew up and married and had babies of their own. One of these children was a little girl named Sarah. Sadly, when Sarah was quite young, maybe six or eight years old, she contracted tuberculosis. Little Sarah had to be isolated from the rest of the family. She spent her last weeks in the house, surrounded by her loved ones, but unable to snuggle up in a welcoming lap. A small closet in the house is still pointed to as the tiny room where Sarah passed away.

The house was eventually bought by a Mr. Skinner, who gave his name to the home. He would die quietly in his sleep in the house. His lady friend was a woman named Florence, who lived in the grand old Victorian house next door. It's said she was a hoarder, and there are still folks in Forest City who can remember the decrepit residence that stood next to the Skinner House. (It's since been torn down.) When that house got filled up with stuff, she just moved in with Mr. Skinner next door.

These former residents of the Skinner house are still very much there. The house mainly serves as a great big dressing room and costume storage closet for the haunt's scare actors, but for the spirits, it is still home. Florence is very protective of the house. She will move from window to window in the second floor, peering out as people wander around in the yard.

It may have been Florence who pushed Molly, a Skinner House volunteer, down the stairs one day. The stairwell near the door is narrow, with a set of steps going up to a landing. The stairs turn 90 degrees, then continue to the second floor. Molly was coming down the stairs one day. She'd just gotten to the landing when she was pushed by an invisible set of hands. She tumbled down the narrow stairs and landed in an awkward tangle of limbs at the bottom. She had to be taken away in an ambulance.

Sarah is also still in the house. Happily, she is no longer restricted to the closet, although she does seem to spend most of her time in the bedroom next to the closet. She likes to play with an antique wooden ball. The ball makes the rounds of the first floor, turning up here and there, not just in Sarah's room. This could be the work of volunteers picking up the ball and setting it somewhere out of the way. But that doesn't explain the incident where the ball came rolling towards Braden, another volunteer - when he was alone in the house.

There's another entity that usually confines himself to the basement of the house, although he has been known to move through various wells on the property, using them as kind of his own personal travel corridor. The management of the haunt has nicknamed him "Walter". Walter seems to be attached to the land rather than the house. He's a darker entity than the others and makes it clear that he wishes to be left alone.

James, Dave, and I investigated the Skinner House for the first time in October 2024. It was daylight out, so our trek through the haunt outside was interesting rather than terrifying. It was the last weekend in October, so the haunt was still in full swing. Just hours after we left, people would be lining up to stumble through the dark labyrinth of the haunt, giggling and shrieking with terror at every turn. With a month's worth of scares stored up, the energy in the place was palpable, even in the daytime.

We wandered through the house, trying to imagine what it looked like when Joel and Mary Barnes, and Sarah, and Florence lived there. It's hard to do with costumes and gory props scattered all around, but this was someone's home once.

The three of us went into the basement. Our guide pointed at a doorway under the stairs. The room beyond, the floor littered with props and debris, was one of Walter's favorite hangouts.

I ducked under the stairs and went into the room, stepping carefully over loose boards and other assorted junk. I stood still for a moment, letting my senses adjust to the tiny room. The atmosphere was heavy and pressed against my face and the small bones inside my sinuses. I didn't feel a sense of dread, just a heavy presence. James came in, too, bending to fit his height under the cobwebby stairs. He reported feeling pressure, too, almost like a sinus headache. He explained his experience: "When I walked down the stairs, it was like being under water. There was just a heavy pressure. Going into the room under the stairs only increased that pressure, so it felt like a super strong sinus pressure pushing up into the bottom of my skull." James reported that after a few moments it became strong enough to make his head ache.

We had such a great time poking around the Skinner House that we decided to come back. This time, we brought friends. With seven of us all trying to investigate the crowded house, it got a bit cramped at times, but we made it work.

We did have an interesting experience that night. James had gone upstairs by himself while everyone else was either poking around the dining room or preparing to do an Estes session in Sarah's bedroom. That was when Ben realized that the door leading upstairs was shut. None of us copped to shutting it, so the guys took turns fiddling with the door, seeing if they could replicate the closing (and trying to debunk it at the same time). While they were doing this, something rather intriguing was going on upstairs.

James had left a camera running in one of the rooms on the second floor. The camera didn't capture anything spectacular ... but the microphone picked something up. It caught the low murmur of voices, and one other word. Reviewing it, I simply heard a long, heavy sigh. But James heard a word, drawn out over the space of a few breaths.

"House."

That does make sense to me. The Skinner House is not only a haunt. It was a beloved family home for many decades.

I guess someone just wanted to point that out to us.

So why are haunted house attractions haunted? You could say that there are already plenty of scares to go around without throwing paranormal activity into the mix. To that I say, why not? Why let the living haunters have all the fun? As a scare actor myself, I can tell you that there's nothing like that rush of energy you get from scaring the paste out of someone and hearing them scream in horrified delight. I have no doubt that the entities left behind at all these places get that same charge.

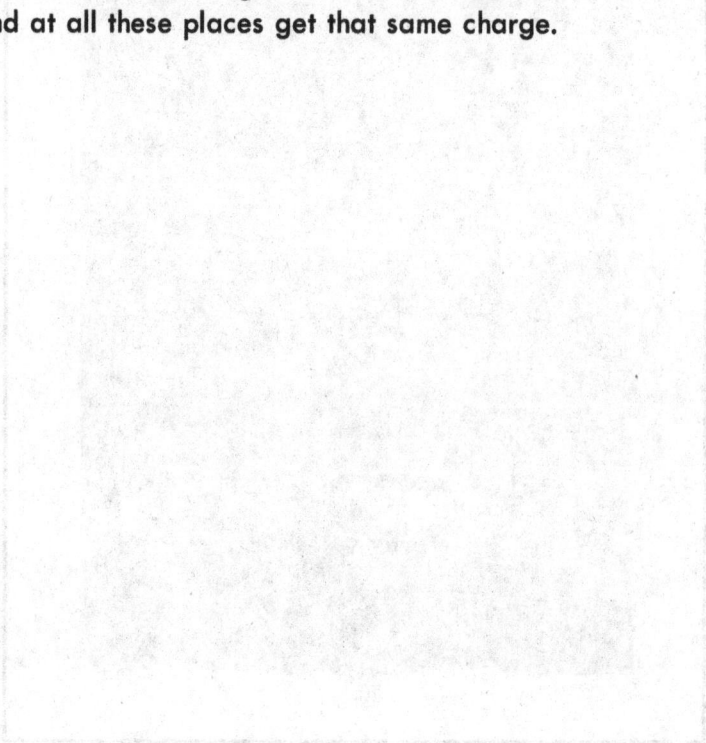

OFF THE
BEATEN PATH:
An Assortment of Spooky Treats

The supernatural can lurk in the most ordinary of places. You might run into a ghost or two when you're least expecting it. The following stories have enough chills to keep you nice and cool on even the most sweltering of summer days.

GHOSTS IN THE GREENERY:
Haunted Botanic Gardens

We're going to start off by looking at, not one, not two, but three botanic gardens. All three of them are gorgeous havens of natural beauty, serene places where people can go to stroll among the tranquility of green glades or riotous displays of vibrant color. And all three of them are quite haunted, but for very different reasons.

Denver Botanic Gardens

The city of Denver, Colorado, began in November 1858 when General William Larimer Jr. staked out a one square mile claim to start the settlement. Larimer was a railroad tycoon, so he was baseline loaded. Then he got even richer by land speculation in the territory of Kansas. He made so much moolah that when he decided to start up a town, people wanted to get in on the action. The community started to grow, with many pioneers ending their

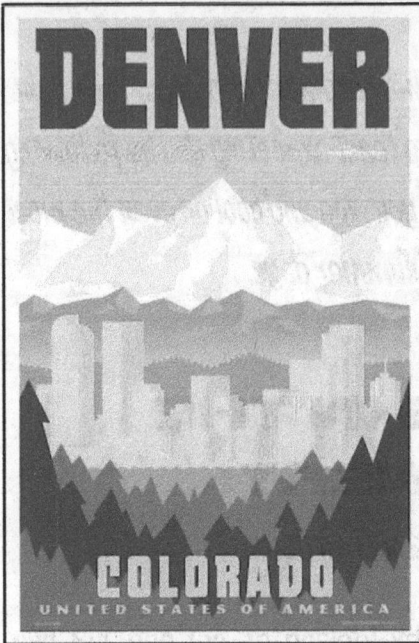

DENVER
COLORADO
UNITED STATES OF AMERICA

westward push in the thriving city. Miners and prospectors also found Denver a good place to put down roots.

Denver was just as dangerous to life and limb as any other frontier town. Larimer, still with dreams of turning Denver into a cosmopolitan attraction, picked out a 160-acre plot of land that would become Mount Prospect Cemetery. The cemetery soon had its first permanent resident: a young man named Abraham Kay died of a lung infection on March 17, 1859, and was buried three days later.

Larimer had dreams that Mount Prospect, situated on a hillside north of the South Platte river (and technically on Arapaho Tribal land, but that didn't concern him much), would become a respectable after-death destination, a lush garden of eternal rest for Denver's elite. Those dreams never did pan out. He pictured elegantly manicured lawns, tastefully dotted with monuments commemorating Denver's high society. The reality was somewhat different: the cemetery looked more like a neglected dust bowl. The cemetery workers just couldn't keep ahead of the weeds, and cows and coyotes wandered through the grounds, leaving piles of crap as calling cards. Adding to this was the fact that there really wasn't much organization in the early days. When someone in Denver happened to kick the bucket, their family members just took the body to Mount Prospect, stuck a shovel into the ground wherever, and started digging a hole.

Eventually, burials began to loosely clump together, with people from various religious groups wanting to be buried in their own sections of the cemetery. In 1865, the Catholics claimed a chunk of land as their own, calling it the Mount Calvary Cemetery. It was on this ground that the botanic gardens would someday be located.

Other factions of society had the same idea. Territorial squabbles soon broke out, and finally the United States government said, if you can't solve this, we'll solve it for you. The government seized the whole cemetery and declared it to be federal land. Uncle Sam eventually relented and sold back the land for $200, on the condition that no residences or city buildings could ever be built there.

In 1876, the Riverside Cemetery opened for business. It was much nicer than Mount Prospect, and soon people were turning up their noses at the old cemetery, preferring to plant their loved ones in the fancier boneyard.

By the 1880s, developers decided it would be quite nice to have a park in Denver. They figured that since Mount Prospect was losing its cachet as a cemetery, they might as well turn that land into a park. This, of course, meant that all those bodies needed to be moved.

Which is when things started to go horrifically, spectacularly, catastrophically wrong.

In 1893, undertaker Edward McGovern was hired by the city of Denver to move the denizens of Mount Prospect to Riverside Cemetery, to the tune of $1.90 "per box of remains." McGovern set his crews to work digging up bodies. He wasn't paying his workers very well, even though he hit on the ingenious idea of padding his expenses by hacking bodies up and distributing the remains into two or three smaller coffins. Some of these containers were little more than packing crates. The boxes regularly ended up being crammed full of parts from several different bodies - a man's skull here, a woman's leg thrown in, a child's ribcage pushed into the box for good measure.

The *Denver Republican* eventually got wind of the dodgy goings-on and wrote a scathing expose of McGovern's shenanigans. "The line of desecrated graves at the southern boundary of the cemetery sickened and horrified everybody by the appearance they presented. Around their edges were piled broken coffins, rent and tattered shrouds and fragments of clothing that had been torn from the dead bodies ... All were trampled into the ground by the footsteps of the gravediggers like rejected junk."

Matt Cole, the botanic garden's director of education, paints a grim picture of the grisly project. He said that the Chinese immigrants kept good records of their burials and were able to have their loved ones' remains exhumed and sent back to China. The same went for the Hebrew section. But many of the dead went unclaimed.

"Some of the open graves were just left as holes, because who's going to fill it back in after you've got your loved one's remains?" Cole said. "There are reports of children playing in the holes or building tree houses [with the coffin wood] and finding metal coffin hinges."

McGovern was duly sacked, but there were still an estimated 2,000 to 3,000 sets of human remains still in the ground. Many of these burials were unmarked because their families couldn't afford a headstone.

Unbelievably, the city of Denver's response to this scandal was quite literally a cover-up. The city gave next of kin ninety days to get their loved ones moved. Any bodies that remained unclaimed after that were just left where they were. By 1907, the cemetery grounds had been smoothed over, with fresh grass planted in the disturbed soil. City workers planted trees in some of the deeper holes. The cemetery became Cheesman Park, with picnickers spreading blankets and opening lunch-filled baskets. Part of the cemetery grounds later became the Denver Botanic Gardens in the 1950s and 1960s.

Many of the park's ghost stories come from Waring House, built in 1923 and donated to the botanic gardens in 1959 by Dr James Waring and his wife, Ruth. Here we have an object lesson on why you shouldn't build your mansion on top of a graveyard.

In addition to the glaringly obvious, it's really not a good idea from an architectural standpoint either. In 1973, a survey was done on the house in response to evidence of structural instability. Cracks were starting to appear in the walls and floors.

Construction on the house was completed in 1923, and the foundation started to shift almost immediately. The damage was so bad, especially in the library and drawing room, that in 1926, the Warings spent $20,000 to reinforce the floors with heavy steel beams. Things were relatively okay until the early 1970s, when the flagstone patio sank twelve inches from its original level, creating jagged rifts in the brickwork around the porch.

The results of the survey were quite enlightening. The engineers drilled three test holes in the areas where the subsidence was most severe and took soil samples as well. Much of the soil turned out to be fill dirt, meaning that it had been disturbed and then put back - exactly what happens when a grave is dug, a casket lowered into it, and the grave refilled with earth.

Several of the test holes yielded samples of redwood, which turned out to be bits of a coffin. One of the test holes was dirt for thirteen feet, then a layer of redwood, then four feet of open space, then more wood. What does that sound like to you? In other words, Waring House was built right over numerous burials. When the wood of the coffins rotted and collapsed, the fill dirt above settled, and the foundation of the house began to sink.

There was another problem that was causing the rapid

subsidence under Waring House. It sat right in the middle of the botanic gardens. Before you say, well duh, what does that have to do with anything? Let me remind you that gardens need to be watered. Gardens as elaborate as those around Waring House *really* need to be watered. This constant irrigation added a lot of water to soil that was already unstable. And water is heavy. This added to the weight of the soil on top of the slowly decomposing coffins.

There really isn't any good solution to this mess. Waring House is literally on shaky ground: no one knows how many coffins are below the foundation, quietly rotting away. It's anyone's guess when any of them will collapse and cause more unseen damage.

With all of this going on - graves carelessly dug up, others simply abandoned - it should come as a surprise to absolutely no one that the Denver Botanic Gardens is ridiculously, dramatically haunted. The venue keeps a logbook of guests' experiences there, and it makes for stimulating reading. Visitors write about the smell of cigar smoke, of hearing a woman's sigh, of having their clothing pulled, of their phones taking pictures without them opening the camera app.

"Outside the carriage house I saw a mist swirling up from the raised garden bed, like a young child turning in a dance."

Apparitions of child ghosts have been seen at Waring House. They've even been caught on camera. A young boy is said to haunt the building, but in 2012, a paranormal investigator named Rose Glenn snapped a photo with an IR (infrared) camera that showed, not a boy, but a little girl. Rose was taking pictures in the hope of capturing something beyond what's possible to see with unaided human vision. IR cameras "see" more of the spectrum than just visible light, so the theory is that perhaps they can capture the energy signatures of spirits and translate them into images that we can actually see.

Rose was standing in the front lobby, taking photos of an elegant staircase. When she looked at the pictures, she was startled, but pleased, to see the figure of a young girl in a dress gazing straight into the camera. According to staff, a coffin was exhumed in the gardens several years ago that contained the mortal remains of a young girl wearing a ruffled dress.

Rose has also had good results with a tool called an Ovilus. That's a gadget that uses the energy levels in the environment to pick out words from its internal database, so spirits can communicate. The words that came up when Rose was using the Ovilus were appropriate for the situation - mostly "buried", but also "help" and "trapped". These are disturbing, but they may represent possible attempts by those whose bodies are still in the ground around Waring House to communicate with the living.

Opinions are divided on the results ghost hunters get with the Ovilus, just as with any spirit box. Words spat out by a device with a whole databases' worth of vocabulary have a pretty decent chance of making sense, even at random. But sometimes, the messages are more personal.

Paula Vanderbilt, a paranormal enthusiast, took an Ovilus with her on one of her visits to the Botanic Gardens, and let it run as she strolled the grounds. She was ambling through Cheesman Park when her Ovilus came up with three words in quick succession, words that formed an intelligible phrase: "Wear the jewelry."

This caught Paula's attention. She did happen to be wearing jewelry that day, that had been left to her by her grandmother. Sometimes, the spirits of a place seem to be quite interested in what's going on around them, and they cheerfully interact with the living.

Chicago Botanic Gardens

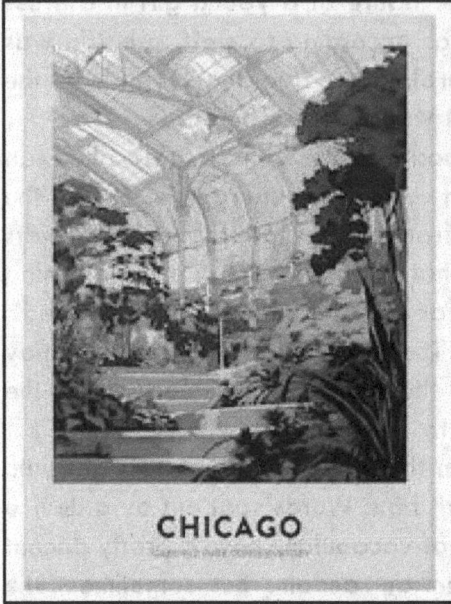

CHICAGO

The energy at the Chicago Botanic Garden, in Glencoe, Illinois, is quite different. It doesn't have quite the ghastly backstory of the Denver Gardens, but spookiness does abound there.

We know what the Denver Gardens were before they were gardens. Now, it's owned by the Cook County Forest Preserves, but before the Chicago Botanic Garden became a destination for nature lovers, it was a swamp, part of the Skokie lagoons. Roger, of the Weird Around Illinois podcast, puts it as delicately as possible.

"Back in the times of Al Capone, mob bosses made interesting use of large marshy areas." In other words, a swamp is a great place to dispose of a suddenly dead body. This area may have been a dumping ground for people who ended up on the wrong end of a mobster's Tommy gun.

Now, though, the former swamp has been turned into around 385 acres of lush, verdant gardens that draw over a million visitors a year. There are spots in these gardens that have taken on an almost ethereal quality. Henry Bort was the former curator of the Japanese Island for several decades. He often spoke reverently of the mystical energy of the gardens.

One of these pockets of wonder is tucked away behind a

maze in an alcove, with a wall of hedges all around it. It's called the "Otter Girl,"; it's a statue of a young girl with an otter curled cozily around her feet. She stands in a shallow fountain, which sometimes has water in it, sometimes not. (This will be of some importance later.)

Roger spoke to a regular visitor to the gardens. She said she came to the Otter Girl alcove to practice astral projection. (The Chicago Botanic Garden has always attracted people who are drawn to the mystical.) She would sit on the bench there, gaze at the statue, and just allow her consciousness to roam free. She did this several times a week.

Once he'd heard of her experiences, Roger decided to investigate this paranormal pocket dimension for himself. He made his way to the hidden little alcove, sat down, and waited for something to happen.

Nothing did.

Roger tried kicking things up a notch. He got out his phone and set an app to broadcast a tone at 172 Hz - a frequency that's known to trigger paranormal activity. After letting the frequency play for several minutes, he took out his EMF meter and went to investigate the pool.

This is when things got interesting. The meter redlined and stayed at its highest setting, but only around the pool. The pool was full of water at the time, and there was an electrical outlet near the pool - but the outlet wasn't registering on the meter. It was the pool itself. He went back a while later, for another investigation. This time, the pool was empty of water, and the meter didn't pick up any energy at all.

"I broadcast at 174 Hz on my phone app," Roger told me, "but here's the thing - I did it every time we went. I set it on a bench nearby while going around with the EMF detector. The only times the meter pegged were when the pool was full of water. When it was empty or even full of frozen water, it gave no reading at all."

Given the ease with which the experiencer was able to slip into astral projection and given that the meter was only registering energy (that seemingly had nothing to do with the electrical outlet) when the pool was full of water, Roger was able to form a working theory. He figures that the water in the Otter Girl fountain acts as a sort of portal. That was the only difference between his two visits. He himself admitted, after the second visit, that this "wasn't a failed expedition, just inconclusive."

Another haunted place in Chicago Botanic Garden is the greenhouse area in the Regenstein Center. Here's the history behind the story: in the early 1990s, a security officer worked at the park, and his mother would bring him his lunch at night. One winter night, she was driving in the park on her way to see her son, and her car got stuck on the slick path. She got out of the car and took off walking but got turned around and became disoriented in the thickly falling snow. She made it to the greenhouse, and pounded on the doors, seeking shelter from the cold. Her son found her while making his rounds in the small hours of the morning. She was barely clinging to life. He brought her inside the greenhouse and called paramedics. Their efforts were ultimately unsuccessful, and she died from exposure at 2:06 AM.

Since then, on the anniversary of her passing, the alarm box near the door of the greenhouse will trigger for no reason. The alarm code will read "unauthorized entry." It doesn't happen every year, but it does happen.

And the alarm sounds at exactly the same time: 2:06 AM.

Missouri Botanical Garden

The history behind the hauntings at Missouri Botanical Garden is gentler still. This haunting also involves a death on the grounds, but the circumstances were quite different.

The garden's motto, splashed over the videos that greet you on the landing page of their website, is "Savor Serenity." And this is the perfect place to do just that. It includes the Garden itself, the 8,000 square foot glass conservatory of the Sophia M. Sachs Butterfly House, and the 2,400-acre Shaw Nature Reserve. It is this last that draws us closer to the man behind all this natural beauty.

Henry Shaw emigrated from England at a young age - he was only 18 when he fetched up in St. Louis, Missouri. In the spring of 1819, he took a horseback ride out into the countryside near his new home. He fell in love with the wild beauty of the prairie in this part of Missouri. He wrote that it was "uncultivated, without trees or fences, but covered with tall luxuriant grass, undulated by the gentle breeze of spring."

Shaw did very well for himself, opening a business selling hardware and cutlery. As St. Louis grew, so did Shaw's fortune. He later expanded his business, and invested in agricultural commodities, mining, real estate, and the fur trade.

Shaw's acute business sense helped him grow an immense fortune, and he was able to retire in 1840, when he was just 39 years old. He didn't let retirement slow him down; he kept on buying land, and eventually owned about 1,000 acres, including the vista that had so enchanted him when he'd first arrived in the

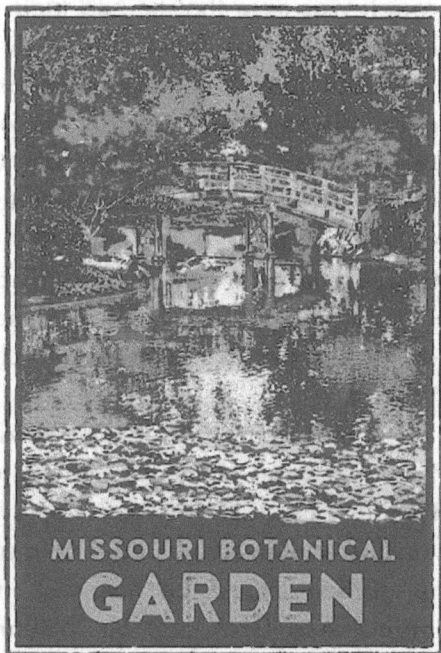

area. It was here that he had built a lovely mansion, a home that become known as Tower Grove House.

But that was some years in Shaw's future. He spent the years between 1840 and 1851 traveling, both in the United States and in Europe. His visits to the Great Exhibition, the massive display of technology of the Industrial Revolution, and to the magnificent gardens at Chatsworth House in Derbyshire, England, inspired him to create a garden for the people of St. Louis. He figured, hey, Europe has all these big gorgeous gardens and estates for the public to enjoy - let's do the same here, in the Midwest.

That's how the Missouri Botanical Garden came into being. Shaw had a bit of help in the project. Dr. George Engelmann, a German botanist who had come to the United States several decades earlier, suggested that in addition to being a public park, the garden should be involved in scientific research. Harvard botanist Asa Gray and Sir William Hooker, the director of the Royal Botanic Gardens at Kew near London, also weighed in. These three heavyweights convinced Shaw to include a library in his garden, along with an herbarium, a collection of botanical specimens for study. In this way, Shaw built his garden on a foundation of scientific exploration and education as well as exquisite natural and architectural beauty.

The Missouri Botanical Garden opened to the public in 1849, and it has been bringing joy and tranquility to its visitors ever since. Henry Shaw devoted the rest of his life to improving and expanding the Garden. Shortly after celebrating his 89th birthday, Shaw caught malaria. He passed away on August 25, 1889, in Tower Grove House, on the grounds. The *Missouri Botanical Garden Bulletin* noted the death of the founder in their November 1924 issue.

"The death, peaceful and painless, occurred in his favorite room on the second floor of the old homestead; by the window of which he sat nearly every night for more than thirty years until the morning hours, absorbed in the reading which had been the delight of his life."

The city of St. Louis was desolate at Shaw's passing. The mayor ordered the flags at government buildings to be flown at half-staff. Shaw lay in state in the Museum Building as hundreds of mourners filed past to pay their respects to the man who'd opened his country estate for the enjoyment of the public.

Henry Shaw loved the Garden so much that he has remained there to this day. And no, this time I'm not speaking paranormally (not yet, anyway). Shaw was rich enough and influential enough that he had a white stone mausoleum built on the grounds, to be his final resting place. Then he changed his mind, and had another mausoleum built out of red granite. This one was placed very near Tower Grove House, the home Shaw loved.

When you're ridiculously rich, you can make arrangements for your final resting place, and basically do whatever you like. Shaw posed for a photograph of himself lying on a funeral bier, his hands clasped in repose, his head propped comfortably up on pillows for all eternity. He sent the photograph to sculptor Ferdinand von Miller II, who created a life-size marble likeness of Shaw. The statue was kept in the basement of Tower Grove House until Shaw's death. Then, after he was laid to rest in the mausoleum, the sculpture was installed over his final resting place. You can still peek through the doors of the mausoleum, and see Shaw lying there, resting in peace.

Shaw's gentle spirit can be felt all over the Garden, but it is Tower Grove House that gets the most attention from paranormal groups. Many groups have investigated there, and have come away with compelling evidence. Some of that evidence backs up experiences shared by staff.

Tower Grove House is an elegant mansion, and part of its

charm is that the flames of battery-operated candles flicker in the windows, welcoming visitors who come to the home after dark. Those candles, needless to say, go through batteries like it's their only job. The candles in the southwest window of the library sit on a pedestal. They have been mysteriously knocked across the room at least three times.

A man's footsteps, hard-soled shoes ringing on the hardwood floors, can be heard walking from the rear of the house to the front. If a staffer calls out "Who's there?", they get no answer. Andrew Dodson, head of security at the mansion, was checking the house one day. He was headed down the staircase when he felt an invisible something pass him on the stairs.

The administration building was once Henry Shaw's townhouse. After his death, it was moved from St. Louis to the grounds of the Garden. People working in the offices on the third floor often hear the elevator arrive when they know they're alone in the building.

Monster Paranormal, headed by Steven LaChance, investigated Tower Grove House in 2015. The RVPs (Radio Voice Phenomena) they caught give good insight into the hauntings at the mansion.

A tour group was visiting the house when a woman heard a clock chime. Charmed by the pleasant sound, she commented on it. Jennifer Wolfe, a staff member, was taken aback at the woman's observation. She knew that none of the clocks had been wound. Not only that, she checked later, and management doesn't even have keys to any of the clocks to wind them. Monster Paranormal heard a clock ticking during their investigation and caught an RVP that said "ticking".

Special Events Technician Kent Barnett was working in the building that was once Shaw's townhouse. He had a couple of run-ins with a shadowy figure. It began with the figure walking in front of him, just moving about the building as Kent was going about his job. A couple weeks later, as Kent was coming into the basement, he became aware of another shadow figure hovering over his right shoulder as he opened a door. He got into the habit of greeting Mr. Shaw; he figured that's who it probably was, and he wanted to be polite. He would tell Shaw goodnight at the end of the day. Monster Paranormal's equipment came up with "goodnight" as well.

Dylan Giadone, a warehouse supervisor, experienced something odd during his first year of working in the office in the gatehouse. The doorbell would ring, he would get up to answer the door, but every time, he would find no one standing there. He and his coworkers thought it must be some park guest looking for information, so they honestly tried to pin down exactly which doorbell the unknown guest was ringing. That's when they realized that none of the doors in the gatehouse *had* doorbells.

The R.V.P. captured at the gatehouse chuckled "joke."

This is a place that is haunted by someone who dearly loved it, and wanted nothing more than to spend eternity among the gardens he enjoyed in life.

He definitely got his wish.

A CHECKERED HISTORY
(Adelaide Zoo, Adelaide, Australia)

You know the saying, if it wasn't for bad luck, I'd have no luck at all? People say that jokingly, but sometimes that dark humor can hide an uncomfortable truth. And places can suffer from bad luck, just as people can.

The Adelaide Zoo opened on May 23, 1883, under the guidance of director Richard Ernest Minchin. Minchin was an Irish transplant to Australia. He had no zoo training, but he went into

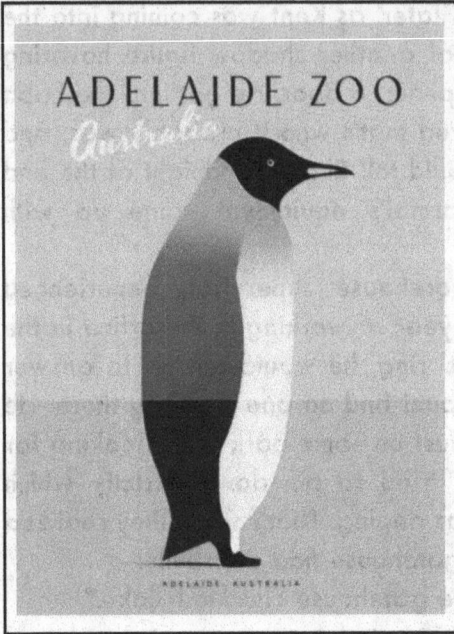

the job with a big heart and a willingness to work. The zoo opened under a shadow; there were concerns about having animals so close to the city. Minchin nonetheless cheerfully plowed ahead, serving as director from 1882 to 1893. He died that year, having caught a virus on a journey to the Far East. He was well-respected and much-loved, and his loss was keenly felt.

His son, Alfred Corker Minchin, took over as director. He had trained at Melbourne Zoo before his father's death. He served for four decades, from 1893 to 1934. By this time, a house had been built on the grounds for the director's residence, and Alfred Minchin lived there with his family. Alfred Minchin was tall and well-liked, and known for his love of lemurs. He led the zoo through some very tough times, including two serious incidents involving his zookeepers. We'll take a look at those in just a moment.

Ronald Minchin was the zoo's third director, and Alfred's second son. He was born at the zoo, in the Director's House, and started working there at the age of 19. When he grew up, he continued to live in the director's house. He brought his wife there when he married, and their child soon joined them. Ronald was passionate about the care and breeding of birds, and added several aviaries to the zoo, concentrating on keeping rare breeds. He stepped into the director's role in 1935, but held the job for only five years. He passed away from cancer in 1940, at the age of 36.

His brother, Alfred Keith Minchin, never rose to the director's position, but made his contribution to the family legacy in another way. Despite being confined to a wheelchair after a bout with polio, Keith traveled the world acquiring animals for the zoo. He also ran a koala farm from 1936 to 1960.

Now let's get to the juicy stories - I know that's why you're here. Our first story took place in January 1902. Bear keeper Richard Henry Dorricott was going about his daily chores. One of the activities of the day's routing was to rattle the grate that separated the bears' daytime and nighttime enclosures. The bears were conditioned to switch enclosures when they heard the rattle. That allowed the keeper to come into the cage to clean it.

Richard had worked at the zoo for eight or nine years and had grown accustomed to being around the big animals. Even though a black bear and a brown bear shared the space, the keeper thought little of the potential danger. It was just his job.

On that January day, Richard came in and rattled the gate as usual. The black bear ambled out of the daytime enclosure, but the brown bear hung back. Richard came into the cage anyway.

The bear lunged at Richard and clamped its powerful jaws down on his shoulder. With one shake of its head, it ripped the keeper's arm off. Richard's screams of pain brought other keepers running, including director Alfred Minchin. Minchin shot the bear dead, and the other men got Richard to the hospital. He was traumatized by the attack and the loss of his arm, but he survived and lived another ten years. Fate (and Minchin) had other plans for the bear. It was stuffed and donated to the Museum of South Australia for display, where it remains to this day.

Alfred Minchin was on hand for another bear incident nearly two decades later, in February 1920. Samuel May was now the bear keeper. Again, he was an experienced employee; May had worked at the zoo for 36 years and was regarded as being very capable with wild animals.

May already bore the scars from an encounter with a sun bear years before. The sun bears had been kept in a pit enclosure, an area dug out for them. May would regularly go down into the pit to clean it and bring food for the bears along with his broom. The bears accepted the treats, but other than that, they didn't pay much attention to him. Minchin warned May to be careful around the predators but May just brushed off the director's concerns.

One day, some sailors were visiting the zoo. As they leaned over the fence to look at the sun bears, one's cap came off and fell into the bear pit. May got his ladder, lowered it down into the pit, and climbed down to retrieve the cap. One of the bears grabbed him by the heel, pulled him down, and mauled him. It was two weeks before he could come back to work.

On this day in February, May was standing outside the polar bear enclosure, spraying the bears with water to keep them cool. (Remember, this was in Australia, so they were in the height of summer.) The zoo had two polar bears, that had been imported from Hamburg, Germany, about ten years before this, when they were just cubs. Now, they were full-grown predators.

Zoo policy was that there should always be two keepers working together to clean the enclosure. But that didn't apply to their duties of feeding and watering them from outside the cage. May was standing there by himself, with the hose aimed at the bears, when one of them reached a massive paw through the bars, grabbed the hose, pulled May close, and tore his arm off below the elbow before letting May go and turning away, disinterested.

May dropped to the pavement, shrieking. Director Minchin was first on the scene. He tried to tie something around the wreckage of May's arm to staunch the bleeding, but the flesh was badly lacerated above the elbow, too torn up for a tourniquet to be of any use. May was rushed to the Royal Adelaide Hospital and died two days later from his injuries.

Minchin was left to explain the tragedy to reporters. He told the press, "[Polar bears] are bad tempered. They are the most treacherous animals in the gardens and cannot be trusted. You know where you are with the lions and tigers, but these fellows will come and take a biscuit out of your hand one day and put their paw out on you the next."

The reporters asked, "What happened to the arm?" Minchin replied, "The animal which attacked May must have eaten it. I had the pond emptied, but it was not there. In the rush to attend to May I did not look at the animals."

Probably swallowing back a mouthful of bile, the reporters went to look at the bear enclosure after interviewing Minchin. "The two large polar bears were walking about with sly unconcern," they wrote.

There was more excitement at the zoo just a few years later, in 1924. A circus elephant escaped from the Exhibition Grounds, across the road from the zoo, and ran loose in the area for a bit. Keith mentioned, the director's son (he of the koala farm), happened to be driving along the road, and saw the escaped elephant. (This had to have been before he contracted polio, as he was not yet wheelchair-bound.)

Thinking quickly, Keith bumped the elephant with his car to knock it off balance. It went sprawling to the ground. Keith got out of his car, calmed the elephant down, and coaxed it back to its feet. Meanwhile, several zookeepers arrived at the scene and took the elephant to a paddock on the zoo grounds. In an interview, Keith told reporters that the elephant was young, and apparently only "out for mischief." He added, "At present it is safely locked up and is amusing itself by battering a bucket."

A much more tragic incident occurred in the zoo decades later. On March 24, 1985, someone climbed over the fence in the middle of the night. Armed with a sheath knife and a double-edged hunting knife, they prowled the zoo searching for havoc.

They went first to the children's zoo and launched into a wholesale slaughter of the animals there. Rabbits, guinea pigs, turkeys, an antelope, a llama named Cynthia, kangaroos - nothing was spared. The criminals cut the throats of every animal they could find. Leaving 64 furry or feathered carcasses in their wake, they moved on, seeking more to destroy.

They found another victim in the alligator habitat. One of the suspects beat a six-foot long reptile to death with an iron bar, then dragged it outside its enclosure to do more damage to the corpse. (I'm not going to go into details here, because I like you and I want you to keep reading.)

Zoo director Dr. Robert Baker was beside himself. "Most of [the animals] were very tame and very easy to catch ... They just went from one enclosure to the next, killing." Detective Sergeant Jeff Lawrence was also heartsick over the gory crime scene. As a police officer, he said, "You can accept a murder scene, but to see innocent animals in a children's zoo slaughtered ... one's got to wonder what type of person this is."

The brutal destruction turned out to be the work of only two people, 18-year-old delinquents. The South Australian Government offered a $5,000 reward, and a private citizen added $1,000 to the pot. The teens were found, arrested, convicted, and sentenced. One got five years in jail, the other got four years and four months.

Sneaking over the fence at Adelaide Zoo has never been a good idea. On June 25, 2005, another 18-year-old kid broke into the zoo to steal some ice cream and tried to climb over the main gates to make his getaway. Karma, in this case, was swifter and more brutal than in 1985. The boy slipped and impaled himself in the groin on the viciously pointed iron bars of the gates, severing an artery. He bled out, and his body slumped off and landed on the foot path. He was found by a police patrol just before 7 am.

There's something about teenagers and animal cruelty at this zoo. The zoo once had a greater flamingo named, appropriately enough, "Greater." He'd been at the zoo since the 1930s. By 2008, he was 78 years old and blind. His senior citizen status didn't help him on October 30 when four teens beat him in broad daylight. Visitors who saw the attack reported it to zoo staff, and the teens were charged. Greater was extremely stressed by the beating, but he survived. He died on January 30, 2014, at an estimated age of 83.

Not all zoo incidents involved death or dismemberment. In 1894, a boa constrictor swallowed a rug that had been laid in its enclosure for comfort. (This is why we can't have nice things.) the rug measured seven feet by six feet and weighed nearly twelve pounds. When the snake yacked it back up almost a month later, the rug was undamaged. (Okay, yes, it had just been disgorged by a boa constrictor, but other than that it was just fine.)

The hauntings at Adelaide Zoo focus mostly on Minchin House, which was built in 1887 and 1888, and used by zoo directors as living quarters until 1970. Nowadays, it's the administration building, but it would seem that some spirits still call the place home.

Steve, a zoo staff member, arrived for work early one winter morning. He came into Minchin house and heard a loud bang from upstairs. He raced up the stairs to see what was going on. Halfway up, he stopped short.

There was a lady standing on the landing at the top of the stairs. She wore a long white dress, and her hair was pulled back in an old-fashioned style. As Steve watched, she simply vanished. Steve is one of several zoo employees who have seen this ghostly woman.

Zoo management is well aware of the hauntings there.

They've invited Adelaide's Haunted Horizons to host Adelaide Zoo After Dark Walking Tours and Paranormal Investigations. The group has been to the zoo many times and has captured some great evidence.

Kag Allwood described some of the encounters the group has had at the zoo. They were doing an investigation at Minchin House. During an EVP burst session, Kag asked, "Are there any children here?" A faint noise was captured, which could have been interpreted as a "yes". (Children's voices have been heard on the staircase.)

The team got more conclusive results in the Boardroom upstairs. They were using the Estes method, and the questioner asked if there was anything the spirit wanted changed at the zoo. The reply "kiwi" came through.

"A few days later we found out that the Head Bird Keeper had been wanting a kiwi for the zoo. Coincidence?" Kag wrote.

The team moved on to the Nocturnal House. A shadowy figure has been seen in this building, a figure that is often mistaken in the darkness for a keeper who is cleaning the exhibits. People have heard disembodied footsteps in the building, and doors slam for no reason. Kag noted, "This dark environment was made even creepier due to the fact that we had to keep very quiet indeed as we didn't want to disturb the animals behind the doors." Some investigation sites do have their unique challenges.

The group did another EVP session and asked if the ghost of Samuel May wanted to communicate. (You'll recall that May was the keeper that was mauled and killed by the polar bear.) A cat ball and an EDI (Environmental Detection Instrument) both began to flash, and the team took that as a yes.

They set up another Estes session. Alison and Dylan were simultaneously using different ghost boxes, listening for answers while blindfolded and wearing noise-canceling headphones. The two investigators spoke up with sentences that had similar meanings at nearly the same time: listening for statements that could be communication from May, Alison said "You make it sound scary," while Dylan blurted "It was frightening!"

The group heard a loud bang at the opposite end of the hallway, so Alison went down to check it out. She didn't know that as she walked around, out of earshot of her team, the others asked if someone could touch her on the head. Shortly after this, as they watched, Alison jumped as if startled, knocking a cat ball flying. A dark shadowy figure had appeared near her, and she turned to find it right next to her.

Adelaide Zoo has seen its share of tragedy. Fortunately, most of the ghostly activity there seems to be on the harmless side, with the spirits of former zoo directors and their families still residing in Minchin House.

LAST OF THE LIONS
(London, England)

An odd thing happened in Regent's Park Zoo in the 1930s. An elderly gentleman was strolling through the zoo, enjoying a day out with his granddaughter. They were walking along, chatting companionably, when the man looked up and realized they were face-to-face with a lion.

It wasn't just any lion, either. The man was a zookeeper himself, and he recognized the beast as one of his charges.

The man locked eyes with the lion. Quietly, he told his granddaughter to back up slowly. It was paramount that the young girl not make any sudden moves to attract the predator's attention. The pair began to move cautiously away from the lion, keeping it in sight all the while. The man was so shaken by seeing his charge out in the middle of the zoo that he barely noticed the odd behavior of the beast. It was standing quite still, not giving any sign that it was about to charge the humans. In fact, it didn't seem to notice them at all.

Also, the lion seemed a bit transparent. Its tawny fur was nearly glowing.

The man got himself and his granddaughter away safely. The next morning, he went into work to find that his lion - the one he'd seen loose in the zoo - had unexpectedly died the day before.

THE DEATH OF HANNAH TWYNNOY
(Malmesbury, England)

We seldom stop to think about the first person to experience something, but we know it happens - it must. Some human being had to be the first person to bake a chocolate cake, or write a poem, or eat a snail.

Hannah Twynnoy, of Malmesbury, holds the dubious honor of being England's first tiger fatality.

Here's what happened. Hannah, who was born in 1669 in Malmesbury, didn't stray far from her birthplace during her life. As a matter of fact, she worked as a barmaid at a pub in Malmesbury called the White Lion Inn. This is about all we really know about the unfortunate Hannah, besides her approximate age (and, of course, the way she exited this world.) We don't know if she was pretty, plain, what her favorite color was, if she preferred fish to beef, if she was skinny or had some meat on her bones, or if she was married, if she was an only child, or if she had siblings.

We do know that she really, really didn't know how to listen to good advice.

In 1703, a traveling menagerie of exotic animals arrived in

town. Malmesbury was a market town, which means that it had a regular market day, and served as a center of business for the area surrounding the town. Since Malmesbury was a center of commerce, the proprietors of the traveling zoo knew it was a good place to set up their display, as folks in the countryside would visit the town on business, and would naturally be drawn to the novel entertainment. Of course, the nobility could visit exotic animals at the Tower of London's menagerie, but this experience was far beyond the means of the common folk. Most of these people would never even have seen drawings of wild beasts, let alone been able to see them up close and personal. A visit to this display would have been a real treat piled on to the excitement of coming into town for the weekly market day. The menagerie was set up in the large rear yard of the White Lion Inn. (A fitting venue, I suppose.)

Hannah was fascinated by the animals on display. Who wouldn't be? Collections of exotic animals were a distinct rarity for the everyday common people of 1703 England. Hannah was so intrigued by the animals, especially the big cats, that she wouldn't stop poking at them through the bars of their cages.

The animals' keeper warned Hannah time and time again not to bother them, but she ignored the warnings. She took particular delight in teasing the huge tiger who paced back and forth in its cage. We don't know how long the menagerie was set up at the pub, but Hannah was told on multiple occasions, over the course of several days, not to mess with the tiger. (Hannah, it seems, was not overburdened with common sense.)

The tiger eventually got tired of being teased and prodded. Enraged, it lunged at Hannah. The iron staple through which its chain was threaded pulled free from its settings with a tortured shriek. The tiger reached out with a paw the size of a dinner plate and snagged Hannah's dress. It pulled the young woman close and mauled her, tearing her body to pieces.

Hannah was buried in a corner of the church yard at Malmesbury Abbey. Her gravestone bears a surprisingly complex epitaph for a simple barmaid; a memorial poem carved into the stone.

"In memory of Hannah Twynnoy, who died October 23rd, 1703 Aged 33 years.

In bloom of life
she's snatched from hence
She had not room to make defence;
For Tyger fierce
took life away.
And here she lies in a bed of clay
Until the resurrection day."

I guess that's more poetic than "mess around and find out."

LIONS AND TIGERS AND BEARS, OH MY!
(Valley of the Kings Sanctuary and Retreat, Sharon, WI)

"When I was young, I thought I could save the world."

Jill Carnegie's voice is wistful as she says this. Jill is a short, compact woman, comfortably stocky. She and her husband Jim Tomasi run an animal sanctuary on ten acres in southern Wisconsin, just over the border from Illinois.

A visit to Valley of the Kings Sanctuary is like strolling around a zoo, but a zoo that's in someone's backyard. There are no concrete sidewalks, just footpaths that wind between huge enclosures. There are no kiosks hawking ice cream or plastic polar bears or pennies you can squish to make a souvenir.

There are just animals.

Most of them are rescues, creatures that spent months or even years in appalling conditions before being brought to this haven. Some were voluntarily re-homed, and some were seized from illegal situations by law enforcement. They have all found refuge here.

And what a menagerie it is! Jill and her staff care for domestic farm animals like horses and cows, more exotic creatures like wolves, llamas, and emus, all the way up to bears and big cats. Barn cats are everywhere. These critters are all part of the VOTK family.

Jill smiles as she watches a tiger lope around in a paddock shaded by trees and littered with tough, sturdy toys. She explains that this tiger, along with a lioness, was rescued from a seizure in Indiana. The two big cats were confined in circus roll cages, kept in a dark barn their entire lives. The tiger walks with a peculiar rolling gait, and Jill explains that she has trouble with her knees. The vet didn't expect the tiger to be able to walk at all, even after being freed from the cage. But now she has the run of her large enclosure.

"Our rescue animals can come in so broken." But here at the sanctuary, "they leap, they play, they don't pace like in zoos." Jill's charges benefit from her devotion to conservation. The predators get whole chicken carcasses or chunks of red meat, not ground beef. The opportunity to chew their food means that their dental health is excellent. These animals radiate strength, power, and the beauty of the natural world.

VOTK once held the record for the oldest living felid in captivity. Sammy, a Sumatran tiger, lived to be 36 years old. When he crossed the Rainbow Bridge, he was cremated and given a headstone in the cemetery on the Sanctuary grounds. "We cremate all the animals, so no one can dig them up 100 years from now like King Tut," Jill says, in a playful nod to the Sanctuary's Egyptian-inspired name.

Oh, didn't I mention it? Yes, there's a cemetery, right there in the middle of everything. It's a quiet, peaceful place, a Zen garden of contemplation in a setting that's already pretty mellow. Jill lost her son to a car accident in 1998. He is buried here. And when the time comes, both Jill and her husband will be laid to rest here, too. They'll spend eternity among the animals, both living and dead, that they love so much.

"I don't want to be buried in a human cemetery," Jill says. "Just doesn't feel right."

Aha, I hear you say, there's a cemetery on the grounds. That must be why Valley of the Kings is in this book.

Not so fast, kiddo. The ghosts of Valley of the Kings have nothing to do with the occupants of this cemetery, human or animal.

There are several spirits on the grounds. One is a protective spirit, an old farmer-type, that is affectionately known as "Hoppy."

Jill tells the story of an encounter she had with Hoppy. At one time, her house was heated with a wood stove, which meant of course that someone had to provide the fuel. Jill would hear someone chopping wood very early in the morning; she assumed it was her son, but he wasn't the one doing it. Determined to get to the bottom of the mystery, she set her alarm for 4:15 am. When she woke up, she waited until she heard the thunk of an axe hitting wood. Then she slowly opened the back door.

She saw a guy dressed in old farmer's overalls. The spirit turned and smiled at her, then was gone.

But VOTK is home to another story, much darker than a kindly old guardian. To hear this story, we have to travel back in time and visit a dance studio in Maine.

Two kids were taking ballet lessons there back in 1954. Ron Guay was 11 years old, and his friend Doris was 7. As their dancing hobby turned into a career, so did their childhood friendship deepen into love. They got married and moved to New York, searching for fame and fortune in the big city. Doris, with hair so blonde it was white, was rather plain. As Ron tells it, she sought advice on her future path from the nuns at her Catholic school. "Mother Superior said, go to New York and dance for God."

They broke onto the stage, performing as a couple, going by the stage names Ron and Joy Holiday. They began their career at Radio City Music Hall, performing as "adagio dancers." This graceful style blends the beauty of classical ballet with the athleticism of acrobatics. Ron and Joy were soon sharing the stage with the likes of Bob Hope, Liza Minelli, and Sammy Davis Jr.

A video from their dancing days showcases the sheer joy of dance that these two performers shared. Ron lifts his partner in a flying arabesque, then gives her a gentle toss into the air. She takes flight for a moment, then lands gracefully in his arms. With the adagio style, trust between the two dancers is an absolute requirement.

As their dance careers began to wane, Ron and Joy never lost that trust. Their travels took them to Las Vegas, where their friend, actor William Holden, set them on a new path. He bankrolled an innovative show that Ron christened "Cat Dancers." Holden even bought them their first feline partner, a baby leopard.

The Holidays pioneered one of the world's first big cat acts, way back in the 1960s. They began adding animal illusions to their stage performances. In one, Joy would get into a huge silver ball. A flash of flame would dazzle the audience - then a big cat, usually a tiger or a leopard, would spring out of the ball in Joy's place. It was all very glamorous and flashy, showmanship at its most spectacular.

This new animal act rocketed them even further into fame. They toured the world and were Johnny Carson's guests on the

Tonight Show. They moved down to Florida, to a large home in St. Petersburg, a place with a big yard for keeping and training the cats.

Fifteen years later, the Holidays moved to a bigger place in Gainesville, with more room for rehearsal, and a bigger yard for their feline co-stars. They also brought another human into their act in 1988, a zoology major and musician named Chuck Lizza. Chuck had literally run away to join the circus when he was younger. Joining the Holidays' Cat Dancer show suited him perfectly.

The trio worked well together: Ron designed the costumes, Chuck wrote the music and trained the cats, and Joy worked out the choreography. Soon, this professional relationship deepened into something more.

Chuck was movie-star handsome, and several decades younger than Ron and Joy, who were both in their late 50s. Chuck was just 24. Chuck became not just a coworker, but also a love interest. The three of them were tight-lipped about the details, but a romantic relationship developed between the trio. Somehow, they made it work.

The show Cat Dancers included some panthers and leopards, but tigers were their primary feline performers. The big cats were trained practically from birth. Chuck, Ron, and Joy used gentle methods of rewards-based training. The secret sauce to their rapport with animals was love and trust.

But love and trust only go so far in a big cat's world. The trio treated the cats like members of their family, forgetting that the massive felines were wild beasts at heart. Jill Carnegie was friends with the threesome and tried to give them the benefit of her years of experience.

"We take precautions. In 44 years, we've never had an injury." Jill is adamant about this. "You always have to remember, they are trained and never tamed. They are who they are, and even a good one can cause serious harm."

In 1995, the Holidays bought a baby white Bengal tiger from a breeder in Alabama. They paid $10,000 for the cub, naming him Jupiter. Jill feared for her friends' safety. She tried to warn them.

"He's going to grow up to be a very dangerous cat."

"Oh, he's just as sweet as can be," Joy protested. One of his tricks was to hold a baby bottle in his paws and drink from it. It was ridiculously cute to watch, and Joy was besotted with the gorgeous creature.

Three years later, by October 1998, Jupiter tipped the scales at 400 lbs. He had been hand-raised by the humans since he was 6 days old, and their bond seemed strong. Jupiter was especially close to Chuck, his trainer.

Jupiter was a well-trained tiger, but he had his quirks. Every once in a while, he would spook if the noise of the audience was too loud, or if he felt something in his environment wasn't quite right. Jupiter and many of the other big cats spent their nights in an 18-wheeler truck trailer; that's where they felt safe and comfortable.

On this October day, Ron was taking Jupiter out to his day area. Workers were due to arrive at the compound to install a fence for a new enclosure. Their van was crunching up the driveway, and Jupiter decided he wasn't happy about it. He started to get worked up.

"Ron should have let him go back to his cage, but he didn't," Jill told me. He got the tiger to the end of the ramp. Here, Jill said, Ron had another opportunity. Jupiter was on a leash. Ron could've clipped Jupiter to the fence, told the driver of the van to leave, then put the tiger safely in the day area. He didn't do that, either.

Instead, he called for Joy, who suggested they get something for the tiger to eat. When a big cat is fixated on something, they get tunnel vision. Even with the promise of a treat, Joy couldn't distract the tiger - he was still freaking out. They decided to bring Chuck out to deal with Jupiter.

Chuck came out of the house, bleary-eyed and still muzzy with sleep. He wasn't wearing his glasses, and he shuffled out in house slippers. As he came toward the big cat, Chuck stumbled over a piece of debris in the yard and fell onto the tiger.

The predator was startled. Instinct took over. He grabbed Chuck by the throat and snapped his neck.

"Jupiter, NO!" Joy shouted in anguish. The tiger dropped his prey, and Chuck fell limply to the ground. Joy knelt by her lover, and Ron gathered his friend's mangled body into his lap. Paramedics worked for about half an hour at the scene to stabilize Chuck, then airlifted him to the hospital. He died at 10:15 am at Shands Medical Center.

Jill heard about the tragedy the next day. "I got down on my hands and knees and I begged Joy not to have any touch - nothing, nothing to do with this cat." She offered Jupiter a home at VOTK. "If you want us to take him, he will live out his days, but you will never be near him."

"No, no, he's our baby, he didn't mean it," Joy sobbed.

"Joy, he meant it," Jill said firmly. "And he's gonna do it again."

Ron and Joy were both devastated at the loss of their friend and lover. Joy spiraled down into a deep depression. She stayed in bed, refusing to eat. Joy, a lifelong dancer, was naturally fit, so when twenty pounds dropped from her already-thin frame in the space of six weeks, Ron became worried.

"Come out, honey. Maybe it would cheer you up if you helped me with the babies tonight." Ron coaxed.

Joy finally relented. She got a handful of treats and went out to the trailer. Jupiter was the last cat to come into the trailer. Jill spoke in a quiet voice as she relayed what happened next.

"Here comes Jupiter. And she just held out her little hand, and said Jupiter, I have a little snack for you. He grabbed her by the throat, lifted her about five feet into the air, and BAM, slammed her down on the floor in the semi-trailer." Joy died instantly.

The couple's friend Russell was there and came running to the scene. Ron wanted to get a gun and kill the tiger himself, but Russell held him down and called the police. All the while, Jupiter was pacing back and forth, circling Joy's body. Ron and Russell couldn't approach Joy, not with Jupiter still agitated. A SWAT team arrived and shot the beautiful, deadly animal. It was November 12, 1998, exactly six weeks after Chuck had been killed.

They had an open casket, Jill tells me. Joy wore a scarf to be buried in, because the mortician couldn't make the mangled meat of her neck presentable.

Two people, killed violently and unexpectedly at the same place. It's a recipe for a haunting. Ron kept hearing Chuck running up the stairs in the house every night, just as he did when he was alive. The home held too many memories, and Ron soon sold it and moved out. The new owners reported hearing the same thing: the sound of someone running up the stairs, night after night.

Jill stepped in to help her friend. She did a clearing ritual and sent Chuck's spirit into the white light. The next day, Russell, who had been Chuck's best friend, called Jill. He'd had a dream about Chuck the night before. Russell told Jill that Chuck had made it home and was now with Joy.

Russell had no idea that Jill had done her crossing-over ritual the evening before.

And after that, the new owners of the house never heard the running footsteps again.

Jill now owns the semi-trailer where Joy was killed. Ghost Research Society is one of the groups that have investigated inside the trailer. Their evidence was scanty and inconclusive, although the Phasma Box did spit out the words "grabbed" and "white tiger."

Joy may very well have moved on, joining her beloved Chuck in the afterlife. Although, I can't think of many more places that would be more pleasant than Valley of the Kings Sanctuary to spend eternity.

MUSIC UNDER THE STARS

(Red Rocks Park and Amphitheater, Denver, Colorado)

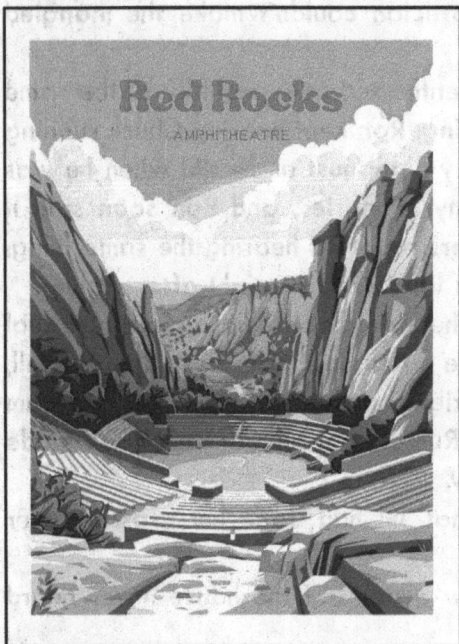

Picture a crowd of nearly 10,000 people waiting with eager anticipation for a concert to begin. The energy swirls and surges, and a happy buzz fills the air, as the audience finds their seats. The first few notes of music yelp out into the air, and the energy crests and breaks over the stage. The musicians bask in the adoration of their audience as they perform, creating the music they were born to make.

Red Rocks Amphitheater is one of the greatest concert venues on Earth. The number of legendary acts who've performed here over the years is staggering: the Beatles, U-2, Rush, Depeche

Mode, Ed Sheeran, Jethro Tull, Stevie Nicks, the list is long and impressive. In 1999, after <u>Pollstar</u> awarded Red Rocks the award for best outdoor venue for the 11th time, the magazine changed its tactics. They simply changed the name of the honor to the "Red Rocks Award" ... and disqualified the famous venue from further competition.

Red Rocks Park, ten miles outside Denver near the town of Morrison, is a stunning wonder of the natural world. The rock formations, carved over millions of years by wind and water, give the amphitheater incredible acoustics. Dinosaurs once roamed this land, too. Fossils of T-Rex and Diplodocus have been found in the Dinosaur Ridge area, east of the venue. The footprints of the huge beasts are still there, captured in mud turned to stone.

The first concert was held here in 1906, when a 25-piece brass band performed the Grand Opening of the Garden of the Titans on May 31. That launched the opening of the natural amphitheater, and performances have been thrilling audiences ever since.

The artists are thrilled, too. The visitor's center is home to the Red Rocks Hall of Fame, filled with memorabilia from well over a century of performance. There's also a secret tunnel under the stage, where the concrete block walls bear the signatures of many of the famous acts who've made Red Rocks ring with their music.

Red Rocks is also home to a variety of supernatural phenomena, including a vortex and a good handful of ghosts.

People who are sensitive to that sort of thing have encountered a strange pull that locals call the "Red Rocks Energy Vortex." This isn't necessarily a bad thing; it just means that all the live music performances over the years have created a really powerful blend of vibes from the artists and the audiences. People are drawn to the rocks and trails for more spiritual reasons, too. People go there to meditate, or to Zen out with an hour of sunrise yoga. All that energy has to go *somewhere*. Many people have reported seeing bursts of anomalous light, hearing strange noises, or feeling unexplained gusts of wind on the trails. It's a weird, wonderful place.

There are ghosts there, too. This was once the territory of the Ute, the Cheyenne, the Arapaho. When hiking the rugged but beautiful trails, people have encountered the wandering spirits of both Native Americans and early settlers. The fact that the Red Rocks Cemetery is at the base of the trail also contributes to the spook factor. The graves here date back to the 1800s. Unfortunately, the strict rule is that only locals can be buried there. Gives new meaning to the phrase "people are dying to get in."

One distinct ghost is known as the Hatchet Lady of Red Rocks. She often appears at the highest point of the rock peaks - and sometimes she's missing her head. Locals say that this is the spirit of "Old Ms. Johnson," a 19th century widow who spent years living in the caves after she lost her husband. It's said she brandished a hatchet to scare away her daughter's suitors. The stories build on this lore, saying that she comes out of her cave riding on a spectral horse, wearing a blood-soaked dress. She's said to prowl through the area, looking for young couples. If she catches them canoodling, she swings her hatchet at them before disappearing into the night air.

It's not only the trails that are home to ghosts. Many of the paranormal reports from Red Rocks come from the Trading Post. (It was originally called the Indian Trading Post, but people wised up.) Employees have seen, heard, and felt some extremely weird things there over the years. These things seem to happen mostly at night - ain't that always the way? Merchandise goes missing overnight, boxes fly across the room as if hurled by an invisible force, doorknobs jiggle, heavy doors open on their own, wind chimes move but make no sound. Interestingly, souvenir mugs with the name "Randy" tend to fall off shelves to shatter on the floor pretty regularly.

Red Rocks Park is a great place to see the stars. And more than a few ghosts.

LONDON BRIDGE IS NO LONGER FALLING DOWN
(Lake Havasu City, AZ)

In the early 1970s, London Bridge was, indeed, falling down. More accurately, the centuries-old bridge was beginning to sink under the weight of modern traffic. The original wooden bridge was built in various stages between AD 50 and 1176. Stonework was added in the medieval period, and the Victorians added more stone in 1831. By the 1960s, the bridge was showing its considerable age. But you can't just tear down London Bridge. The City of London decided to auction off the historic landmark in 1968.

Robert McCulloch, an American entrepreneur, made the winning bid. The bridge was dismantled block by block, and each stone was numbered. The blocks were shipped via the Panama Canal to Long Beach, California, then trucked 300 miles inland to Lake Havasu City,

Arizona.

It took three years of careful reconstruction, working from the coded diagram and from plans from 1824, but in 1971, the bridge was fully restored. It was officially dedicated on October 10, to great fanfare: fireworks, a parade, and a visit by the Lord Mayor of London.

Adorably, an English village was built next to the bridge. Exports from the UK abound - transplanted English grass, a red telephone box, an iconic double-decker bus, and a London taxi. City planners also added an English restaurant and a pub, Ye Hog In Armour.

Those aren't the only things that came over to keep the bridge company. London Bridge has its own complement of Old World ghosts.

The lamps on the bridge are made from melted-down cannons from Napoleon's warships, captured in the Battle of Waterloo. So if you think about it, those lampposts have killed a lot of people. Other energy comes from victims of the Black Death in the mid-1300s. Corpses of plague victims were stacked on the riverbank to be picked up by a ferry for burial.

There are individual ghosts that haunt the bridge too. One is a London bobby, still patrolling his beat. People say the ghost of Jack the Ripper hangs out at the bridge too - he killed seven girls in 1888 in Whitechapel, which was within one mile of the bridge when it stood in London.

Other ghosts include a couple in Victorian dress who walk along as if enjoying an evening stroll. And why not? They probably think they're still in foggy London, not in the Arizona desert. Or maybe they do know where they are and are glad for the change in scenery.

One lucky witness was thrilled to see four ghosts wandering the bridge in Victorian garb. She thought it was absolutely ingenious of the organizers to add a touch of London spooky to the bridge by creating realistic holograms, or projections, or ... whatever ...

After searching for a projector, and not finding anyone who could answer her questions about the ghosts, she realized that the Victorian "ghosts" that so enthralled her were not, in fact, projections for the delight of tourists visiting London Bridge.

They were real.

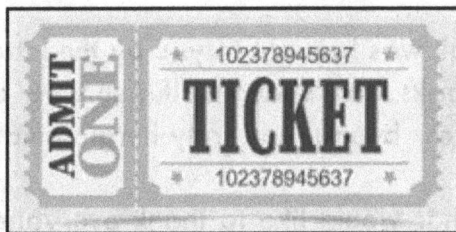

CONCLUSION
Home Again

Thanks so much for coming along with me on another road trip in search of the spooky, the historic, and the just plain fun. Soon we'll be pulling into the driveway, safely home. We'll unpack our suitcases, shake the sand out of our towels, and hang the wet bathing suits to dry.

But happily, another vacation is always around the corner.

ACKNOWLEDGEMENTS

This book was brought to you by the letters A through Z, four notebooks, ten and a half pens, 98 cans of fizzy water (and a few beers), and truly heroic amounts of tea.

The author would like to thank everyone who shared their stories for your enjoyment - it's truly appreciated. You'll meet them in these pages. Huge thanks go to Miriam Zethmayr, for creating another drawing of our little ghostie travel buddy. Look for him in the back of the book!

Special thanks are due to James Brija, who turned his guest room into a writing haven for the creation of this book, and many more to come. He also did a whole lot of typing for me, so you all owe him a steak dinner. I've already paid up.

ABOUT THE AUTHOR

Sylvia Shults has been a paranormal investigator for many years, and a fan of the supernatural all her life. She has worked as a librarian for the past 25 years, slowly smuggling out enough words in her pockets day by day to build several books of her own. She sits in dark, spooky places so you don't have to. She lives in Illinois with a certifiably insane Husky, and far too many books.

Spectral locomotives wait for no man, or ghost ... Tenny may need to hitch a ride with you! Take a picture with him on your summer holiday and use the hashtag #endlesssummer so he can go traveling!

www.ingramcontent.com/pod-product-compliance
Lightning Source LLC
Chambersburg PA
CBHW010043090426
42734CB00018B/3239